CRITICAL ACCLAIM
FOR *TRAVELERS' TALES*

"The *Travelers' Tales* series is altogether remarkable."
—Jan Morris, author of *Journeys*, *Locations*, and *Hong Kong*

"For the thoughtful traveler, these books are an invaluable resource. There's nothing like them on the market."
—Pico Iyer, author of *Video Night in Kathmandu*

"This is the stuff memories can be duplicated from."
—Karen Krebsbach, *Foreign Service Journal*

"I can't think of a better way to get comfortable with a destination than by delving into *Travelers' Tales*...before reading a guidebook, before seeing a travel agent. The series helps visitors refine their interests and readies them to communicate with the peoples they come in contact with...."
—Paul Glassman, Society of American Travel Writers

"*Travelers' Tales* is a valuable addition to any predeparture reading list."
—Tony Wheeler, publisher, Lonely Planet Publications

"*Travelers' Tales* delivers something most guidebooks only promise: a real sense of what a country is all about...."
—Steve Silk, *Hartford Courant*

"The *Travelers' Tales* series should become required reading for anyone visiting a foreign country who wants to truly step off the tourist track and experience another culture, another place, firsthand."
—Nancy Paradis, *St. Petersburg Times*

"Like having been there, done it, seen it. If there's one thing traditional guidebooks lack, it's the really juicy travel information, the personal stories about back alleys and brief encounters. The *Travelers' Tales* series fills this gap with an approach that's all anecdotes, no directions."

TRAVELERS' TALES BOOKS

Country and Regional Guides
America, Australia, Brazil, Central America, Cuba, France, Greece,
India, Ireland, Italy, Japan, Mexico, Nepal, Spain, Thailand, Tibet,
Turkey; American Southwest, Grand Canyon, Hawai'i,
Hong Kong, Paris, San Francisco, Tuscany

Women's Travel
Her Fork in the Road, A Woman's Path, A Woman's
Passion for Travel, A Woman's World, Women in the Wild,
A Mother's World, Safety and Security for Women
Who Travel, Gutsy Women, Gutsy Mamas

Body & Soul
The Spiritual Gifts of Travel, The Road Within,
Love & Romance, Food, The Fearless Diner, The Adventure
of Food, The Ultimate Journey, Pilgrimage

Special Interest
Not So Funny When It Happened,
The Gift of Rivers, Shitting Pretty, Testosterone Planet,
Danger!, The Fearless Shopper, The Penny Pincher's
Passport to Luxury Travel, The Gift of Birds, Family Travel,
A Dog's World, There's No Toilet Paper on the Road
Less Traveled, The Gift of Travel, 365 Travel, Adventures in Wine

Footsteps
Kite Strings of the Southern Cross, The Sword of Heaven,
Storm, Take Me With You, Last Trout in Venice, The Way of
the Wanderer, One Year Off, The Fire Never Dies

Classics
The Royal Road to Romance,
Unbeaten Tracks in Japan, The Rivers Ran East,
Coast to Coast, Trader Horn

TRAVELERS' TALES

TIBET

TRUE STORIES

TRAVELERS' TALES

TIBET

TRUE STORIES

Edited by
JAMES O'REILLY AND
LARRY HABEGGER

TRAVELERS' TALES
SAN FRANCISCO

951.5
T433

Copyright © 2003 Travelers' Tales, Inc. All rights reserved.
Introduction copyright © 2003 by Heinrich Harrer.

Travelers' Tales and *Travelers' Tales Guides* are trademarks of Travelers' Tales, Inc.

Credits and copyright notices for the individual articles in this collection are given starting on page 293.

We have made every effort to trace the ownership of all copyrighted material and to secure permission from copyright holders. In the event of any question arising as to the ownership of any material, we will be pleased to make the necessary correction in future printings. Contact Travelers' Tales, Inc., 330 Townsend Street, Suite 208, San Francisco, California 94107. www.travelerstales.com

Art Direction: Michele Wetherbee
Interior design: Kathryn Heflin and Susan Bailey
Cover photograph: © China Tourism Press/gettyimages. Potala Palace, Lhasa.
Map: Keith Granger
Page layout: Patty Holden using the fonts Bembo and Boulevard

Distributed by: Publishers Group West, 1700 Fourth Street, Berkeley, California 94710.

Library of Congress Cataloguing-in-Publication Data

Travelers' Tales Tibet: true stories / edited by James O'Reilly and Larry Habegger.—1st ed.
      p. cm. — (Travelers' Tales)
   ISBN 1-885211-76-7 (pbk. : alk. paper)
    1. Tibet (China)--Description and travel. I. O'Reilly, James. II. Habegger, Larry. III. Series: Travelers' Tales guides.
DS786.T698 2003
951'.5059--dc21

                       2002151658

First Edition
Printed in the United States of America
10 9 8 7 6 5 4 3 2 1

For Robbie and Kim,
lanterns in the cold dark night.

'03/ $18.95

Why is it that the fate of Tibet has found such a deep echo in the world? There can only be one answer: Tibet has become the symbol of all that present-day humanity is longing for, either because it has been lost or not yet realized or because it is in danger of disappearing from human sight: the stability of a tradition, which has its roots not only in a historical or cultural past, but within the innermost being of man, in whose depth this past is enshrined as an ever-present source of inspiration.

—LAMA ANAGARIKA GOVINDA,
*THE WAY OF THE WHITE CLOUDS:
A BUDDHIST PILGRIM IN TIBET*

Table of Contents

Introduction   xv
  HEINRICH HARRER

Map   xviii–xix

Part One
ESSENCE OF TIBET

A Tibetan Picnic   3
  BARBARA BANKS

Chasing Monks   7
  MARIA MÖLLER

The Pilgrims' Way   10
  EDWARD WONG

Tutor to the Dalai Lama   16
  HEINRICH HARRER

Around the Jokhang   32
  ALEC LE SUEUR

The Realm of the Clouded Leopard   40
  WADE DAVIS

The Sew-Tel Hotel   59
  BROUGHTON COBURN

Tibet through Chinese Eyes   63
  PETER HESSLER

Part Two
SOME THINGS TO DO

Like a Rolling Stone   87
    TIM WARD

On the Sacred Mountain   96
    CHARLES ALLEN

A Meeting with a Monk   105
    KEVIN ENGLISH

The Holy Lake   113
    SVEN HEDIN

Bicycles to Burang   120
    JEREMY SCHMIDT

The Lost Kingdom of Guge   131
    MICHAEL BUCKLEY

At the Norbulingka   143
    KAREN SWENSON

Part Three
GOING YOUR OWN WAY

The Space Between   151
    TOM JOYCE

Instant Karma   163
    MARK JENKINS

Red River Valley   173
    MICHAEL BUCKLEY

Approaching Lhasa   184
    ALEXANDRA DAVID-NEEL

Mondays Are Best   193
    PICO IYER

Journeys with a Buddhist Pilgrim   196
    LAMA ANAGARIKA GOVINDA

The Visions of the Dead   212
    FOSCO MARAINI, TRANSLATED BY ERIC
    MOSBACHER AND GUIDO WALDMAN

Part Four
IN THE SHADOWS

Zone X in Zhangmu 227
SANGITA LAMA WITH RAJENDRA S. KHADKA

A Day in the Life of Ghang Sik Dondrup 235
JEFF GREENWALD

Rebuilding Palpung 247
PAMELA LOGAN

A Walk on the Wild Side 255
RALPH WHITE

Part Five
THE LAST WORD

Mestizo 277
ROBBIE BARNETT

Recommended Reading 285

Index 289

Index of Contributors 291

Acknowledgments 293

Tibet: An Introduction
by Heinrich Harrer

Heinrich Harrer, an Austrian now in his tenth decade, has had a life for the history books. He was an Olympic skiing champion, a first-class mountaineer who on the first successful ascent of the "unclimbable" North Face of the Eiger (which he recounted in his unforgettable book, White Spider*), got caught up in World War II and was interned by the British in India, fled to Tibet where he became tutor to the teenage Dalai Lama, about which you can read in these pages, wrote* Seven Years in Tibet *based on his extraordinary time there, fled with the Dalai Lama to India in 1959, returned to Tibet many years later, a journey he recounted in* Return to Tibet, *and now lives at home in a village in Austria.*

Literature about Tibet is flooding the book market, I can't cope or read it all. It is therefore a welcome task for me to write the introduction for *Travelers' Tales Tibet,* which respects the cause of Tibet and is accepted by the Tibetans themselves.

When I try to write about my second homeland, the reader will understand that I am not always objective, that in my memory all unpleasant encounters are forgotten and I remember only the compassionate habits of my ever-ebullient friends. I never succeeded in depicting the vast landscape—its colors were always more beautiful than I could possibly describe. When God created our world, he gave preference to the country beyond the horizon. The Tibetans respected and thanked the Divine for this generous gift by being the greatest conservationists of nature.

Every human builds his successes upon the shoulders of others, and I am no different. In Lhasa one of my great mentors was Trijang Rinpoche, by far the most learned Tibetan and teacher of the Dalai Lama. He took me under his umbrella, as the Tibetans say, and approved of my seeing the Dalai Lama in Norbulingka. With Gyayum Chenmo, the great mother of His Holiness, I had a kind of conspiracy. As loving mother for her holy son she was often outspoken and realized, or even foresaw, that hearing of the Western World might be useful to the young Dalai Lama.

When Peter Aufschnaiter and I gradually advanced deeper into the "forbidden country," we encountered a thousand-year-old culture. In Tsaparang, the ancient city of the old kingdom of Guge, we admired Tibetan art in its highest completion. And also in Kyirong, where virtually milk and honey were flowing and the most popular Yogi Milarepa was born, who wrote poems and songs about gods and nature a thousand years ago.

The merry Tibetans, devoted to their Buddhist religion, worked hard on the barley fields, which were cultivated even above 4,000 meters.

On the way to Lhasa, it was already the second winter, we often heard them saying "*Nying je*"—meaning, they felt compassion and sympathy for our poor outfit in temperatures of minus 40 degrees. It was touching when crossing the 6,000-meter-high Pass Guringla, a nomad gave us some precious dried apricot from Gilgit, where we had been eight years earlier on the Nanga Parbat expedition.

Lhasa hoards many memories, one of which I will narrate because it shows how informal and leisurely Tibetans behave.

I was just drawing on a map when my faithful servant Nyima breathlessly announced that a group of Kutras (noblemen) was approaching my house near the holy river Kyichu. They were my best friends Wangdü, Wangchuk, and Lobsang Samten, the elder brother of the Dalai Lama. Nyima was handed the trunk of a sheep of which the mutton had the much appreciated *sor-nyi*, two-finger-thick fat. Nyima immediately prepared Tibetan tea, which is very often falsely described, because not even in mysterious Tibet do oxen give milk. (The females are called *dri* and the castrated bull is the yak, the ox. Most writing about Tibet, however, uses the generic yak, so we better just say "yak," which has become the synonym for bull, ox, and *dri*.) My friends sat down, turned the radio on, and searched for their house on the map, which was lying on the drawing table.

After some time Nyima came with the steaming pot, the smell of mutton-fat and yak dung fire filled the room. Everybody took a piece of meat with his fingers, dunked it in a sauce of hot peppers, and rather noisily the meal began. My memory is so vivid that my mouth waters when I describe it. The horses were not forgotten and got a sack full of peas, and the servants got a share of boiled mutton. After strong burps, tea was served, which came from Darjeeling, once Tibetan territory with the beautiful name Dorjeling—"Thunderboltgarden."

After some time Wangchuk, as the oldest, said, "We enjoyed the meal and tea, we thank you very much, but now we request permission to go." This expression I also use jokingly at home in Austria after an invitation. It is a sensible expression which relieves the host as well as the guest. The horses were saddled, Nyima stood with his family in front of the kitchen, and devotedly accepted the generous tip with both hands.

I have many more anecdotes to describe the open and merry character of Tibetans, and it still can be experienced today. This unforgotten time is not gone forever, because one of their great virtues is the concept of time, the strength to wait, wait until they are free again.

And until then, you the traveler or reader can learn much more about this extraordinary land and people in *Travelers' Tales Tibet*.

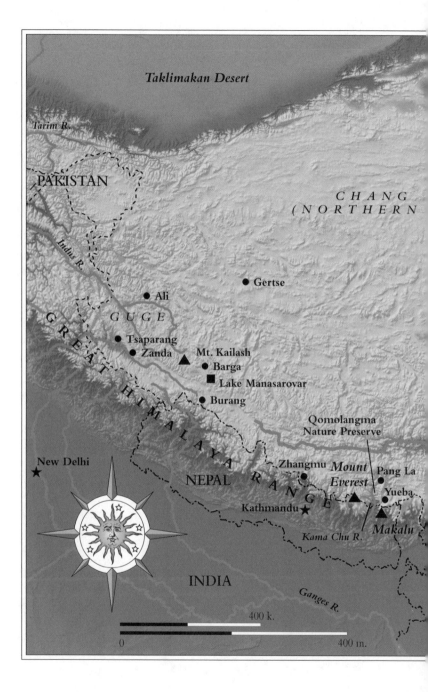

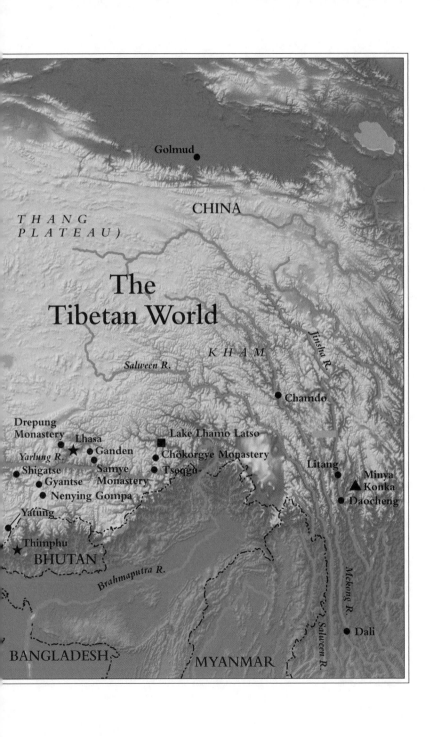

Golmud

CHINA

THANG
PLATEAU)

The
Tibetan World

KHAM

Salween R.

Jinsha R.

Chamdo

Drepung
Monastery   Lhasa   Lake Lhamo Latso
Yarlung R.   Ganden   Chokorgye Monastery
  Shigatse   Samye   Tsoqgu·   Litang
      Gyantse   Monastery   Minya
       Nenying Gompa   Konka
Yatung   Daocheng
    Thimphu
  BHUTAN

Brahmaputra R.

Mekong R.

BANGLADESH   MYANMAR   Salween R.

Dali

PART ONE

ESSENCE OF TIBET

A Tibetan Picnic

As the belly fills, so does the heart.

THE LAND CRUISER LABORS ITS WAY ACROSS THE COUNTRYSIDE, followed by the baby blue supply truck. We are in the remote stretches of Tibet to do field work, and it is two 16,000-foot passes since breakfast. Time is of little consequence in this immensity, and the decision to eat will be made by place, not by the clock. Open pasture stretches out on either side of the dirt road that passes for Tibet's major highway out here, and in the distance a girl is collecting yak dung in a basket to bring back to her village for fuel. Suddenly the Land Cruiser veers off the road and bumps across the sparse grass towards the river we have been following for hours, the blue truck lurching behind like a drunken dinosaur. We have arrived.

Dawa is out of the truck in moments, and climbs up the side bars to unlash the canvas top. He is a giant of a man, with a heart as huge as the sky and a wacky, Jackie Gleason sense of humor that can shake the road weariness out of us in moments. He reaches into the hold of the truck and drops three lumpy burlap sacks and the wooden tea churn to waiting arms below. Small fireplaces sprout across the grass like mushrooms, built of round stones packed with clay from the nearby river, and you realize why this spot was chosen above all the other promising sites you had passed, although

how they could tell this or remember the distinguishing characteristics that mark this particular bend in the road remain a mystery, to
be stored with many others that have filled your head since entering this beautiful enigma of a place. Phurbu the cook bends over
the sticks and dried grasses he has gathered in one of the fireplaces,
coaxing flames into life, and within moments the blackened tea
kettle is set on the fire. Life does not continue without tea.

We are in a campsite used by countless people before us; nomads
following their flocks down from summer pasture, traders walking
their goods to the town that lies two days to the east, families making the long pilgrimage to Lhasa to honor the deities that protect
their country. The sacks are untied; from one comes a full leg of a
sheep. Refrigeration is both unavailable and redundant here; the
dry air and the cold of the high plateau take care of it for you.
From another sack a plump pillow of roasted barley flour and a
large wooden bowl are pulled out, from the third a small rosewood
bowl, its top tied with a leather lace. These are the ingredients for a
Tibetan picnic.

We sit on the sun-warmed grass, sweaters around our shoulders
against the promise of winter that haunts the wind. Shamba returns
from the riverbank, his face and hands bright red from their scrubbing in the frigid water. He holds the tiny branch of a bare bush,
which he sets down gently beside the teapot without saying a word,
then joins our circle on the grass. Phurbu is kneading the barley
with the first of the tea, working the flour around the edges of the
bowl to make a dough. As each handful comes to the right consis-
tency, he squeezes it in his fist and passes it to one of us, a tube of
roasted grain imprinted with the mark of his sure hand. Dawa is at
work on the leg of the sheep; he draws the dagger-like knife which
every Tibetan man and most Tibetan women keep hanging from
their waists for just such occasions. Everyone else pulls their daggers
out as well; Dawa's is simply a big flattened steel bar, ground to an
edge, with a massive handle fitted on the end. We will make do with
our Swiss Army knives, which look as fragile as matchsticks in the
company of all this serious metal. Dawa slices off chunks of mutton,
throwing most of them onto the grass in the center of the circle; the

irresistible chunks he pops directly into his mouth. When he has cut a good-sized heap he sets the leg down beside him. The rosewood bowl has been opened to reveal ground red pepper, which we tip into the lid as a serving bowl. There isn't a fork in sight, nor a plate or napkin for that matter. However, it is time to eat.

We fall onto the food as if it is the first we have seen in days, or the last we will see for days to come, and in truth you never know up here. Between bites of *tsampa*—the roasted barley flour dough— we reach into the pile of meat, dipping our pieces into the red pepper either on just one side or two, depending on how hot you like it. As the meat pile diminishes, the leg of mutton is passed around and we take turns cutting off more and throwing it into the pile, usually while we are both chewing and talking. Manners do count out here, but they are a different set of manners, and you get to break every rule that was drummed into you as a child. (This may be the real reason that people fall in love with Tibet.)

Meanwhile, Phurbu has poured the black tea into the wooden churn, and hooks his leg around it as a brace. He adds a knife-blade full of yak butter and a small handful of salt, then with the gesture that is rhythmic and graceful and

We were hungry, tired, and cold as we stumbled through the moonlit, ruined monastery into a low room where an amazing sight awaited us: our Tibetan companions were cooking dinner with blowtorches, goggles firmly in place. I forget what we ate, but I'll never forget the making of the feast.

—James O'Reilly, "Notes from the Roof"

practiced a thousand times over, he churns the *sö cha*, or butter tea, regular as a metronome. The tea is poured, thick as cream and the color of caramel, back into the black kettle, its smoky flavor interwoven with the scent of melted yak butter. Phurbu reaches over to the twig that Shamba had brought back from the river and fits it into the spout, a perfect strainer. Our cups are ready, always ready for tea: there are silver-lined traditional wooden tea bowls alongside plastic thermal mugs, and the kettle is lifted time and again—no cup gets drunk to the bottom before being refilled, and the brothy mixture is warming from deep within. Here it is quite proper, expected even, that you will make a lot of noise when you eat. In fact, if you have no appetite but don't want to offend your hosts you can get by with a lot of smacking of your lips and swallowing sounds; they don't notice as long as you keep drinking your tea.

And so we sit, nine human beings in a circle, encircled by a wall of mountains that swallow up our laughter and tiny voices. We tell jokes and stories while we eat, tossing any unwanted bits over our shoulders until we are surrounded by a necklace of gristle and bone. Amidst the talk and jokes there is a sudden sharp crack. Dawa raises his dagger arm again and slices across the bone, taking the whole top off this time. For all their congeniality, Tibetan picnics can have a decidedly Neanderthal flavor to them. With the point of his ten-inch blade Dawa reaches into the bone for the marrow, eating it straight off the knife tip, the yellow sash swinging like a jaunty exclamation point from the handle. We wait our turn, knives ready.

Suddenly, without a spoken signal, the picnic ends. Burlap sacks are cinched closed and tossed back into the belly of the truck. Jackets are folded to once again provide seat cushions against the rutted road. The last of the tea is swung in an arc across the grass; the twig strainer is carefully removed from the spout and left by the fireplace for the next set of pilgrims. We pile into the vehicles and set off in silence, the spell of our meal together still hovering over that tiny spot in the immense Tibetan land.

Barbara Banks has been traveling since age five, when she ran away from home because her brother ate all of the ice cream. She has built wooden boats in France, driven a freight train across Turkey, and sailed across the North Sea. More conventional work has been as a documentary filmmaker and writer for an adventure travel company. She lives in Berkeley, California.

MARIA MÖLLER

Chasing Monks

*The author glimpses a world of mischief beyond
the close-cropped heads and maroon robes.*

I AM CHASING MONKS. DOWN THE CROOKED STREETS OF OLD
Tibetan Lhasa, along the wide avenues of new Chinese Lhasa, I
compile my list of "best monk" sightings. Some monks wear emer-
ald green bowler hats, like inexplicably misplaced leprechauns.
Others sport gold brocade visors, the long square brims shading
their faces. Some are ancient and weathered, clutching prayer beads
and avoiding my female eyes. Others are just teenagers and bouncing off the walls with adolescent excitement. Maroon imitation-
Nike windbreakers over their matching maroon-colored robes, they
suck on Popsicles and ask if they can practice their English with me.
On the street corner, in the temple, at a café, I open my Tibetan-
English phrasebook and teach them to say "How are you?" and
"Thank you very much."

One day, out on the hunt, I turn down an ancient lane behind
the Jokhang temple and find yet another English-seeking monk. No
older than sixteen, he leads me up a flight of stairs to a balcony,
through a doorway, and into a tiny temple.

A huge golden deity fills up half the room. On a raised platform
next to the statue sits an older monk. He pounds a drum with a
long curved drumstick, and at the same time chants a mantra, and

clangs giant cymbals, and accepts offerings of yak butter from visitors, and smiles in greeting to me.

The young monk sits me down at a low table below the older monk's platform, brings me a cup of yak butter tea, and opens up his English textbook. It is in Chinese, of course, but he has written the Tibetan translations of the Chinese characters in the margins. But even if it wasn't in Chinese, I could guess that's where it came from: the exercises run along the lines of "Are you an artist? No, I am a worker." I teach him to say "I am a monk" instead.

Before I know it, the yak butter has congealed on the top of my cup and five other young monks have heard that I am captive in the temple. They all gather around, trying to teach me some Tibetan, and they all laugh heartily at my attempts. The old ladies of the neighborhood continue to stream in with their bags of yak butter, and glare at me with the disapproving look of old ladies everywhere. The older monk continues to chant, to bang the drum, and to clang the cymbals right above my head.

I've somehow slid into antiquity, with only the English textbook stringing a Maoist lifeline to the present. I could sink into this place, give in to the flickering butter lamps and the drone of the monk above my head. I could sit here for an eternity and no one but the old ladies would mind; everyone here is used to eternity, after all. But then, without even meaning to, I glance at my watch. My young monks let out a gasp of collective excitement: it's an Adidas sports watch. As each one grasps my wrist in turn, taking a look at its glowing face and multiple settings, I discover that just like

> With protestations failing under her insistence, I take the bowl with one hand, the other resting on the edge as custom demands. I am full. I have had five bowls of tea already this morning but refusal, although *de rigueur*, is only a formality. Genuine refusal is insulting. Only enemies refuse a bowl of tea. And only enemies, I remember with a sinking heart, refuse the second—and the third.
>
> —Catriona Bass, "A Most Maligned Drink"

there is a worldwide "disapproving old lady glare," there is also a worldwide "look of glee on a young man's face when examining a gadget." And with this I've slid decidedly out of my romantic antiquity and into reality. Eventually I pull myself—and my watch—away.

The older monk gives me a final smile, and the young monks follow me out onto the balcony. As I walk down the stairs and continue down the lane, they line up along the railing, waving and laughing, jostling each other and shouting goodbye.

Despite the maroon robes, they don't seem like monks at all. I was a Catholic schoolgirl and I'm used to men of the cloth. But these are teenage boys, not men, and I feel like their favorite high school teacher—the cool one whom some of the kids have a crush on. And they are even more excited about the novelty of me, the little peek I gave them into my world, than I am about the glimpse I've gotten into theirs.

But then again, they're also excited because they've sent me down a dead-end street. After a minute or two I reach a wall and have to turn back the way I came. The monks are waiting on the balcony for me. One of them has dressed himself up in a Chicago Bulls cap. There is a hint of reckless excitement in the air. My English-lesson friend is holding a bucket full of water and I can see right away what he's about to do. As I start to run he follows above me along the balcony, and then hurls the water wildly. The monks collapse in laughter.

The water misses me by a wide margin. I smile at them and giggle good-naturedly, assuming that this cannot possibly be as strange as it seems. And then I scurry down the lane before they can get me for real.

So the next time I go chasing monks, I'll forget about eternity. I'll leave my watch behind. Instead I'll pack a loaded water pistol and be ready to fire, just in case the monks decide to turn the tables and chase me.

Maria Möller is a theater artist, writer, and photographer based in Philadelphia. She has performed "The Tourist Police," an original monologue about traveling in Tibet and India, at Chicago's Rhinoceros Theatre Festival and at the Philadelphia Fringe Festival.

EDWARD WONG

The Pilgrims' Way

*The trek to the monastery of Samye, sacred
for many, can also be demanding.*

LIFE IS ABOUT SUFFERING. YOU SUFFER AND THEN YOU DIE. THAT
was one of the central teachings of the Buddha. Maybe I had not
taken it to heart before, but I certainly understand it now.

I was suffering. My friend Mary was suffering. We were walking
with thirty-pound backpacks above 13,000 feet in the high desert
of central Tibet. Our pain would end soon enough. We were in the
final hours of a five-day trek (to cover about fifty miles) that we were
trying to do in four; we would reach our destination or collapse.

Less than ten miles away lay the eighth-century monastery of
Samye. Its gilded spires glittered above a green oasis surrounded by
sand dunes. But we were sputtering along like cars running on gasoline fumes. Visions of a bed and hot meal taunted us. (Another of
the Buddha's teachings: desire leads to suffering.)

I had bought bad gas for my camp stove in Lhasa, the capital of
Tibet, and breakfast that morning had consisted of cocoa powder
mixed with cold, iodine-treated water. The same was dinner the
previous night.

We both had diarrhea. Mary was limping because she had aggra-
vated a running injury. On top of that, the hip belt on her pack had
snapped apart.

Neither of us had expected to carry our packs. But our yak driver fell ill the previous day and returned to his village. We were left standing alone on a 16,700-foot pass with our gear. We were also left to find the trail, which disappeared for hours at a time.

We gingerly navigated through a hamlet guarded by vicious dogs. We raced through a village we were told was infested with plague. Now we found ourselves down in the desert by the Yarlung River with snow-capped peaks far to the south. The sun beat down and the wind kicked up dust clouds.

Collapsed next to our packs, we stared with longing at Samye. Around the bend came a monk in scarlet robes and two shaggy nomads wearing fur-lined coats. They grinned. Maybe they pitied us. Maybe they were laughing at us.

They nodded toward the monastery. Keep going, they were saying. Like many Tibetans, they appeared to be pilgrims who spent months wandering from one sacred site to another, sleeping on the ground and cooking with campfires.

Mary and I were embarrassingly sedentary by contrast. We had spent too many hours hunkered down in office cubicles. Our bodies were out of sync with the earth. To get them in tune would take no small amount of suffering. So as the pilgrims turned toward Samye, we put on our packs and fell in step behind them, grimacing.

I had traveled about 8,000 miles, surveyed 3,417 miles during the geographically important part of the journey, crossed sixty-nine passes, all of them rising over 14,500 feet above sea level. I had taken a series of sextant observations at 100 points, made 300 photographs, collected between 300 and 400 ethnological, botanical, and geological specimens. For two months we had lived soaked by the rains and blinded by snow and hail, with little or nothing to eat, and tea as our only beverage; and yet not one of us had a moment's illness from the day we left till we reached our homes again.

—William Rockhill,
American Explorer (1892)

The trek was only a small part of our time in Tibet, but we had intended it to be one of the highlights, a chance to leisurely drink in the spectacle of the Himalayas. This trail was also a pilgrimage route between the Ganden and Samye monasteries, allowing us to experience the rigors of the sacred journey. Samye is the oldest monastery in Tibet. Ganden was the first to train followers of the Gelugpa sect, led by the Dalai Lamas.

The route traversed several desolate valleys and crossed the Yartö Drak range via two passes above 16,000 feet. We understood too well the dangers of altitude sickness. Mary had become severely ill on an earlier trek. After two nights, we had tried evacuating her on a horse, only to have her fall off when the horse bolted. We spent two days recovering and acclimatizing in Lhasa.

From there, we took a pilgrim bus to Ganden that left at dawn. We squeezed into the back beside disheveled nomads who had left behind their yaks and tents to tend to their spiritual obligations. Pilgrimages brought good karma.

The white-walled buildings of the fifteenth-century monastery at Ganden were built into a spectacular bowl at the top of a cliff face twenty-five miles east of Lhasa. The monastery had once been a world unto itself, with more than 2,000 monks living and studying above 14,700 feet. Then the Chinese invaded, eventually destroying most of Ganden during the Cultural Revolution.

Mary and I spent an hour following some families on a high pilgrimage path that circled the monastery. Later, a man sitting outside the monastery guest house yelled out to me. His name was Tsering. He was forty-four and as thin as a stalk of barley. He had two boys, two girls, and ten yaks.

Using hand signals and a few words of Mandarin, he asked whether Mary and I wanted to hire a yak for the pilgrimage to Samye. We settled on $7.50 a day.

After breakfast, Tsering lashed our packs to his yak. I was worried about the beast. It was scrawny. Mucus ran from its eyes. It looked more fit for a slaughterhouse than for crossing mountain passes.

The air was warm, the sky a sharp blue as we set off. The path from the monastery led up to a saddle next to the sacred mountain of Wangku Ri. Far below, clusters of houses dotted the banks of stream beds.

We crossed the ridge and descended to a village, Hebu. A pair of yaks driven by a farmer tilled a barley field. Smoke curled up from several other fields that had been set on fire after a recent harvest.

Winter was arriving. Three black nomad tents had been set up by a small river, neatly spaced out like suburban tract housing.

The nomads had uprooted themselves from a tributary valley to live out the season at a lower elevation. A caravan of a dozen yaks laden with bulging sacks came lumbering down, but we climbed upward.

We made camp in a dry meadow where the nomads lived in warm weather. Rings of stones marked their tent sites, and discarded shoes were scattered about. The Chinese government had once tried to collectivize the nomads, forcing them onto plots of land. But when that policy ended, many of them returned to the rhythm of wandering, stopping, moving on.

By morning, a layer of frost had covered our tent. The

Sour or not, filthy or not, the hospital floor looks pretty good as we take our bed for the night. The evacuation from Lhasa caused by the onset of pulmonary edema was nothing less than miraculous. The day has been one of non-stop phone calls organizing the onward evacuation to Hong Kong. It seems tomorrow we will be fortunate enough to take the cheap route—a commercial carrier will remove three seats, install a stretcher, an M.D. and nurse will arrive in the morning from Hong Kong to escort her out— all for only US$10–12,000. Private evacuations from Lhasa cost between US$60–70,000. Our fortune lies in having found a foreign company which has entered into a joint venture with the People's Liberation Army. That explains why they can get her out so quickly. The PLA can re-designate airspace in minutes if it has to, and there is no incentive like hard cold cash.

—Tim Norris, "Tibet Journals"

streams were iced over. Frozen scrub crunched beneath our boots.

It took about three hours to march up to the Zhukar La, a pass at more than 17,000 feet. While mountain sheep pranced effortlessly on the rock walls, we clambered to the top gasping for breath. Prayer flags fluttered in the wind. We were ecstatic, but Tsering started down immediately, wary of lingering on an exposed pass.

We felt more insignificant than ever in the next valley, dwarfed by the expanse of earth and sky. It was like a scene from old photographs of the American West, with dozens of grazing yaks resembling herds of bison. We had seen no one the entire day.

We made camp in a grassy clearing a few hours short of the second high pass. Snow began falling lightly after dark. Shivering, Mary and I curled up in our sleeping bags. Tsering formed a makeshift shelter near our tent with a plastic tarp and some large rocks. Maybe he knew something we did not, about how to live off the land and survive above 16,000 feet with the barest necessities. But in the morning, he pointed to his head and clutched his stomach. Then he threw up. I gave him some aspirin.

He and Mary were shivering uncontrollably, unable to stay warm as temperatures had dropped below freezing overnight. The valley was still bathed in shadow when we started on the three-hour walk up to the Chetur La, at about 16,700 feet. Tsering stopped several times, sometimes to lie down and rest.

Tsering sat down as soon as we reached the top of the pass. He cradled his head between his hands. Samye was another two days' march. Tsering wanted to leave us with our backpacks and return to Ganden by a shortcut through the valley.

We paid him and gave him a full bottle of water, a pair of gloves, and a rain poncho. He handed us our backpacks. Then he turned around and walked back down the trail that we had just climbed, leading the scrawny yak that still had mucus-covered eyes.

They got smaller and smaller until they disappeared in the distance. We were left alone among the snowcapped peaks. Silence followed. Just like that, we would never see Tsering again. All things passed, nothing remained. The only thing to do was to keep walking, feet firmly on the earth.

We slung our packs over our shoulders and began our journey.

Edward Wong is a business reporter for The New York Times.

Tutor to the Dalai Lama

In 1946, the author of Seven Years in Tibet *became
a teacher in Lhasa—with an extraordinary pupil.*

I WAS RIDING SLOWLY HOME WHEN, A LITTLE WAY OUT OF LHASA, I
was overtaken by an excited soldier of the bodyguard, who told me
that they had been looking for me everywhere and that I must at
once ride back to the Summer Garden. My first thought was that
the cinema apparatus was out of order, as I could hardly imagine
that the young ruler, still a minor, would override all conventions
and summon me directly to see him. I immediately turned round
and was soon back at the Norbulingka, where everything was now
peaceful and still. At the door of the yellow gate a couple of monks
were waiting. As soon as they saw me they signaled to me to hurry
up and when I reached them they ushered me into the Inner
Garden. There Lobsang Samten awaited me. He whispered something to me and put a white scarf in my hand. There was no doubt
about it. His brother was going to receive me.

I at once went towards the cinema, but before I could enter the
door opened from the inside and I was standing before the Living
Buddha. Conquering my surprise, I bowed deeply and handed him
the scarf. He took it in his left hand and with an impulsive gesture
blessed me with his right. It seemed less like the ceremonial laying-
on of hands than an impetuous expression of feeling on the part of

a boy who had at last got his way. In the theater, three abbots were waiting with bowed heads—the guardians of His Holiness. I knew them all well and did not fail to observe how coldly they returned my greeting. They certainly did not approve of this intrusion into their domain, but they had not dared openly to oppose the will of the Dalai Lama.

The young ruler was all the more cordial. He beamed all over his face and poured out a flood of questions. He seemed to me like a person who had for years brooded in solitude over different problems, and now that he had at last someone to talk to, wanted to know all the answers at once. He gave me no time to think over my answers, but pressed me to go to the projector and put on a film which he had long been wanting to see. It was a documentary film of the capitulation of Japan. He came with me to the apparatus and sent the abbots into the theater to act as spectators.

I must have seemed slow and clumsy in handling the projector as he impatiently pushed me to one side and, taking hold of the film, showed me that he was a much more practiced operator than I was. He told me that he had been busy the whole winter learning how to work the apparatus and that he had even taken a projector to pieces and put it together again. I observed then, for the first time, that he liked to get to the bottom of things instead of taking them for granted. And so, later on, like many a good father who wishes to earn the respect of his son, I often spent the evening reviving my knowledge of half-forgotten things or studying new ones. I took the utmost trouble to treat every question seriously and scientifically, as it was clear to me that my answers would form the basis of his knowledge of the Western world.

His obvious talent for technical things astonished me at our first meeting. It was a masterly performance for a boy of fourteen years to take a projector to pieces and then to reassemble it without any help, for he could not read the English prospectus. Now that the film was running well, he was delighted with the arrangements and could not praise my work too highly. We sat together in the projection room and looked at the picture through the peepholes in the wall and he took the greatest pleasure in what he saw and heard, often clasping my hands excitedly with the vivacity of youth. Although it was the first time in his life that he had been alone with a white man he was in no way embarrassed or shy. While he was putting the next film on the reel, he pressed the microphone into my hands and insisted on my speaking into it. At the same time he looked through the peepholes into the electrically lit theater in which his tutors sat on carpets. I could see how keen he was to observe the wondering faces of the worthy abbots when a voice should suddenly come out of the loudspeaker. I did not want to disappoint him so I invited the nonexistent public to remain in their seats as the next film would present sensational scenes from Tibet. He laughed enthusiastically at the surprised and shocked faces of the monks when they heard my cheerful, disrespectful tones. Such light, unceremonious language had never been used in the presence of the Divine Ruler, whose gleaming eyes showed how he enjoyed the situation.

He made me turn the film which I had made in Lhasa while he looked after the switches. I was as curious as he was to see the results, as this was my first full-length picture. An expert could have picked out faults in it, but it seemed quite satisfactory to us. It contained my shots of the "small" New Year Festival. Even the formal abbots forgot their dignity when they recognized themselves on the flickering screen. There was a burst of laughter when a full-length picture appeared of the Minister who had gone to sleep during the ceremonies. There was no malice in their laughter, for each of the abbots had sometimes to struggle to keep awake during these endless festivities. All the same, the upper classes must have got to know that the Dalai Lama had witnessed his Minister's weakness, for afterwards whenever I appeared with my camera, everyone sat up and posed.

The Dalai Lama himself took more pleasure than anyone in the pictures. His usually slow movements became youthful and lively and he commented enthusiastically on every picture. After a while I asked him to turn a film which he had made himself. He very modestly said that he would not dare to show his apprentice efforts after the pictures we had already seen. But I was anxious to see what subjects he had chosen for filming and persuaded him to put his roll on to screen. He had not, of course, had a large choice of subjects. He had done a big sweeping landscape of the valley of Lhasa, which he turned much too fast. Then came a few under-lighted long-distance pictures of mounted noblemen and caravans passing through Shö. A close-up of his cook showed that he would have liked to take film portraits. The film he had shown me was absolutely his first attempt and had been made without instructions or help. When it was over he got me to announce through the microphone that the performance was over. He then opened the door leading into the theater, told the abbots that he did not need them any more and dismissed them with a wave of the hand. It was again clear to me that here was no animated puppet, but a clear-cut individual will capable of imposing itself on others.

When we were alone we cleared away the films and put the yellow covers on the machines. Then we sat down on the magnificent carpet in the theater with the sun streaming through the open windows. It was fortunate that I had long acquired the habit of sitting cross-legged, as chairs and cushions are not included in the Dalai Lama's household furniture. At the start I had wished to decline his invitation to sit down, knowing that even ministers were not supposed to sit in his presence, but he just took me by the sleeve and pulled me down, which put an end to my misgiving.

He told me that he had long been planning this meeting as he had not been able to think of any other way of becoming acquainted with the outside world. He expected the regent to raise objections but he was determined to have his own way and had already thought up a rejoinder in case of opposition. He was resolved to extend his knowledge beyond purely religious subjects, and it seemed to him that I was the only person who could help him to do so. He had no idea that I was a qualified teacher, and had he known this it would probably not have influenced him. He asked my age and was surprised to learn that I was only thirty-seven. Like many Tibetans he thought that my "yellow" hair was a sign of age. He studied my features with childish curiosity and teased me about my long nose, which, though of normal size as we reckon noses, had often attracted the attention of the snub-nosed Mongolians. At last he noticed that I had hair growing on the back of my hands and said with a broad grin: "Henrig, you are as hairy as a monkey." I had an answer ready, as I was familiar with the legend that the Tibetans derive their descent from the union of their god Chenresi with a female demon. Before coupling with his demon-lover Chenresi had assumed the shape of a monkey, and since the Dalai Lama is one of the Incarnations of this god, I found that in comparing me with an ape he had really flattered me.

With remarks such as this our conversation soon became unconstrained and we both lost our shyness. I now felt the attraction of his personality, which at our earlier fleeting contacts I had only guessed at. His complexion was much lighter than that of the average Tibetan. His eyes, hardly narrower than those of most Europeans, were full of expression, charm, and vivacity. His cheeks glowed with excitement, and as he sat he kept sliding from side to side. His ears stood out a little from his head. This was a characteristic of the Buddha and, as I learned later, was one of the signs by which as a child he had been recognized as an Incarnation. His hair was longer than is customary. He probably wore it so as a protection against the cold of the Potala Palace. He was tall for his age and looked like reaching the stature of his parents both of whom had striking figures. Unfortunately, as a result of much study in the seated posture with his body bent forward, he held himself badly. He had beautiful aristocratic hands with long fingers which were generally folded in an attitude of peace. I noticed that he often looked at my hands with astonishment when I emphasized what I was saying with a gesture. Gesticulation is entirely foreign to the Tibetans, who in their reposeful attitudes express the calm of Asia. He always wore the red robe of a monk, once prescribed by Buddha, and his costume differed in no way from that of the monastic officials.

Time passed swiftly. It seemed as if a dam had burst, so urgent and continuous was the flood of questions which he put to me. I was astounded to see how much disconnected knowledge he had acquired out of books and newspapers. He possessed an English work on the Second World War in seven volumes, which he had

had translated into Tibetan. He knew how to distinguish between the different types of airplanes, automobiles, and tanks. The names of personages like Churchill, Eisenhower, and Molotov were familiar to him, but as he had nobody to put questions to, he often did not know how persons and events were connected with each other. Now he was happy, because he had found someone to whom he could bring all the questions about which he had been puzzling for years.

It must have been about three o'clock when Sopön Khenpo came in to say that it was time to eat. This was the abbot whose duty it was to look after the physical welfare of the Dalai Lama. When he gave his message, I immediately rose to my feet meaning to take my leave, but the God-King drew me down again and told the abbot to come again later. He then, very modestly, took out an exercise book with all sorts of drawings on the cover and asked me to look at his work. To my surprise I saw that he had been transcribing the capital letters of the Latin alphabet. What versatility and what initiative! Strenuous religious studies, tinkering with complicated mechanical appliances, and now modern languages! He insisted that I should immediately begin to teach him English, transcribing the pronunciation in elegant Tibetan characters. Another hour must have passed, when Sopön Khenpo came in again and this time insisted that his master should take his dinner. He had a dish of cakes, white bread, and sheep's cheese in his hands which he pressed on me. As I wanted to refuse it, he rolled the food up in a white cloth for me to take home with me.

> Right from the moment of our birth, we are under the care and kindness of our parents. And then later on in our life, when we are oppressed by sickness and become old, we are again dependent on the kindness of others. And since at the beginning and end of our lives, we are so dependent on others' kindness, how can it be in the middle that we neglect kindness towards others?
>
> —H.H. the Dalai Lama

But the Dalai Lama still did not want to end our conversation. In wheedling tones he begged his cup-bearer to wait a little longer. With a loving look at his charge the abbot agreed and left us. I had the feeling that he was as fond of the boy and as devoted as if he had been his father. This white-haired ancient had served the thirteenth Dalai Lama in the same capacity and had remained in the service. This was a great tribute to his trustworthiness and loyalty, for in Tibet when there is a change of masters, there is a change of servants. The Dalai Lama proposed that I should visit his family who lived in the Norbulingka during the summer. He told me to wait in their house till he should send for me. When I left him he shook my hand warmly—a new gesture for him.

As I walked through the empty garden and pushed back the gate bolts, I could hardly realize that I had just spent five hours with the God-King of Tibet. A gardener shut the gate behind me and the guard, which had been changed more than once since I came in, presented arms in some surprise. I rode slowly back to Lhasa and, but for the bundle of cakes which I was carrying, I would have thought it was all a dream. Which of my friends would have believed me if I had told him that I had just spent several hours alone in conversation with the Dalai Lama?

Needless to say I was happy in the new duties that had fallen to my lot. To instruct this clever lad—the ruler of a land as big as France, Spain, and Germany put together—in the knowledge and science of the Western world, seemed a worthwhile task, to say the least.

On the same evening I looked up some reviews which contained details of the construction of jet planes about which I did not know the answers. I had promised to give him full explanations at our next meeting. As time went on I always prepared the material for our lessons, as I wanted to introduce some system into the instruction of this zealous student.

I had many setbacks on account of his insatiable curiosity, which drove him to ask me questions that opened up whole new regions. Many of these questions I could answer only to the best of my lights. In order, for example, to be able to discuss the atom bomb, I had to tell him about the elements. That led to a disquisition on metals, for which there is no generic word in Tibetan, so I had to go into details about the different sorts of metals—a subject which, of course, brought down an avalanche of questions.

My life in Lhasa had now begun a new phase. My existence had an aim. I no longer felt unsatisfied or incomplete. I did not abandon my former duties. I still collected news for the Ministry; I still drew maps. But now the days were all too short and I often worked late into the night. I had little time for pleasures and hobbies, for when the Dalai Lama called me, I had to be free. Instead of going to parties in the morning, as others did, I came late in the afternoon. But that was no sacrifice. I was happy in the consciousness that my life had a goal. The hours I spent with my pupil were as instructive for me as they were for him. He taught me a great deal about the history of Tibet and the teachings of Buddha. He was a real authority on these subjects. We often used to argue for hours on religious subjects and he was convinced that he would succeed in converting me to Buddhism. He told me that he was making a study of books containing knowledge of the ancient mysteries by which the body and the soul could be separated. The history of Tibet is full of stories about saints whose spirits used to perform actions hundreds of miles away from their physical bodies. The Dalai Lama was convinced that by virtue of his faith and by performing the prescribed rites he would be able to make things happen in far-distant places like Samye. When he had made sufficient progress, he said, he would send me there and direct me from Lhasa. I remember saying to him with a laugh: "All right, Kundün, when you can do that, I will become a Buddhist, too."

> This is my simple religion, There is no need for temples; no need for complicated philosophy. Our own brain, our own heart is our temple....
> —H.H. the Dalai Lama

✳

Unfortunately we never got as far as making this experiment. The beginning of our friendship was darkened by political clouds. The tone of the Peking radio became more and more arrogant and Chiang Kai-shek had already withdrawn with his government to Formosa. The National Assembly in Lhasa held one sitting after another; new troops were raised; parades and military exercise were carried out in Shö, and the Dalai Lama himself consecrated the army's new colors....

In these difficult times the state oracle was frequently consulted. His prophecies were dark and did not help to raise the morale of the people. He used to say, "A powerful foe threatens our sacred land from the north and the east." Or, "Our religion is in danger." All the consultations were held in secret but the oracular utterances seeped through to the people and were spread abroad by whisperers. As is usual in times of war and crisis, the whole town buzzed with rumors like a beehive, and the strength of the enemy was swelled to fabulous dimensions. The fortunetellers had a good time, for not only was the fate of the country in the balance but everyone was interested in his own personal welfare. More than ever men sought counsel of the gods, consulted the omens, and gave to every happening a good or bad meaning. Far-sighted people already began to send away their treasures to be stored in the south or in remote estates. But the people as a whole believed that the gods would help them and that a miracle would save the country from war.

The National Assembly had more sober views. It had at last become clear to them that isolationism spelt a grave danger for the country. It was high time to establish diplomatic relations with foreign states and to tell the whole world that Tibet wished to be independent. Hitherto China's claim that Tibet was one of her provinces had remained without contradiction. Newspapers and broadcasters could say what they liked about the country: there was never an answer from Tibet. In conformity with their policy of complete neutrality, the government had refused to explain themselves to the world. Now the danger of this attitude was recognized and people began to grasp the importance of propaganda. Every day Radio Lhasa broadcast its views in Tibetan, Chinese, and English. Missions were appointed by the government to visit Peking, Delhi, Washington, and London. Their members were monastic officials and young noblemen who had learned English in India. But they never got farther than India, thanks to the irresolution of their own Government and the obstruction by the great powers.

The young Dalai Lama realized the gravity of the situation but he did not cease to hope for a peaceful outcome. During my visits I observed what a lively interest the future ruler took in political events. We always met alone in the little cinema-theater, and I was able to understand often from trifling indications how much he looked forward to my coming. Sometimes he came running across the garden to greet me, beaming with happiness and holding out his hand. In spite of my warm feelings toward him and the fact that he called me his friend, I always took care to show him the respect due to the future king of Tibet. He had charged me to give him lessons in English, geography, and arithmetic. In addition, I

If you care about the fate of modern Tibet, consider a donation to the Tibet Information Network. TIN (www.tibetinfo.net) is the only independent comprehensive news and research service in the world specializing in Tibet. TIN monitors and reports on the political, social, economic, environmental, and human rights situation in Tibet today. Based in London, TIN has been providing this service for more than fourteen years and is a world leader in its field.

TIN's main objective is to provide an accurate, impartial news and information service for journalists, development agencies, human rights groups, governments, and international organizations, balancing official statements from Beijing, Lhasa, and Dharamsala, with reliable first-hand testimony from Tibetans themselves.

—JO'R and LH

had to look after his cinema and keep him conversant with world events. He had my pay raised on his own initiative, for though he was not yet constitutionally entitled to give orders, he had only to express a wish for it to be executed.

He continually astonished me by his powers of comprehension, his pertinacity, and his industry. When I gave him for homework ten sentences to translate, he usually showed up with twenty. He was quick at learning languages, as are most Tibetans. It is quite common for people of the upper class and businessmen to speak Mongolian, Chinese, Nepalese, and Hindi. My pupil's greatest difficulty was to pronounce the letter "F", which does not occur in Tibetan. As my English was far from being perfect, we used to listen to the English news on a portable radio and took advantage of the passages spoken at dictation speed.

I had been told that in one of the government offices there were a number of English schoolbooks stored in sealed cases. A hint was given to the Ministry and on the same day the books were sent up to the Norbulingka. We made a little library for them in the theater. My pupil was delighted at this discovery, which was something quite out of the ordinary for Lhasa. When I observed his zeal and thirst for knowledge I felt quite ashamed at the thought of my own boyhood.

There were also numerous English books and maps from the estate of the thirteenth Dalai Lama, but I noticed that they looked new and had obviously not been read. The late ruler had learned much during his journeys in India and China, and it was to his friendship with Sir Charles Bell that he owed his knowledge of the Western world. I was already familiar with the name of this Englishman and had read his books during my internment. He was a great champion of Tibetan independence. As political liaison officer for Sikkim, Tibet, and Bhutan, he had gotten to know the Dalai Lama on his flight to India. This was the beginning of a close friendship between the two men which lasted for many years. Sir Charles Bell was, doubtless, the first white man to come into contact with a Dalai Lama.

My young pupil was not yet in a position to travel, but that did not diminish his interest in world geography, which was soon his favorite subject. I drew for him great maps of the world and others of Asia and Tibet. We had a globe, with the help of which I was able to explain to him why Radio New York was eleven hours behind Lhasa. He soon felt at home in all countries and was as familiar with the Caucasus as with the Himalayas. He was particularly proud of the fact that the highest summit in the world was on his frontier, and like many Tibetans was astonished to learn that few countries exceeded his kingdom in area.

Our peaceful lessons were disturbed this summer by an untoward event. On August 15th, a violent earthquake caused a panic in the Holy City. Another evil omen! The people had hardly got over their fright caused by the comet, which in the previous year had been visible by day and night like a gleaming horsetail in the heavens. Old people remembered that the last comet had been the precursor of a war with China.

The earthquake came as a complete surprise, without premonitory tremors. The houses of Lhasa began suddenly to shake and one heard in the distance some forty dull detonations, caused no doubt by a crack in the crust of the earth. In the cloudless sky a huge glow was visible to the east. The aftershocks lasted for days. The Indian radio reported great landslides in the province of Assam, which borders Tibet. Mountains and valleys were displaced and the Brahmaputra, which had been blocked by a fallen mountain, had caused immense devastation. It was not till a few weeks later that news came to Lhasa of the extent of the catastrophe in Tibet itself. The epicenter of the earthquake must have been in South Tibet. Hundreds of monks and nuns were buried in their rock-monasteries and often there were no survivors to carry the news to the nearest district officer. Towers were split down the middle, leaving ruined walls pointing to the sky, and human beings, as if snatched by a demon's hand, disappeared into the suddenly gaping earth.

The evil omens multiplied. Monsters were born. One morning the capital of the stone column at the foot of the Potala was found lying on the ground in fragments. In vain did the Government send monks to the centers of ill-omen to banish the evil spirits with their prayers, and when one day in blazing summer weather water began to flow from the gargoyle on the cathedral, the people of Lhasa were beside themselves with terror. No doubt natural explanations could have been found for all these happenings, but if the Tibetans lost their superstitiousness they would at the same time lose an asset. One has to remember that if evil portents can demoralize them with fear, good omens inspire them with strength and confidence.

The Dalai Lama was kept informed of all these sinister events. Though naturally as superstitious as his people, he was always curious to hear my views on these things. We never lacked matter for conversation and our lesson time was all too short. He actually spent his leisure hours with me, and few people realized that he was using his free time for further study. He kept punctually to his program, and if he awaited my coming with pleasure, that did not prevent him from breaking off as soon as the clock told him that our conversation time was over, and that a teacher of religion was waiting for him in one of the pavilions.

I once learned by chance what store he set by our lessons. One day, on which many ceremonies were to take place, I did not expect to be called to the Norbulingka and so went with friends for a walk on a hill near the town. Before I started, I told my servant to flash me a signal with a mirror if the Dalai Lama sent for me. At the usual hour the signal came and I ran at top speed back into the town. My servant was waiting with a horse at the ferry but, fast as I rode, I was ten minutes late. The Dalai Lama ran to meet me and excitedly grasped both my hands, calling: "Where have you been all this time? I have been waiting so long for you, Henrig." I begged him to pardon me for having distressed him. It was only then that I realized how much these hours meant to him.

On the same day his mother and youngest brother were present, and I showed them one of the eighty films which the Dalai Lama possessed. It was very interesting for me to see the mother and son together. I knew that from the moment of the official recognition of the boy as the Incarnate Buddha the family had no more claim on him as a son or brother. For that reason his mother's visit was a sort of official event, to which she came in all her finery and jewels. When she left, she bowed before him and he laid his hand on her head in blessing. This gesture well expressed the relation of these two persons to one another. The mother did not even receive the two-handed blessing which was accorded only to monks and high officials.

It very seldom happened that we were disturbed when we were together. Once a monk of the bodyguard brought him an important letter. The huge fellow threw himself three times to the ground, drew in his breath with a panting sound as the etiquette demands, and delivered the letter. He then withdrew from the room, walking backwards, and closed the door silently behind him. In such moments I was very conscious how greatly I myself offended against the protocol.

The letter I have mentioned came from the eldest brother of the Dalai Lama, the abbot of Kumbum in the Chinese province of Chinghai. The Reds were already in power there and they were now hoping to influence the Dalai Lama in their favor through his brother Tagtsel Rimpoche. The letter announced that Tagtsel was on the way to Lhasa.

On the same day I visited the Dalai Lama's family. His mother scolded me when I arrived. Her mother's love had not failed to

As you enter a temple or shrine, angle to the left in the respectful, clockwise manner. Keep prayer walls and offering cairns to your right, and walk clockwise around the pilgrim circuits. If monks are chanting or involved with a religious service, it's not a problem to walk quietly around the room. If they ask you to join them on the rows of cushions where they are sitting, go right ahead. Take your shoes off first, then sit cross-legged. Get into the habit of carrying a cup in your daypack, for you'll undoubtedly be offered butter tea. If you don't like butter tea or have had enough, politely say *me*, which means no, and put your hand over the cup. They will still try hard to serve you more.

—Gary McCue, *Trekking in Tibet: A Traveler's Guide*

notice how much he depended on me and how often he had looked at the clock as he waited for my coming. I explained why I had not come in time and was able to convince her that my unpunctuality had not been due to casualness. When I left her she begged me never to forget how few chances of enjoying himself in his own way her son had. It was perhaps a good thing that she had seen herself how much our lesson hours meant to the Dalai Lama. After a few months everyone in Lhasa knew where I was riding about noon. As was to be expected, the monks criticized my regular visits, but his mother stood up for her son's wishes.

The next time I came through the yellow gate into the Inner Garden I thought I noticed the Dalai Lama looking out for me from his little window, and it seemed as if he was wearing glasses. This surprised me as I had never seen him with spectacles on. In answer to my question he told me that he had for some time been having difficulty with his eyes and had therefore taken to wearing glasses for study. His brother had procured him a pair through the Indian Legation. He had probably damaged his eyes when he was a child, when his only pleasure was to look for hours through his telescope at Lhasa. Moreover, continuous reading and study in the twilight of the Potala were not exactly calculated to improve his sight. On this occasion he was wearing a red jacket over his monastic robe. He had designed it himself and was very proud of it, but he allowed himself to wear it only in his leisure moments. The chief novelty about this garment was the fact that it had pockets. Tibetan clothes do not have any, but the designer had noticed the existence of pockets in the illustrated papers and in my jackets and had realized how useful they might be. Now, like every other boy of his age, he was able to carry about with him a knife, a screwdriver, sweets, etc. He also now kept his colored pencils and fountain pens in his pockets and was, doubtless, the first Dalai Lama to take pleasure in such things. He was also much interested in his collection of watches and clocks, some of which he had inherited from the thirteenth Dalai Lama. His favorite piece was an Omega calendar-clock which he had bought with his own money which was left as an offering at the foot of his throne. Later on the treasure vaults of the Potala and the

Garden of Jewels would be open to him and, as ruler of Tibet, he would become one of the world's richest men.

Heinrich Harrer, Austrian mountaineer and Olympic skiing champion, was climbing in the Himalayas when, caught up in the outbreak of World War II, he was interned by the British in India. With a companion, he escaped and crossed the Himalayas into Tibet. After many hardships and adventures, they reached the Forbidden City of Lhasa, where they were eventually allowed to live and work. They found a new appetite for Western knowledge and ideas, and soon were in great demand as advisers on many subjects. Eventually Harrer was presented to the young Dalai Lama and became the boy's friend and tutor. After the end of the war, Harrer stayed on, but after the Communist Chinese invaded Tibet he accompanied the Dalai Lama in flight to India, and then returned to Europe.

Around the Jokhang

It's the very heart of Lhasa, and all things Tibetan.

I FOLLOWED THE DIRECTION IN WHICH BARBARA HAD POINTED AND found myself on the edge of the square at the opening to the Jokhang temple. Deep behind the whitewashed walls of the opening passage, red painted pillars, the width of stout men, support a balcony draped in yak haircloth. Two gilded deer and a dharma wheel shine down from over the balcony on all who pass beneath. But your attention is not held by any of the interesting structural technicalities or adornments of the building, instead it is focused on the people who crowd the forecourt.

The granite paving stones are worn to a polish that no hotel housekeeper could ever produce. Apart from the lapse during the Cultural Revolution, every day for hundreds of years has seen many thousands of prostrations over these slabs. With hands first clasped together in front of the head, the chest and the waist, each prostrater then lies flat down on the ground with arms outstretched in the direction of the temple.

Merit is what Buddhism is all about. At least that is what I had gathered so far from my meager research into the subject. I had found most books on Buddhism terribly difficult to digest—all those incomprehensible names and anatomically impossible beings.

I could guess that the Eleven-Headed One Thousand-Armed Avalokitesvara would not be a bodhisattva to take on at table tennis, but I had yet to consider any of the more complex ideologies of Buddhism.

Without going into tiresome detail and very long names, the simple formula to follow is that the more merit you have gained during this lifetime, the better your chance of being reincarnated as something higher than an earwig in the next. If you are really pious and score high numbers of merit points, you could come back as a human being again and if you earn just those few more points you could come back as a rich nobleman or a high lama, instead of having to be a down-trodden peasant again. It's a bit like collecting air miles.

Hitting the jackpot, in terms of merit, would be to score so many points that you could leave the endless cycle of rebirths and achieve nirvana. Once you have reached this Buddhist's bingo there are no more worries about who or what you are going to come back to.

The first-time walker around the Barkhor is momentarily mystified by the sound of prostrating pilgrims. Their mumbled *"Om Mani Padme Om"* prayers are rhythmically punctuated by the combined sounds of their heavy exhalations—almost like someone being punched in the gut—and the sliding of their wood-shod hands as they hit and skate across the stony deck of the Barkhor. It is a sound that one never forgets.

—Mike Gill, "Lhasa Notes"

With this clear incentive to keep prostrating, some manage to keep going for over a thousand prostrations per day. Others stick to the holy number of 108, which is quite difficult enough. To ease the pain of sliding outstretched across the granite, special gloves fashioned in the shape of small clogs are often worn. Aprons can be used to protect clothing from wearing out and women prostrating will often tie their long dresses close around their ankles if they are going in for a lengthy session.

Around the temple entrance is also where the first-time visitor to Tibet has his initial encounter with an unfamiliar odor: yak butter. Or the more fragrant variety: rancid yak butter. It is brought into the temple by devout pilgrims who carry blocks of the yellow grease in yak bladder bags. They scoop the butter out by the spoonful into each of the stone and silver vessels of yak butter which burn in the holy chambers of the temple. Yak butter is not an easy odor to forget. It clings to every person in the Barkhor, to every item sold in the stalls, to every piece of clothing. Even when you think that you have left Tibet far behind, the smell of yak butter will still be lingering in your suitcases, waiting to hit you when you open them to pack for next year's holiday.

Fortunately, two holy incense burners are within a few yards of the temple entrance, and a step towards them brings the very pleasing fragrance of a blend of burning juniper and a finely scented artemisia. Piles of dried herbs and small bundles of wood collected from high in the hills around Lhasa are offered for sale to those who did not bring their own supplies for the burners.

We'd seen the prostrating pilgrims in animal skins and callused foreheads, the whirling prayer wheels and flapping prayer flags, but nothing prepared us for the scene inside the Jokhang. It was the destination of thousands who had inchwormed hundreds of miles, and now they all seemed to be here at once. The dark room glowed with the light of yak-butter lamps, the scent of burning butter rising sweet and rancid, the space filled with the guttural chant of monks. The pilgrims scraped butter from jars onto altars before Buddhas, spooned barley flour from pouches onto piles in silver bowls, wedged supplications into woodwork. We were wraiths in their single-minded path to worship; the best we could do was marvel at a scene that has not changed in hundreds of years.

—Larry Habegger,
"Glimpses of Tibet"

Starting from the entrance to the Jokhang temple, the market street continues clockwise in a half-mile perimeter circuit right around the temple and back to the entrance again. By no small coincidence the market street is also a holy walk. Every temple, monastery, holy mountain, holy lake, and holy entity is surrounded by a holy walk known as a *kora*, and by walking this *kora* in a clockwise direction you gain merit. All these merit points keep adding to your running total of merit to give you a better chance for a good reincarnation next time around. The beauty of the Barkhor bazaar is that you can gain merit and do your shopping at the same time.

A ramshackle collection of metal stalls lines each side of the street selling a mixture of imports, antiques, fakes, and forgeries. Trinkets from Kathmandu and nylon clothes from China share stands with Tibetan rugs and traditional jewelry. Bulky silver rings studded with beads of red coral or turquoise, heavy-set earrings of gold, old Indian coins made into brooches, and any amount of religious paraphernalia are all on offer for sale.

The word "antique" is used for anything which dates from pre-1959, when the Dalai Lama went into exile. Customs laws are strict in China and they declare that anything that is "antique" or a "cultural relic" cannot be removed from the country.

"Holy turquoise!" called out a Khampa girl, thrusting a piece of blue plastic in my face and then running off down the street giggling to her friends. I followed, caught up in the clockwise stream of bodies that flows continually around the Barkhor. Only the most ignorant tourist and a few belligerent Chinese attempt to walk against the flow.

Just past the Jokhang entrance on the main Barkhor street I was attacked by a small child. A boy of no more than five years of age grabbed my right leg and clung on as hard as he could while launching into his sales pitch in perfect English: "I have no money. I have no parents. I have no money. I have no parents. I have no money. Please give me money. I have no parents. I have no money. Please give me money…"

The "Rapper," as we called him, was the most persistent of all the Barkhor beggars. His ruthlessly pitiful approach was used to great effect. He could only be shaken off with either a considerable amount of force or a large contribution to his funds which he would then take back to his parents who eagerly awaited him at the front of the temple.

One of the favorite claims by the Chinese is that they eradicated begging when they liberated Tibet in 1951 and that they turned the beggars into "the new proletariat of the New Tibet."

I pictured the Rapper clinging to the leg of a die-hard Communist and wondered who would win: the lecture on the no-begging policy of New Tibet, or a contribution to the Rapper's welfare funds?

For the Tibetans, there has never been anything unwholesome about begging. There are claims that before the Chinese entered Tibet there were some 20,000 beggars making their living across the country. In the constant search throughout life to gain merit, giving money to beggars scores high points and giving money to beggars in the Barkhor scores some of the highest merit points of all. For some pilgrims the walk to Lhasa, their spiritual capital, was the accomplishment of a

---

Tribesmen and traders have come from the far corners of Tibet and beyond to be at this place, and everyone is curious. There's a group of big Khampa men from the east standing transfixed, watching the local dentist bang on a man's front teeth with a large hammer and chisel. Up ahead looks like Yak World. Several herdsmen sit on the edge of the street displaying huge bloody chunks of freshly quartered yak meat. Next to them is the dairy section. Big blocks of yak butter sit waiting to be used for cooking, candle-making, moisturizer, whatever. There's a slow natural transition as you move down the boulevard from fresh butter, to older ripening butter, to kilo chunks of hard cheese. Across the street is a fine selection of yak pelts, yak bones, and yak sinew. The yak is their buffalo, their provider.

—William Eigen, "At Large in the Common World"

lifetime which had taken their entire life savings to achieve. They would beg in the Barkhor to raise enough money to see them through the trip home.

Colonel Waddell, who accompanied the British invasion of Tibet in 1904 and who may well have had the Rapper's great, great grandfather around his leg, described the Barkhor beggars as "repulsively dirty." It is a description which could be used very accurately today and after removing the Rapper and his sticky lollypop from my trouser leg, I set off down the side streets for some relief from the bombardment of sensations at the Barkhor.

In the narrow streets behind the Barkhor I would find my favorite part of Lhasa, where time has stood still for hundreds of years. Streets twist and turn, sometimes thirty feet wide, sometimes six feet wide, veering off at right angles between old whitewashed stone buildings three to four stories high with black trapezoid windows. Here you only see Tibetan faces—the Chinese do not venture alone down these little alleyways.

One street corner always has a ram tethered to a door post. He has a very short rope and can only stand or sit on the large granite doorstep. There is never any food visible yet he is permanently chewing something, sitting on his doorstep gazing at the world going by. Sheep are often saved from the slaughterhouse by Tibetans who take them on as pets. It is thought that this saving of a soul from death is a very merit-worthy action and therefore adds to the running total of merit of the new sheep owner. It is quite common to see Tibetans walking around the Barkhor with a sheep on a lead, or taking a couple of sheep on a long pilgrimage.

At least I used to hope that this ram was one of the saved ones. It did dawn on me one day that perhaps it was a different ram there every time and that they were just being fattened up for slaughter.

In a dimly lit doorway across from the ram, an old Tibetan lady in full Tibetan dress slices a turnip on a chopping board across her lap. Another spins wool into thread. Small girls lean out of first floor windows calling, "Hello, *tashi delai*, hello!" to passersby. Everyone has time to greet you, whether by a smile, a nod, a *tashi delai*, or occasionally by the really traditional greeting of sticking a tongue out at you. This is the Tibet of the past that so many wish was still here today.

Trying to find my way back to the Barkhor market, I found myself trapped between two narrow streets filled with excrement and the decaying carcasses of dogs. The pungent stench of rotting flesh and maggot-infested pools sent me scrambling for the fresh air of the open square. Even rancid yak butter was perfume compared with this. Halfway down the narrow alley, at a point where the path consisted of stepping stones through the sewage, two men came out of a doorway, their eyes wide with excitement and their breath heavy with a strong alcohol. They stopped in front of me, blocking the only dry path through the nauseous street. Both had the distinctive profiles of Khampas. They stood tall and proud with red braid wrapped across their matted black hair. One was bare-chested with his *chuba*, the Tibetan cloak, tied around his waist. They stared at me in silence for some time, looking me up and down. Their surly expressions did not change and they held firm their position blocking the only dry exit. There was no one else around. There were no old ladies in the doorways, no little children smiling and waving from the windows. Alone in excrement alley face-to-face with two alcohol-steaming Khampas, I was a long way up the creek without a paddle.

"*Do drigey rey?*" the bare-chested one broke the silence.

I had no idea what he was saying.

"*Do drigey rey?*" he shouted.

I smiled at him but to no avail. He pulled a sword from its sheath, stooped over me and held it up to my chest. Why had I been so mean to the Rapper? Is this what happens if you don't earn merit? Where was a Chinese soldier when you needed one?

The other Khampa looked over his shoulder and moved in closer to me. "*Katse rey?*" he called out with a nod of his head. The bare-chested one waved the sword closer to my face. Sunlight flashed in my eyes as he tilted the steel blade towards me. I could even see every detail of the intricate engravings running along the center of the blade between the two razor edges.

He withdrew the sword, pointed to the space beside us and made a series of cuts in the air to demonstrate a nifty disemboweling motion. He shook it in front of my face again.

"*Katse rey? Katse rey!?*" he shouted.

The bare-chested one frowned in thought, recalling the only English words which he must have heard from his wife.

"You how much?" he called to me.

It was with an enormous sense of relief that I suddenly realized they were not threatening to decapitate me if I crossed their path, but were merely trying to sell me the sword. Their scowls turned into broad gold-capped grins as I took the sword and examined it closely. The swirling engravings of the steel blade ended abruptly inside a gaping dragon's mouth of silver which formed the base of the handle. The body of the dragon curled around on itself to provide the bulk of the grip. It was newly made, perhaps one of the imports from Kathmandu, and certainly practical for the man about town. But disemboweling daggers were not high on my shopping list and I had no intention of buying it, I just wanted to get out of the place with dry feet and in one piece.

I shook my head and passed the sword back to him. Recalling Tashi's words of greeting at the airport, I ventured the only Tibetan words that I knew: "*Tashi delai.*" This earned me a great slap on the back that pushed me dangerously close to the edge of the excrement area. My two new Khampa friends strode off down the lane howling with laughter.

There are only so many smells and sensations that the body can take on the first day of reaching an altitude of 12,000 feet, so after I had found my way back to the Barkhor I haggled for another rickshaw to return to the hotel.

Alec Le Sueur graduated with a degree in hotel management and worked for several of the world's top hotels before making the strangest decision of his career—to work as sales manager for the Holiday Inn in Lhasa. He spent five years there, working and traveling and spawning the book, Running a Hotel on the Roof of the World, *from which this story was excerpted. He has since moved back to his native Jersey in the U.K. and now works as the marketing manager for Jersey Tourism.*

The Realm of the
Clouded Leopard

*A small group of men search for a beast
as mythical as the spirit of Tibet.*

OUR PURPOSE WAS NOT TO CLIMB EVEREST BUT RATHER TO explore the hidden drainage of the Kama Chu, the river that begins in the ice at the base of the East Face. There, in what the British described as the most beautiful valley in the Himalayas, amid meadows and rocky ledges overlooking the Kangshung Glacier, live snow leopards and blue sheep. Beyond the river to the south soars a wall of ice mountains—Lhotse, sister to Everest, Chomo Lönzo, and Pethangtse, each higher than anything in North America, and finally Makalu, by all accounts the most stunning peak on Earth, fifth in height but unmatched in beauty. In twenty-three miles, the Kama Chu falls 14,000 feet, dropping over a spectacular series of waterfalls into the deepest ravine on Earth, the canyon of the Arun, a river older than the Himalayas.

Beneath the cliffs and ice fields of Makalu, a mere fifteen miles from the base of Everest, thrive immense forests of juniper and fir. Further downstream, in thickets of bamboo and rhododendron, mountain ash and birch, we hoped to find the most elusive cat of all, the clouded leopard, a creature so rare and mysterious that early observers traced its lineage to the saber-toothed tiger. Secretive and solitary, possibly nocturnal, it had never been photographed in the wild in Central Asia. Local legend describes it as a tree dweller, half human, and capable of leaping twice its body length as it moves through the branches hunting monkeys and pheasants, falling like a shadow to the ground to kill musk deer and red pandas.

Weighing no more than sixty pounds, far less than a snow leopard, with a total length of perhaps six feet, including the tail, the clouded leopard is relatively small, but its upper canines are especially prominent, larger in relationship to the skull size that those of any other cat, hence the comparison to the saber-toothed tiger. Photographs of the animals in captivity reveal penetrating eyes, enormous paws, and for balance an unusually long tail, thick to the tip. The chest is a blaze of white, the dense coat mottled with dark rosettes that float like clouds in the rich yellowish fur. Whereas the snow leopard generally lives above treeline close to the ice, the clouded leopard lives in the forests below 12,000 feet. Once found throughout Asia from the foothills of the Himalayas to the islands of Borneo and Sumatra, its range has been much reduced and the animal has become a true avatar of the wild.

To seek the clouded leopard in the valley that leads to the base of Qomolangma [the Tibetan name for Everest] was a quixotic idea, the dream of two Americans, father and son, Daniel and Jesse Taylor-Ide. Fluent in Hindi, Daniel grew up in the foothills of the Himalayas, the son and grandson of medical missionaries.

Jesse, like his father, was born in America but nursed in the Himalayas. At the age of six months he was taken by his parents in a canoe through the jungles of Nepal as they sought and found the mythical Octagon Well, the sacred Hindu site where Rama and Sitamet met and loved. At two, he was carried on his father's back for two months through the jungles of the Barun Valley, as a team of adventurers and scholars sought proof of the existence of the yeti, the hairy manlike beast known to the West as the abominable snowman. At five, he first saw the Potala Palace in Lhasa, home of the Dalai Lama, and climbed up the narrow passageways that opened into dark chambers where placid Buddhas were illuminated by tiny candles. In rooms full of treasure, he watched as old wizened pilgrims placed coins into heaps of yak butter. When he was nine he slept in the meadows of the Kyirong, a member of the first foreign party to enter the valley since Heinrich Harrer had departed to write his book, *Seven Years in Tibet*. That same season Jesse walked around Kailash, the mountain sacred to Hindu and Buddhist alike, the source of the Indus and Brahmaputra. At fifteen, he first entered the Kama Valley, and with his father made the second ascent of Kartze, a 21,700-foot peak climbed first by George Mallory in 1921 as he sought a route to the summit of Everest. Unlike Mallory, Jesse hauled a snowboard to the top and slipped off the mountain to complete the second-highest run ever made.

"Isolation was in our blood," the Dalai Lama once wrote. Distilling several thousand years of history into a single phrase, His Holiness perfectly captured the Tibet of Western imagination, a serene and lofty kingdom, hidden behind a veil of myth and mountains, a peaceful people disengaged from time, living alone on the roof of the world. Such an image is easy to embrace in the dawn light on the summit of the Pang La, a 17,000-foot pass on the dirt road that runs south from Shekar 130 kilometers toward Kharta and the northern approaches to Everest. In bitter cold, amid a small forest of rock cairns, we watched the sun rise over the Himalayan range, a solid wall of mountains, including four of the five highest on Earth, each soaring above 26,000 feet. Running from Kanchenjunga in the east through Makalu, Lhotse, Everest, Nuptse, and Cho Oyu is the planet's greatest geological panorama, the slow drama of two worlds in collision. Forty million years ago

---

I remember Pang La as a stark, stony place where I spent an eternity shaking like a leaf in an inadequate sleeping bag, kept awake by helpless crescendos of clattering teeth and the gulping of air by my oxygen-starved tent-mate. The only relief was getting up and urinating under an astonishing sky, at once the darkest and brightest I'd ever seen.

—James O'Reilly,
"Notes from the Roof"

the Indian subcontinent drifted away from Africa and slipped beneath Asia, crushing the face of a continent and rolling back the Earth's crust like a carpet to form mountains that to this day grow skyward at a rate of half an inch per year. Such was the force of impact that an area of land half the size of the United States was lifted from sea level to 15,000 feet, thus forming the Tibetan plateau. As the mountains rose, the Arun River, flowing south since the dawn of time, cut a deeper and deeper canyon, through sediments laden with fossil seashells and valleys that reached to the sky.

Coming out of the Pang La, descending rapidly through a series of switchbacks, the road passes through small settlements into valleys and canyons lined with marbled stones and contorted cliffs. Near the village of Phagdruchi the road forks, with one branch heading for Rongbuk and the base camp of Everest, the other heading for Kharta and the passes leading to the Kama Chu. Following this route, dropping to the drainage of the Arun, we drove along a narrow dirt track through a landscape dominated by ruins, all that remains of the dozens of ancient fortifications that once guarded the approaches to Nepal. Here was the image of another Tibet, less a land of isolation, hermetically sealed from the winds of time, than a crossroads of trade and empire sitting atop the heart of Asia.

Westerners, of course, knew little of old Tibet. Until 1979 fewer than two thousand had entered the nation, and most of these were members of the British invasion force of 1904, under the command of Sir Francis Younghusband. But if Europeans had trouble reaching Lhasa, others did not. In the eighteenth century the streets of the Tibetan capital were crowded with Tartars, Muscovites, Chinese, Kashmiris, and Nepalese, merchants and traders who came from all parts of central Asia. Monasteries drew monks and pilgrims from as far away as the Black Sea. Elements of Tibetan dress are found in the court costumes of Persia.

Nor were Tibetans always peaceful. Their armies fought the Ladhakis in 1681, took on the Mongols in 1720, rallied against Nepalese invaders in 1788-1792 and again in 1854. Younghusband had to fight his way to Lhasa in 1904, killing more than 1,000 Tibetan soldiers in pitched battles. Indeed, the ebb and flow of warfare has swept over Tibet for centuries. The image of the land as an earthly paradise, the culture a cosmic meritocracy, is an illusion.

Like any complex society, Tibet had great inequalities. Power was concentrated in the hands of an aristocratic elite, dominated by the great Gelugpa monasteries. The selection of the Dalai Lama was an awesome event, inspired by oracles and infused with magical and cosmological significance, all derived from the Buddhist belief that a bodhisattva chooses the moment and place of reincarnation. But the process was not removed from politics. The entire ritual complex, the dispatching of search parties, the interpretation of signs, the very notion that the memory and spiritual authority of an elder could be reborn in the soul of a child, was, at least in part, a seventeenth-century invention. In subsequent years several young boys, ordained by divination and anointed as gods, failed to reach maturity, their lives severed by intrigue and deception. At least one Dalai Lama was poisoned. Another died in bed when an enemy sawed away the posts supporting the roof of the room. A third dispensed with Buddhist vows altogether to revel in love and sensual trysts on an island in a lake at the foot of the Potala Palace.

The kids are on us before we have our tents staked, swarming like flies. Medicine and candy are the most requested items. One woman in a striped *panden* (the apron of a married woman) hits up our guide, Gary McCue, for eye drops; when he politely declines, her seven-year-old daughter begins to pummel him with her little fists. He backs away with a grin and calls her a nasty little marmot. No one has greater love and respect for these complex people than Gary, but his policy is firm: "I don't give food, or money, or medicine when they beg or demand it. And I *never* give out pictures of His Holiness. It can get us all in big trouble—and put them in prison."

—Tom Joyce, "Yeti, Flying Saints, and Boys with Guns"

The fact that Tibetans are mortal, a people of politics and power as well as the spirit, in no way belittles their legacy. To the contrary, a realistic knowledge of their history and traditions reinforces the legitimacy of their sovereignty. The roots of the current conflict between China and Tibet go back to the thirteenth century and the Mongol conquest of Asia. Tibetans submitted to Genghis Khan in 1207 and within forty years were providing religious instruction to the invaders. In 1279 the Mongols under Kubla Khan conquered China, founding the Yuan dynasty and bringing the ancient land into an empire that already included Tibet. The Chinese today trace their claims to this moment, when both nations succumbed to the Mongols. The Tibetans, by contrast, remember that distant era as the time when two sovereign nations fell in succession to a single enemy. When the Yuan dynasty collapsed, Tibet reclaimed its independence.

The country that emerged over the centuries was not a perfect society, but its failures and complexities were its own. Looking south and east, fending off invasions, struggling with civil strife and intrigue from within, Tibetans engaged the sordid realities of nationhood. When the Nepalese invaded in 1788, reaching Shigatse and looting the sacred

---

The term "Tibet" generally refers to the entire Tibetan Plateau (geographic Tibet), an area encompassing over 800,000 square miles or about one-quarter the size of the continental United States. This includes the four traditional regions of Tibet: Ü and Tsang (Lhasa and Shigatse were the original capitals, respectively), which together comprise Central Tibet; Ngari-korsum, the westernmost land of nomadic herders in the northeast; and Kham, the forested, easternmost edge of the Plateau. The Chinese province of Tibet, the Tibet Autonomous Region (TAR), is a political entity created in 1965 that makes up half the geographic area of the Tibetan Plateau, covering 470,000 square miles.

—Gary McCue, *Trekking in Tibet: A Traveler's Guide*

monastery of Tashilhunpo, Tibet forged an alliance with China. The Qing emperor dispatched an army that vanquished the Nepalese and then, in the wake of victory, refused to leave. The Chinese maintained a modest presence in Lhasa until Qing influence faded in the late nineteenth century. By then China faced its own enemies, European powers descending on Asia from the eastern sea. In the early years of this century, Chinese authority in Tibet was symbolic, marginal at best. Whatever claim they had ended in 1911 with the overthrow of the Qing dynasty. From 1913 until the invasion of the Red Army in 1949, Tibet was again an independent nation, albeit a complex land on the cusp of change. The very idea of China today claiming Tibet, a land and people unique by any ethnographic or historical definition, is as anachronistic as England laying claim to America simply because it was once a British colony.

Our road ended at a wooden footbridge over the Kharta Chu, a rushing mountain stream draining a broad treeless valley strewn with boulders. Across the way, on a rise overlooking the river, was the small village of Yueba, a cluster of stone houses emerging from the earth. The land was beautiful—the brown and russet of fields, the pale yellow of barley stalks, a distant copse of juniper around a small monastery on the flank of a mountain dusted with snow. Within minutes of our arrival at the trailhead, villagers appeared, herdsmen in sheepskin coats and homespun woolen trousers, old men and women thumbing dark beads and spinning silver and copper prayer wheels, mothers and young children with faces blackened by yak butter and charcoal.

Under their watchful eyes, we set up camp and awaited the rest of our party. There were eleven of us, including local officials, traveling in three Land Cruisers. The bulk of the supplies and gear followed in a larger truck, along with three Sherpas hired as cooks in Kathmandu. Our translator was a government employee named Lhakpa, a Tibetan from Shegar who had been raised in Dharamsala. Tall and handsome, with a gentle manner and easy smile, he seemed ill cast in his role as a forest warden. His green uniform hung loosely on his long limbs. The military cap, a size too large, tilted at an angle that appeared either rakish or clumsy depending on the moment. Like the local farmers and herders, he wore canvas sneakers made in China, miserable footwear for a march through ice and snow.

While Daniel and Lhakpa met with the villagers and settled on a price for hiring yaks to continue our journey, the rest of us stayed in camp, taking care of the last-minute preparations that invariably mark the eve of an expedition. Talk for the most part was about the strange turn of the weather. November in the Himalayas is normally a month of clear skies, warm days, and cold nights, ideal for trekking. This year the winter had come early, and snow already blanketed the three high passes leading from the Kharta Valley south into the Kama Chu. When the British first scouted Everest from the east in 1921, they moved through this very camp, up the Kharta River and over the distant Langma La, an 18,000-foot pass that leads to the Kangshung or East Face of the mountain. Our plan was to climb the Samchung La, the first of the passes, and then traverse the splendid valley of the fourteen lakes to drop into the Kama farther downstream. En route we would set cameras, above and below the treeline, and in the dense forests of the lower river. Then, proceeding up valley toward the East Face, we would establish more traps on the rocky ledges and in the meadows frequented by snow leopards and blue sheep. After ten days, Daniel and I, with the rest of our party, would return to Kharta over the Langma La. Jesse, accompanied by a guide, would retrace our journey, retrieving the cameras, and meet us in Kharta.

It was a fine plan that dissolved in the reality of the season. The yak herders, once hired, informed Daniel that two of the passes, the Langma La and Samchung La, were too deep in snow to permit safe passage. That left the Shao La, the route the British had taken in August of 1921 when they retreated from Everest, having abandoned the East Face. Howard-Bury had led the way, climbing in thick rain, through juniper growing at the edge of snowfields, past beautiful lakes and covens of Himalayan snowcocks feeding in open grass beneath the ice. With luck, Daniel was told, we might traverse the Shao La, follow the Kama Chu to the base of Qomolangma, and return before the snows became too deep to cross back over the pass.

With few options, we embarked in the morning, our ranks swollen by a dozen yak herders, each pushing two animals, laden with supplies, up the narrow track that rose along the south bank of the Kharta Chu. Jesse went ahead, and I enjoyed walking with him. The previous day we had slipped away from camp and scrambled up a steep ridge. There on the summit, in a ruined fortress, he had told me an interesting story about his father. In India, near the family home at Mussoorie, Daniel's grandfather, a devout Christian, had met a Hindu sadhu, a wandering holy man. A mutual fascination with spiritual mysteries forged an unlikely friendship. "There are senses beyond science," Grandpa Taylor had told young Daniel, "beyond the five that we acknowledge. These we can develop. Prayer is one, but there are others. A hunter senses impending danger. All of these senses lead to knowledge."

Encouraged by his family, Daniel as a child sought out the sadhu, and whenever possible sat beside him, unperturbed by his naked body, the filthy loincloth and trident, the shaggy hair, ashes, and beard to the waist. In time the sadhu took the boy under his wing, sharing certain mysteries, techniques of meditation and insight....

According to Jesse, his father still practices the techniques taught him by the sadhu. One morning in 1985, in the midst of a blizzard at their mountaintop home in West Virginia, Daniel emerged from a night of reflection and meditation with an idea for an entirely new kind of protected area, an international nature preserve, centered on Qomolangma. The ultimate goal was the preservation of the entire Himalayas.

A month later he was in Kathmandu, scheduled to deliver a speech. At the opening banquet, attended by King Birenda, his roommate at Harvard, he met the official in charge of the Chinese geological survey of the borderlands. When Daniel gently encouraged him to experience Qomolangma, the bureaucrat offered to go if passage could be arranged by air, an impossible task, or so it seemed. Daniel excused himself, strolled over to the king, and borrowed the royal helicopter, on the condition that he would pay for the gas.

Airborne at dawn, the Chinese geologist sat stunned by the wonder of the vista, not just the mountains but the lush valleys that

reached into Tibet. Joining forces with Daniel, he carried the story
to Beijing, and a month later negotiations began in earnest for the
creation of a nature preserve not administered by distant bureaucrats
but guarded by the people who dwell within its boundaries. It was
a bold idea, so novel that at every meeting Daniel was able to
increase the size of the proposed park, until ultimately it embraced
6 million acres, an area larger than Massachusetts, straddling the
heart of the Himalayas. As Jesse wound up his story, I looked east to
distant mountains, white with snow. The entire horizon was within the cordon of the Qomolangma Nature Preserve. His father's
dream had become reality.

During the day, we climbed some 2,000 feet, leaving the fields
and villages behind, and made camp on the snow at the foot of the
Shao La. As soon as the sun went down, the temperature dropped
well below freezing. The bright stars were promising, but the signs
of winter ominous. Even at this elevation, the barberry and rhodo-
dendrons lay beneath deep drifts that swept over the frozen streams.
From a ridge above camp, in snow to the knee, I watched the
herders drive the yaks up the slope to graze; already they had
expressed concern about the availability of feed. Later I followed
them back to their fire, where they joked and laughed, huddled
together, sharing dried yak meat, *tsampa* (flour ground from barley),
and *rakshi* (raw spirits distilled from grain). Though by morning ice
would cling to their clothes, they made no effort to put up tents,
preferring to sleep beneath sheepskins in the open air, curled alongside the fire.

It snowed during the night, but the sun broke through soon after
dawn, and the air was warm by the time we set out ahead of the
yaks, heading for the pass. The trail rose gradually at first, and then
climbed steeply to a high treeless valley, enveloped in cloud. Skirting
the edge of a beautiful lake, past stone corrals and walled shelters
piled across the mouths of caves, the route approached the base of
the pass, a 1,000-foot climb on a trail through deep snow. From the
valley bottom, I glimpsed three tiny figures on the summit, darting
in and out of view. An hour later they walked silently past me on

the trail. Young women in wool skirts and bright aprons, bent low
beneath illicit loads of lumber, their eyes shielded from the sun by
long braids entwined with
turquoise. The wood was silver fir, the only Himalayan
tree that splits easily into
boards and beams with
wedges and hammers made
from rhododendron limbs.
Harvested in spring in the
depths of the Kama Chu, the
timber is stacked to dry until
the last possible moment in
the fall, when, fighting the
season, the woodcutters haul
100-pound loads over the pass
to Kharta. Used mostly for
window and door frames,
with as much as 90 percent of
the source tree wasted on the
forest floor, the wood eventually makes its way to Shegar
and beyond. There is a construction boom under way in
Tibet, as tens of thousands of
ethnic Chinese flood the country. In Lhasa the once quiet lanes that
linked the sacred sites are now awash in noodle shops and karaoke
bars. Less than half the population is Tibetan, and the Chinese own
more than 80 percent of businesses. The Tibetan capital has become
a Chinese outpost.

Cloud cover obscured the top of the pass, and the wind blew
fiercely from the south. Everything was sheathed in ice—the red
and yellow prayer flags marking the summit, the small piles of mani
stones inscribed with invocations at the foot of the rock cairn, the
trail itself as it fell way through deep snowdrifts toward the Kama
Chu. Seeking shelter in the lee of a rocky ledge, I stumbled upon

> ─────── ✳ ───────
>
> Last night I read some lovely
> stories written by Pema
> Bhum about one Tibetan's view
> of the Cultural Revolution. He
> says in his book, *Six Stars with a
> Crooked Neck: A Tibetan Memoir
> of the Cultural Revolution*, that
> because of the way it sounded
> when translated into his
> home Amdo dialect, he loved
> Chairman Mao's *Little Red Book*
> long before he ever saw it. He
> thought everyone was talking
> about "Chairman Mao's Baby
> Goat" and was genuinely sur-
> prised to discover it was a book.
> —Tim Norris,
> "Tibet Journals"

other woodcutters, asleep in the snow, apparently unfazed by the cold. Their only protection was a thin patchwork of Chinese army jackets, tattered pants, and sodden sneakers without socks. Startled, they leapt to their feet, hoisted their loads, and scrambled down the slope, just in time to catch sight of Jesse sweeping down the draw on his snowboard.

As our yaks slowly and steadily lumbered their way toward the pass, Daniel and I waited in the rocks, somewhat stunned by the severity of the season. Already two passes into the Kama were sealed. The Shao La, at 16,500 feet, was the middle of the three. But with so much snow falling and the visibility reduced by violent gusts, the possibility of becoming trapped for the winter in Kama Chu skirted our thoughts.

"Tibetans," Daniel said, his voice barely audible above the wind, "consider a pass to be a place of energy, marking the transition between worlds. Prayer flags bring luck, as do the small bits of paper, inscribed with blessings, that travelers toss into the air as they cross a divide. But snow is the work of demons, a blizzard the test of a pilgrim's sincerity. This snow will not melt. It will only get deeper."

As we marched out of the pass, beginning a long gradual descent, the yak herders started to chant, one by one, without thought, as they moved the animals forward. Away from the summit, the wind died, and all that could be heard was the sound of their voices, the tinkling of yak bells, and the slow scuffle of boots on a rocky trail that ran to the valley below. A shaft of light cut through the clouds, which slowly opened to reveal black cliffs the height of mountains. To the south emerged a row of peaks as impressive as any in the Americas. Then, as the clouds lifted higher, the unearthly sight of the Himalayas was revealed, Makalu and Chomo Lönzo, a range so grand as to reduce the icy crags in the foreground to mere foothills. Exhilarated by the sight, I noticed one of the herders, a man named Tandu, standing to one side, staring back at the pass. Perhaps it was cruel coincidence, or possibly he sensed something. But two weeks later, when we returned to Kharta, we would learn that even as we had walked out of the Shao La, an avalanche had swept off the slope not 300 meters from the pass, leaving a solitary woodcutter to die, buried to the neck in snow.

It was late by the time we reached the bottom of the pass, and the last few miles to camp were a race against the failing light. Even in the darkness, one could discern the absence of snow amidst the fragrance of rhododendron and wild rose. Exhausted, we pitched tents in a damp meadow just beyond the flood plain of the stream we had followed since first dropping into the valley. Hot lemon tea and a dinner of rice and curry lifted morale, and in the cold night air I wandered beyond the camp, climbing in and about a nest of massive boulders. A forest of juniper spread up one side of the valley to rock bluffs, silver in the moonlight. Though I was aware of the distance we had come and felt the looming presence of Everest, it was the subtle beauty of the plants that was most impressive: mountain ash and birch, willows, spiraea and poppies, a score of familiar genera and species growing at such a height. The British, upon first entering the Kama Chu, had been similarly impressed. George Mallory described it this way: "When all is said about Chomolungma, the Goddess Mother of the World, I come back to the valley, the valley bed itself, the broad pastures, where our tents lay, where cattle grazed and where butter is made, the little stream we followed up to the valley head, wandering along its well-turfed banks under the high moraine, the few rare plants, saxifrages, gentians and primulas, so well watered there, and a soft, familiar blueness to the air which even here may charm us. Though I bow to the goddesses I cannot forget at their feet a gentler spirit than theirs, a little shy perhaps, but constant in the changing winds and variable moods of mountains."

The British had seen the Kama Chu in August. Now it was November. Walking back to camp, I noticed that the yak herders had put up their tents, black shadows against the stones.

The snow began to fall soon after midnight and did not stop for three days. By morning the yaks stood belly deep in fresh powder, and the valley and forest had been transformed. Leaving the others in camp, Jesse, Daniel, and I set off just before noon, during a slight break in the storm, and walked to the edge of the hanging valley, where the route divided: one trail stayed high, climbing steeply to the east toward Everest, and the other dropped through juniper and birch to the canyon of the Kama Chu. Within an hour we reached the river, just below the point where the channel broadened to a wide glacial bar, which we followed for some time, scouting for signs of game, pugmarks that might reveal the presence of cats. A wooden footbrige drew Jesse's attention. Leopards avoid water, and this was the only dry crossing within miles. On the far side of the bridge he found a faint track, perhaps that of a snow leopard pushed below its normal range by the early onset of winter. But the scat discovered a moment later suggested otherwise. Snow leopard feces smells sweet. This had a pungent odor, not unlike that of the common house cat. It was, according to Daniel, the stool of a clouded leopard.

"How can you be sure?" I asked.

"I can't," he replied with a broad grin. "But then nothing is certain with this cat. Every bit of data is anecdotal. I don't know a damn thing about the creature, but no one else does either. That's what makes it so great."

As Daniel struggled to rig a camera beneath the bridge, Jesse and I set the laser monitor between two stones, camouflaged the connecting wires with wood and bark, then checked the angle to make sure that anything crossing would trigger the shutter.

"With these woodcutters passing through," remarked Jesse, "we'll probably just get thirty shots of somebody's legs."

"With all this snow you may be lucky to get that," said his father.

For the rest of the afternoon we followed the valley downstream and set a series of photo traps along the trail, wherever we encountered signs of leopard prey: tracks or scat of red pandas, musk deer, or pheasant. Daniel, in particular, worked with a wild intensity, as if effort alone might conjure the cat. Then, after a long day, and with the storm building upon the face of Makalu, we retraced our steps upriver and climbed back through the forest to camp, arriving just as the blizzard began in earnest. Snow fell throughout the night.

A day in camp, relieved only by a short outing to establish a camera on the high trail to Everest, followed by another night and day of heavy snow, left all of us wondering whether we might be forced to retreat. By the third morning, when we woke to gray skies still swirling with snow, the yak herders themselves seemed fearful. Their animals had not eaten in three days, and the storm showed no signs of letting up. With winter coming on, not one of them was keen to climb thousands of feet higher to the East Face of Qomolangma. While Daniel, Lhakpa, and the others sat in the cook tent, talking things over, I noticed Tandu, the quiet leader among the Tibetans, placing a large flat stone on the snow. Kindling a fire with dried juniper, he burned incense and green boughs, then added offerings of *tsampa*, yak butter, and tea, all the while singing a deep melodious chant that drew everyone out of the tents into a wide circle around the flames. The ritual puja, a ceremonial prayer, in this case for good weather, had two immediate and gratifying effects. First, it brought our group together, dispelling in a moment any thoughts of retreating over the pass. Second, the sky cleared. Within an hour the clouds lifted, and the sun emerged. A day later, having fed the yaks with bamboo gathered low in the valley of the Kama Chu, we began our climb toward the East Face of Everest.

The following days took us past the dazzling cliffs of Makalu and Chomo Lönzo, rising 10,000 feet above the river, as we climbed through juniper forests and beyond the treeline to snowfields that stretched for miles across the flanks of impossibly vast mountains. By day the sun was hot and luminous. At night the temperatures fell to 20 degrees below freezing, and the only sounds were those of yak bells, ringing in perfect clarity. Mornings began with the thunder of avalanches tumbling like clouds down the sheer face of the mountains. For three days our route followed the tracks of a snow leopard, while overhead bearded vultures soared, and ravens and black-eared kites darted in the wind.

Everest first came into view as we crested a ridge and happened upon a number of rock cairns, Buddhist tombs deliberately placed within sight of the sacred mountain. At first its peak seemed almost lost, overshadowed by Lhotse and Chomo Lönzo and the two glaciers, Kangshung and Kangdoshung, that flow into the valley. But the closer we came, the more astonishing the mountain appeared. By the time we reached our highest camp, in the snow overlooking the Kangshung, just below a series of ledges frequented by blue sheep, the mountain dominated every thought. To be this close, just shy of Pethang Ringmo, the gentle meadows celebrated by the British climbers of 1921, was to feel something of their spirit. George Mallory first saw Everest from the north as he climbed the Rongbuk glacier, having paid homage to the lama of the legendary Rongbuk monastery, a simple monk who found the passions of the English somewhat difficult to understand. "I was filled with great compassion," the lama later reflected, "that they underwent such suffering in unnecessary work."

But for Mallory and his comrades, all inured to death, the mountain was an exalted radiance, immanent, vast, incalculable. He described his first sighting: "We had mounted perhaps a thousand feet when we stopped to wait for what we had come to see. As the clouds rolled asunder before the heights, gradually, very gradually, we saw the great mountainsides and glaciers and ridges, now one fragment, now another, through the floating rifts, until, far higher in the sky than imagination dared to suggest, a prodigious white fang—an excrescence from the jaw of the world—the summit of Everest, appeared."

Though the lama was puzzled as to why one would tread upon sacred ground and disturb the spirit of the mountain, the British, in fact, approached the peak with a reverence that even Tibetans might find difficult to match. To placate the monks, Mallory and Howard-Bury described their expedition as a group of mountain worshippers embarked on pilgrimage. Cryptic as they intended the message to be, it, in fact, perfectly encapsulated who they were, climbers willing to sacrifice all to reach the summit of the unknown. The word sacrifice, of course, means to make sacred, and when Mallory in his famous retort explained that the reason for climbing Everest was nothing more than the fact that it was there, he distilled the perfect notion of emptiness and pure purpose.

In the spacious silence of Pethang Ringmo, we looked up at the mountain's entire profile, including the northern approach, where perhaps Mallory's body lies. With binoculars, I could just make out the first and second steps, the rock ledges where on June 8, 1924, Mallory and his companion, Sandy Irvine, were last seen going strong for the top.

Like the rest of their expedition, they were pathetically under-dressed, wearing simple wool vests, flannel shirts, Shackleton smocks, gabardine knickers, soft elastic cashmere puttees, and fur-lined leather motorcycle helmets. They knew nothing of the death zone, the altitude above which oxygen deprivation reduces any climb to a pure and horrendous act of will. They had no idea that the peak of the mountain lay in the jet stream, where winds of 150 miles per hour drive ice crystals in dark plumes off the summit. They had oxygen to breathe but disdained its use, and had no faith in the primitive apparatus, which kept breaking down in the cold. At 27,000 feet, they read Shakespeare in the snow, in flimsy tents designed for the mud of Flanders.

As the mist rolled in, enveloping their memory in myth, there was one witness, a brilliant climber in support, Noel Odell, who never doubted that they had reached the top. Nor did he question the sublime purpose that had taken them all, 400 miles on foot from India and across Tibet just to reach the base of the mountain. Odell wrote of Mallory: "My final glimpse of one, whose personality was of that charming character that endeared him to all and whose nat-ural gifts seemed to indicate such possibilities of both mind and body, was that he was 'going strong,' sharing with that other fine character who accompanied him such a vision of sublimity that it has been the lot of few mortals to behold; nay, few while beholding have become merged into such a scent of transcendence."

From the base of Everest, thinking about these men, I stared sky-ward at a mountain that has killed one climber for every four that have reached the summit. It was an awesome sight. Though I was standing on ground higher that any in North America, the moun-tain rose two miles above, fluted ribs and ridges, gleaming balconies and seracs of blue-green ice, shimmering formations ready to col-lapse in an instant. "We must remember," Mallory once wrote, "that the highest of mountains is capable of severity, a severity so awful and fatal that the wiser sort of men do well to think and tremble even on the threshold of their high endeavor."

Once it became known that Mallory and Irvine had died in their summit attempt, the other British climbers, waiting in their advance camp, retreated from the valley. "We were a sad little party," wrote Teddy Norton, leader of the 1924 expedition, who himself had reached 28,128 feet without oxygen, "but from the first we accepted the loss of our comrades in the rational spirit which all of our generation had learnt in the Great War, and there was never a tendency to a morbid harping on the irrevocable. But the tragedy was very near."

On May 1, 1999, mountaineer Conrad Anker finally found the mummified body of George Mallory at 27,000 feet. His book about the discovery, written with fellow mountaineer David Roberts, is must reading for every Everest-o-phile: *The Lost Explorer: Finding Mallory on Mount Everest.*
—JO'R and LH

"There was something Homeric about those men," Daniel said one evening as he and I walked along the ridge above our camp, downwind from a band of blue sheep grazing on the windswept terraces. "After that war, when so many had died, life became less precious than the moments of life. I think that explains Mallory's willingness to climb on, accepting a degree of risk that might have been unimaginable before the war. They were not cavalier, but death was no big deal. They had seen so much that it had no hold on them. What mattered was how one lived. It always seemed fated to me that they would meet their end in the Himalayas, and not just because of that one mountain."

"What do you mean?" I asked.

"Well, I think that's why we all come here, why the landscape and the religion hold such an attraction for people from the West. I started with the yeti. I was desperate to find it, to prove that it existed.

But then gradually the creature ceased to be a physical mystery and became instead a symbol of the unknown, an image that allowed me to tie together things that were known, and things I merely sensed. That's why I turned to conservation. We all need a place on Earth to hide the wild parts of ourselves. With land preserved, each generation can search again for the yeti and discover the science of life, which is ecology, and participate in the art of science violated, which is magic. In the end what we discover is a greater sense of who we are, and a knowledge that what we are is just what is."

In the end the clouded leopard eluded us. After several days at the foot of Everest, we retraced our steps only to find our cameras buried deep in snow. Two months later, however, word came from Delhi that in the forests of India, Jesse had indeed caught the elusive creature on film, the first photograph of the clouded leopard ever recorded in central Asia.

Wade Davis holds degrees in anthropology and biology and received his Ph.D. in ethnobotany from Harvard University. His books include The Serpent and the Rainbow, Nomads of the Dawn, Passage of Darkness, *and* One River. *Davis's writing has also appeared in many magazines, newspapers, and journals, including* Outside, Premiere, Fortune, *and* Condé Nast Traveler. *This piece was excerpted from his book,* Shadows in the Sun: Travels to Landscapes of Spirit and Desire.

The Sew–Tel Hotel

A foreigner is drawn into a Communist
business intrigue.

SOME YEARS AGO, THE TIBETAN STAFF OF THE BANAKSHÖL SEWING commune in Lhasa arrived at work to find their sewing machines gone.

"The building has been converted into a hotel," one of the young seamstresses announced to the latecomers, "and now *we* have to operate it." They stood idly watching carpenters divide the two long factory floors into cubicles. The Chinese government had finally opened Tibet to independent travel, and the seamstresses had two days to prepare for the arrival of guests, some of whom were expected to be "foreign friends."

I arrived at the Banakshöl Hotel the day before it opened. The seamstresses checked me in anyway.

I filled in my travel permit, then one of the seamstresses leaned over the plywood transom of the reception booth. "Now...what's a hotel?" she asked, smiling but serious, convinced I would know; a hotel was something meant for people like me. Several other women lounging in the reception booth listened in, giggling, equally curious. I spoke passable Tibetan, and suddenly realized they were recruiting me to show them how to operate and manage the beast.

"Well, you provide clean rooms, soft mattresses, wash water, showers, towels, and drinking water, to start with. Do you have a budget for that stuff?"

They did. I joined them in counting the rooms and making a list of supplies. The women scattered into the market, each assigned to purchase twenty-four pieces of a single item.

They placed me in the room directly above the reception, for easy access in the event of a hotel management crisis. The street sounds and the ambience of the reception booth were noisy enough, but even these were drowned out by the telephone; Chinese and Tibetans shouted into it insanely throughout the day and night, especially when making trunk calls. Their phones didn't handle ranges of tone, tough for those speaking a tonal language. I slept with earplugs.

Mingma, a slim and exuberant young seamstress, opened my door without knocking. "Inji Tenzing?" she said, using the nickname she and the other staff had given me. Her provocative lean against the doorway was natural, uncultivated. "A European woman here wants a towel. What do we do?"

"Why not just give her one?"

"What if she gets it dirty?" she protested.

Urbanized Tibetans must have picked up their obsession with cleanliness from the Chinese. They swept religiously and aggressively each morning, then followed it with abrasive facial scrubbing at the local water tap. In the countryside, nomads bathed once a year.

"She probably *will* get it dirty," I said, "especially with all the dust in this town."

"And, Inji Tenzing, why don't you watch her while she bathes, to see that she doesn't run off with it?"

"If you'll come with me," I suggested.

"Sure—you go there and take your clothes off, and I'll get naked and join you in a minute...."

The single shower room was configured with four shower heads in a line, and I had already advised them to schedule separate shower times for men and women travelers. The first few days had been a free-for-all. Modesty wasn't a custom the Tibetans had picked up with modernization.

Sunflower seed hulls hung from Mingma's lower lip, a fashion accessory common among unmarried Tibetan girls. It appears slovenly and distracting to Westerners at first, then becomes unusually seductive, an invitation to reach up and gently clean them off.

"Do you have any boyfriends?" I asked.

"Not a single one, and I probably never will."

"Someone as cute as you—why not?"

"Because I don't have the equipment boys want—it's not there, it's just smooth where the equipment should be."

Mingma carried on about the European woman. "You know, she wants some drinking water, too." I sensed a certain pride of self-sufficiency. Tibetan women weren't so needy. Or, the concept of the customer being right was perhaps too foreign to their Communist training to work here, though the seamstresses' boisterous Tibetan business sense was still intact.

One afternoon when I returned to the hotel, Mingma jumped into the hallway. "Oh, Inji Tenzing—a very beautiful Western woman has checked in, but we can't communicate with her very well. She says she knows you and wants to see you right away. She's in Room 7."

"*You're* the beautiful one," I responded with a playful smile. Then I casually moved in the direction of Room 7. Mingma stood quietly at the end of the hallway, a tinge of jealousy seeming to betray her curiosity. Behind her, the women in the reception booth half-stifled their laughter, no doubt making fun of her girlish infatuation.

Confidently, I knocked on the door, then winked at Mingma. The door opened.

Standing before me was a thin Chinese man wearing a stained singlet, blue pants, and rayon socks, smoking a cigarette, a Public Security uniform and stiff-brimmed hat with an oversized badge hung from the bedpost. Glossy black patent leather shoes poked rudely from beneath the bed. The room was filled with smoke, the window closed.

"Uh...." I looked again at the number on the door—7.

The man took a noisy drag on his cigarette, sucking air around his fingers, annoyed at being disturbed. In practiced English he said, "Passport please."

I turned and looked down the hall. The seamstresses had piled out of the reception booth and joined Mingma, laughing so hard that they tottered against the walls, writhing, clutching each other for support.

I swallowed my saliva, slowly reached into my shoulder bag and pulled out my passport. Cigarette dangling from his lip, the officer scrutinized it, riffled through the pages, handed it back to me, then closed the door with a grunt. He had done his job.

My job at the Banakshöl, I realized, would never end. And, if I were to hang there much longer I was headed for trouble with Mingma or the other saucy seamstresses. It was time to head to Nepal, for work. The route overland to Kathmandu was opening up, rumor said, and it was possible to hitchhike.

The day I left the Banakshöl, Mingma and two others jumped me from behind, trying to restrain me. It wasn't easy to leave, but the gravitational force of obligations and a more mundane life were pulling me to lower elevations.

Broughton Coburn is the author of five books, including Nepali Aama, Aama in America, *and the national bestsellers* Everest: Mountain Without Mercy *and* Touching My Father's Soul: A Sherpa's Journey to the Top of Everest *(with Jamling Tenzing Norgay).*

PETER HESSLER

Tibet through Chinese Eyes

There are no easy answers in this
heartbreaking part of the world.

POLITICAL VIEWS ON TIBET TEND TO BE AS UNAMBIGUOUS AS THE
hard blue dome of sky that stretches above its mountains. In Western
opinion, the "Tibet question" is settled: Tibet should not be part of
China; before being forcibly annexed, in 1951, it was an independent country. The Chinese are cruel occupiers who are seeking to
destroy the traditional culture of Tibet. The Dalai Lama, the traditional spiritual leader of Tibet, who fled to India in 1959, should be
allowed to return and resume his rule over either an independent or
at least a culturally autonomous Tibet. In short, in Western eyes
there is only one answer to the Tibet question: Free Tibet.

For Han—ethnic Chinese—who live in Tibet, the one answer
is exactly the same and yet completely different. They serve what
the Chinese call "Liberated Tibet." Mei Zhiyuan is Han, and in
1997 he was sent by the Chinese government to act as a "Volunteer
Aiding Tibet" at a Tibetan middle school, where he works as a
teacher. His roommate, Tashi, is a Tibetan who as a college student
was sent in the opposite direction, to Sichuan province, where he
received his teacher training. Both men are twenty-four years old.
They are good friends who live near Heroes Road in Lhasa, which
is named after the Chinese and Tibetans who contributed to the

63

"peaceful liberation" of Tibet in the 1950s. This is how Mei Zhiyuan sees Tibet—as a harmonious region that benefits from Chinese support. When I asked him why he had volunteered to work there, he said, "Because all of us know that Tibet is a less developed place that needs skilled people."

I went to Tibet to explore this second viewpoint, hoping to catch a glimpse of the Tibet question through Chinese eyes. Before coming to Tibet, I had spent two years as a volunteer English teacher at a small college in Sichuan, which made me particularly interested in meeting volunteer teachers like Mei Zhiyuan. I also talked with other young government workers and entrepreneurs who had come to seek their fortunes, and for four weeks that was my focus, as I spent time in Lhasa and other places where there are large numbers of Han settlers.

> The Chinese know Tibet as *Xizang*, the Western Treasure House. Treasures are usually defined in terms of gold and jewels. However, the real treasure of Tibet is the land— with its golden vistas, its snow leopards and blue poppies, and its resilient people.
>
> —George B. Schaller, Foreword,
> *Trekking in Tibet: A Travelers'*
> *Guide* by Gary McCue

Of all the pieces that compose the Tibet question, this is by far the most explosive: the Dalai Lama has targeted Han migration as one of the greatest threats to Tibetan culture, and the sensitivity of the issue is evident in some statistics. According to Beijing, Han make up only 3 percent of the population of the Tibet Autonomous Region, whereas some Tibetan exiles claim that the figure is in fact over 50 percent and growing. Tibetans see the influx of Han as yet another attempt to destroy their culture; Chinese see the issue as Deng Xiaoping did in 1987, when he said, "Tibet is sparsely populated. The 2 million Tibetans are not enough to handle the task of developing such a huge region. There is no harm in sending Han into Tibet to help.... The key issues are what is best for Tibetans and how can Tibet develop at a fast pace, and move ahead in the four modernizations in China."

Regardless of the accuracy of the official Chinese view, many of the government-sent Han workers in Tibet clearly see their role in terms of the Tibet question, and yet they are also the most often overlooked. Why did they come to Tibet? What do they think of the place, how are they changing it, and what do they see as their role?

Gao Ming, a twenty-two-year-old English teacher, told me, "One aspect was that I knew we should be willing to go to the border regions, to the minority areas, to places that are *jianku*—difficult. These are the parts of China that need help. If I could have gone to Xinjiang, I would have, but I knew that Tibet was also a place that needed teachers. That was the main reason. Another aspect was that Tibet is a natural place—there's no pollution here, and almost no people; much of it is untouched. So I wanted to see what it was like."

Shi Mingzhi, a twenty-four-year-old physics teacher, said, "First, I'd say it's the same reason that you came here to travel—because it's an interesting place. But I also wanted to come help build the country. You knew that all of the volunteers in this district are Party members, and if you're a Party member, you should be willing to go to a *jianku* place to work. So you could say that all of us had patriotic reasons for coming—perhaps that's the biggest reason. But I also came because it was a good opportunity, and the salary is higher than in the interior of China."

Talking with these young men was in many ways similar to talking with an idealistic volunteer in any part of the world. Apart from the financial incentive to work in Tibet, many of the motivations were the same—the sense of adventure, the desire to see something new, the commitment to service. And government propaganda emphasizes this sense of service, through figures like Kong Fansen, a cadre from eastern China who worked in Tibet and became famous as a worker-martyr after his death in an auto accident. Han workers are exhorted to study the "old Tibet spirit" of Kong and other cadres as they serve a region that in the Chinese view desperately needs their talents.

Central to their task is the concept of *jianku*. I heard this term repeatedly when the Chinese described conditions in Tibet, and life is especially *jianku* for Volunteers Aiding Tibet who commit in advance to serving eight-year terms. Most government-sent Han workers fall into the category of Cadres Aiding Tibet—teachers, doctors, administrators, and others who serve for two or three years. Having graduated from a lower-level college, Mei Zhiyuan could not qualify for such a position, and as a result was forced to make an eight-year commitment. The sacrifice is particularly impressive considering that he assumed it would have serious repercussions on his health. Many Chinese believe that living at a high altitude for long periods of time does significant damage to the lungs, and a number of workers told me that this was the greatest drawback to living in Tibet. "It's bad for you," Mei Zhiyuan explained, "because when you live in a place this high, your lungs enlarge, and eventually that affects your heart. It shortens your life." During my stay in Tibet I heard several variations on this theory (one from an earnest young teacher who was smoking a cigarette), but generally it involved the lungs expanding and putting pressure on the heart. There is no medical evidence to support such a belief; indeed, in a heavily polluted country like China, where one of every four deaths is attributed to lung disease, the high, clean air of Tibet is probably tonic. Nevertheless, this perception adds to the sense of sacrifice, and it is encouraged by the government pay structure, which links salary to altitude: the higher you work, the higher your pay.

The roughly 1,000 yuan a month that Mei Zhiyuan earns is half what the local cadre teachers make. Even so, his salary is two to three times what he would make as a teacher in rural Sichuan, and he is able to send half his earnings home to his parents, who are peasants. It's good money by Chinese standards but seems hardly a sufficient incentive for a young man to be willing to shorten his life. Leaving before his eight years are up would incur a heavy fine of up to 20,000 yuan—nearly two years' salary, or, for a peasant family like Mei Zhiyuan's, approximately twenty tons of rice.

★

From the Chinese perspective, Tibet has always been a part of China. This is, of course, a simplistic and inaccurate view, but Tibetan history is so muddled that one can see in it what one wishes. The Chinese can ignore some periods and point to others; they can cite the year 1792, when the Qing Emperor sent a Chinese army to help the Tibetans drive out the invading Nepalese, or explain that from 1728 to 1912 there were Qing *ambans*, imperial administrators, stationed in Lhasa. In fact, the authority of these *ambans* steadily decreased over time, and Tibet enjoyed de facto independence from 1913 to 1951. An unbiased arbiter would find Tibetan arguments for independence more compelling than the Chinese version of history—but also, perhaps, would find that the Chinese have a stronger historical claim to Tibet than the United States does to much of the American West.

Most important, China's reasons for wanting Tibet changed greatly over the years. For the Qing Dynasty, Tibet was important strictly as a buffer state; *ambans* and armies were sent to ensure that the region remained peaceful, but they made relatively few administrative changes, and there was no effort to force the Tibetans to adopt the Chinese language or Chinese customs. In the Qing view, Tibet was a part of China but at the same time it was something different; the monasteries and the Dalai Lamas were allowed to maintain authority over most internal affairs.

In the early twentieth century, as the Qing collapsed and China struggled to overcome the imperialism of foreign powers, Tibet became important for new reasons of nationalism. Intellectuals and political leaders, including Sun Yat-sen, believed that China's historical right to Tibet had been infringed by Western powers, particularly Britain, which invaded Tibet in 1904 to force the thirteenth Dalai Lama to open relations. As Tibet slipped further from control, a steady stream of nationalistic rhetoric put the loss of Tibet into the familiar pattern—the humiliation by foreign powers in the nineteenth and early twentieth centuries, as Hong Kong went to the British, Manchuria and Shandong to the Japanese, Taiwan to the U.S.-funded Kuomintang. By the time Mao Zedong founded the People's Republic of China, in 1949, Tibet had figured into the nation's pre-eminent task: the reunification of the once-powerful motherland.

Tibet thus changed from buffer state to a central piece in Communist China's vision of itself as independent and free from imperialist influence. Orville Schell, a longtime observer of China, says that even today this perception is held by most Chinese. "I don't think there's any more sensitive issue," he says, "with the possible exception of Taiwan, because it grows out of the dream of a unified motherland—a dream that historically speaking has been the goal of almost every Chinese leader. This issue touches on sovereignty, it touches on the unity of Chinese territory, and especially it touches on the issue of the West as predator, the violator of Chinese sovereignty."

The irony is that China, like an abused child who grows up to revisit his suffering on the next generation, has committed similar sins in Tibet: the overthrow of the monasteries and the violent redistribution of land, the mayhem of the Cultural Revolution, and the restriction of intellectual and religious freedom that continues to this day. And as in any form of imperialism, much of the damage has been done in the name of duty. When the Chinese speak of pre-1951

The law of unintended consequences is at work in the ever-larger Tibetan diaspora. As Lama Surya Das says in his book, *Awakening the Buddha Within*: "With the Chinese invasion of Tibet, it was as if a dam had burst: Suddenly Tibetan wisdom began to flow freely down from the roof of the world and to the West. Nuns, monks, lamas, and teachers who had never left their cloistered monasteries and hermitage retreats were confronted with a new world—filled with men and women eager to learn the Dharma. Tibetan teachers say that if it's possible for any good to have come from the Chinese invasion, that good has been found in the dissemination of the teachers to so many new students."

—JO'R and LH

Tibet, they emphasize the shortcomings of the region's feudal-theo-cratic government: life expectancy was thirty-six years; 95 percent of the population was hereditary serfs and slaves owned by monasteries and nobles. The sense is that the Tibetans suffered under a bad system, and the Chinese had a moral obligation to liberate them. Before traveling to Tibet, I asked my Chinese friends about the region. Most responded like Sai Xinghao, a forty-eight-year-old photographer: "It was a slave society, you know, and they were very cruel—they'd cut off the heads of their slaves and enemies. I've seen movies about it. If you were a slave, everything was controlled by the master. So, of course, after Liberation the rich lords opposed the changes [instituted by the Chinese]. It's like your America's history, when Washington liberated the black slaves. Afterward the blacks supported him, but of course the wealthy class did not. In history it's always that way—it was the same when Napoleon overthrew King Louis, and all of the lords opposed Napoleon because he supported the poor."

My friend is not an educated man, but many Chinese intellectuals make the same comparison. President Jiang Zemin made a similar remark during his 1997 visit to the United States (although he correctly identified Lincoln as the Great Liberator). The statistics about Tibetan illiteracy and life expectancy are accurate. Although the Chinese exaggerate the ills of the feudal system, mid-century Tibet was badly in need of reform—but naturally the Tibetans would have much preferred to reform it themselves.

> The Chinese fight with their weapons but we don't have any of those. It's not that we can't fight back for all those killed. We won't get anything through violence. We won't get to the truth by taking someone's life. Buddhism and truth have their end. There is no truth if something is taken by force.
>
> —A Tibetan Nun

Another aspect of the Chinese duty in Tibet is the sense that rapid modernization is needed, and should take precedence over cultural considerations. For Westerners, this is a difficult perspective to understand. Tibet is appealing to us precisely because it's not modern, and we have idealized its culture and anti-materialism to the point where it has become, as Orville Schell says, "a figurative place of spiritual enlightenment in the Western imagination—where people don't make Buicks, they make good karma."

But to the Chinese, for whom modernization is coming late, Buicks look awfully good. I noticed this during my first year as a teacher in China, when my writing class spent time considering the American West. We discussed western expansion, and I presented the students with a problem of the late nineteenth century: the Plains Indians, their culture in jeopardy, were being pressed by white settlers. I asked my class to imagine that they were American citizens proposing a solution, and nearly all responded much the way this student did: "The world is changing and developing. We should make the Indians suit our modern life. The Indians are used to living all over the plains and moving frequently, without a fixed home, but it is very impractical in our modern life…. We need our country to be a powerful country; we must make the Indians adapt to our modern life and keep pace with the society. Only in this way can we strengthen the country."

Virtually all my students were from peasant backgrounds, and like most Chinese, the majority of them were but one generation removed from deep poverty. What I saw as freedom and culture, they saw as misery and ignorance. In my second year I repeated the lesson with a different class, asking if China had any indigenous people analogous to the Plains Indians. All responded that the Tibetans were similar. I asked about China's obligation in Tibet. The answers suggested that my students had learned more from American history than I had intended to teach. One student replied, "First, I will use my friendship to help [the Tibetans]. But if they refuse my friendship, I will use war to develop them, like the Americans did with the Indians."

Regardless of China's motivations, and regardless of its failures in Tibet, the drive to develop the region has been expensive.

According to Beijing, more than 200,000 Han workers have served in Tibet since the 1950s. Taxes in Tibet are virtually nonexistent; Tibetan farmers, unlike those in the interior, receive tax-free leases of land, and a preferential tax code has been established to encourage business. Low-interest loans are available, and business imports from Nepal are duty-free. Despite the dearth of local revenues, government investment is steadily developing a modern infrastructure. From 1952 to 1994 the central government invested $4.2 billion in the region, and in 1994 Beijing initiated sixty-two major infrastructure projects for which the eventual investment is expected to be more than $480 million.

This investment of both human and financial capital complicates the issue of Tibet in ways that few outsiders realize. Foreign reports often refer to the exploitation of Tibetan resources as a classic colonial situation, which is misleading. Although Beijing is certainly doing what it can with Tibet's timber and mineral reserves, China spends an enormous amount of money in the region, and if self-sufficiency ever comes, it will not come soon. Tibet does have significant military value: the Chinese do not want to see it under the influence of a foreign power such as India, but not even this would seem to merit the enormous investment. In 1996 China spent some $600 million in Tibet. One foreign observer who has studied the region puts this in perspective: "For that same year the United States gave a total of $800 million in aid to all of Africa. That's all of Africa—we're talking about hundreds of millions of people. In Tibet there are only 2½ million. So if they become independent, who's going to be giving them that kind of money?"

"Unless you're a complete Luddite," Orville Schell says, "and don't believe in roads, telephones, hospitals, and things like that, then I think China must be credited with a substantial contribution to the modern infrastructure of Tibet. In this sense Tibet needs China. But that's not to diminish the hideous savageness with which China has treated Tibet."

Almost every aspect of Chinese support has two sides, and education illustrates the point well. I met a number of young Han teachers like Mei Zhiyuan, who were imbued with a sense of service: they were conscientious, well-trained teachers, and they were working in places with a real need for instructors. One volunteer was teaching English at a middle school where the shortage was so acute that many students had to delay the start of their English studies until the following year, when additional Han teachers were expected to arrive. I visited one district in which out of 230 secondary-school teachers, 60 were Han, and many of the Tibetan instructors had been trained in the interior at the Chinese government's expense. Such links with the interior seem inevitable, given that the Chinese have built Tibet's public education system from scratch. Before they arrived, in 1951, there were no public schools in Tibet, whereas now there are more than 4,000.

Likewise the schools I saw were impressive facilities with low student fees. In one town I toured the three local middle schools; two of them were newly built, with far better campuses than I was accustomed to seeing in China. The third school, whose grounds featured massive construction cranes fluttering with prayer flags, was being refurbished with the help of a $720,000 investment from the interior. Unlike students at

---

For better or worse, "development" has arrived in Tibet. The information superhighway is paved with bureaucrats, development experts, and well-meaning do-gooders with little or no practical expertise speeding along in Land Cruisers loaded with sacks full of money. Local hires have adopted terminology suited to the times: "joint adventure," "healthy department," "expensive reports." In one location after severe snowstorms, funding for yak replacement was provided, but the money was instead pocketed. When the donor's inspection team notified local officials that visitors would be arriving soon, animals were borrowed and placed alongside the road where they could be pointed to as the evaluators drove by. After the foreigners left, the herds were returned to their owners. Working here is like living in a Gary Larson cartoon.

—Tim Norris, "Tibet Journals"

most Chinese schools, those at the local No. 1 Middle School paid no tuition, and even high school students, who generally pay substantial amounts in China, had paid at most seventy dollars a semester, including board. Everything possible was being done to encourage students to stay in school: a student's tuition and boarding charge were cut in half if only one parent worked, and transportation to and from the remote nomad areas was often free.

In a poor country such policies are impressively generous; essentially Tibetan schools are better funded than Chinese schools. And this funding is sorely needed: the adult illiteracy rate in Tibet is still 52 percent. Only 78 percent of the children start elementary school, and of those only 35 percent enter middle school. But Chinese assistance must be considered in the context of what's being taught in the schools—a critical issue for Tibetans.

One morning I visited an elementary school on a spacious, beautiful campus, with new buildings and a grass playground that stretched westward under the shadow of a 14,000-foot mountain. Most of the school's 900 students were Tibetan. I paused at the central information board, where announcements were written in Chinese.

The board detailed a $487,800 investment that had been made by a provincial government in the interior, and displayed a short biography of Zu Chongzhi, a fifth-century Chinese mathematician. Next to this was a notice telling students to "remember the great goals." They were urged to work on doubling China's GNP from its 1980 level, and they were reminded that by 2050 China needed to achieve a GNP and a per capita income ranking in the middle of developed countries. Beside these goals was a long political section that read, in part:

> We must achieve the goal of modern socialist construction, and we must persevere in building the economy. We must carry out domestic reform and the policy of opening to the outside world.... We must oppose the freedom of the capitalist class, and we must be vigilant against the conspiracy to make a peaceful evolution toward imperialism.

*

It was heavy stuff for elementary school students (and indeed, if I were a Chinese propagandist, I would think twice before exhorting Tibetan children to resist imperialism), and it indicates how politicized the climate of a Chinese school is. Despite all the recent economic changes in China, the education system is still tied to the past. This conservatism imbues every aspect of education, starting with language. Two of the schools I visited were mixed Han and Tibetan, and classes were segregated by ethnicity. The reasons here are linguistic: most Tibetan children don't start learning Mandarin until elementary school, and even many Tibetan high school students, as the Han teachers complained, don't understand Chinese well. This segregation leads to different curricula—for example, Tibetan students have daily Tibetan-language classes, whereas Han students use that time for extra English instruction. To the Chinese, this system seems fair, especially since Tibetan students have the right to join the Han classes.

But Tibetans feel that there is an overemphasis on Chinese, especially at the higher levels, which threatens their language and culture. All the classes taught by Han teachers are in Chinese or English, and most of the Tibetan teachers in the middle and high schools are supposed to use Mandarin (although the ones I spoke with said they often used Tibetan, because otherwise their students wouldn't understand). In any case, important qualifying exams emphasize Chinese, and this reflects a society in which fluency is critical to success, especially when it comes to any sort of government job. Another, more basic issue is that Tibetan students are overwhelmed. One Han teacher told me that his students came primarily from nomad areas, where their families lived in tents; yet during the course of an average day they might have classes in Tibetan, Chinese, and English, three languages with almost nothing in common.

Political and religious issues are paramount. In Lhasa I met a twenty-one-year-old Tibet University student who was angered by his school's anti-religious stance, which is standard for schools in Tibet. "They tell us we can't believe in religion," he said, "because we're supposed to be building socialism, and you can't believe in both socialism and religion. But of course most of the students still believe in religion—I'd say that 80 to 90 percent of us are devout." One of his classmates, a member of the Communist Party, complained about the history courses. "The history we study is all Chinese history [of Tibet]," he said. "Most of it I don't believe." These students also adamantly opposed existing programs that send exceptional Tibetan middle and high school students to study in the interior, where there is nothing to offset the Chinese view of Tibet.

Such complaints reflect the results of recent education reforms. A series of them made in 1994, characteristically, represent both the good and the bad aspects of Chinese support. On the one hand, the government stepped up its campaign against illiteracy, and on the other, it resolved to control the political content of education more carefully, in hopes of pacifying the region. There has certainly been some success with this approach: I met a number of educated Tibetans who identified closely with China. Tashi, Mei Zhiyuan's roommate, seemed completely comfortable being both Tibetan and Chinese: he had studied in Sichuan, he had a good job, and he had the government's support to thank. When I asked him what was the biggest problem in Tibet, he mentioned language—but not in the way many Tibetans did. "So many [Tibetan] students can't speak Chinese," he said, "and if you can't speak Chinese, it's hard to find a good job. They need to study harder."

Most Tibetans seemed less likely to accept Chinese support at face value. But it was clear that politically they were being pulled in a number of directions at once, and my conversations with educated young Tibetans were dizzying experiences. Their questions ranged from odd ("Which do you think is going to win, capitalism or socialism?") to bizarre ("Is it true that in America when you go to your brother's or sister's house for dinner, they charge you money?"), and the surroundings were often equally unsettling. One Monday morning I watched the flag-raising ceremony at a middle school, where students and staff members lined up to listen to the national anthem, after which, in unison, they pledged allegiance to the Communist Party, love for the motherland, and dedication to studying and working hard. With the Tibetan mountains towering above, it was a surreal scene—and it became all the more so when the school's political adviser, a Tibetan in his early thirties with silver teeth, walked over and asked me where I was from. After I told him, he said, "Here in Tibet we already have a lot of influence from your Western countries—like Pepsi, Coke, movies, things like that. My opinion is that there are good and bad things coming from the West. For example, things regarding sex. In America, if you're married and you decide that you want another lover, what do you do? You get a divorce, regardless of how it affects your wife and child. But the people here are very religious, and we don't like those kinds of ideas."

> E xpressions heard in Tibet these days:
> 1. Under the Communists, man exploited man. With capitalism, it's the other way around.
> 2. The Chinese are defeated by their suspicion. The Tibetans are defeated by their hope.
> —Tim Norris, "Tibet Journals"

I heard a number of comments like this, and undoubtedly the education system included a great deal of anti-America propaganda. I felt that here the Chinese were almost doing the Tibetans a service; nothing depressed me more than my conversations with less-educated Tibetans, who invariably had great faith in American support and believed that President Clinton, who was then in China on a state visit, had come in order to save Tibet. Considering that China's interest in Tibet is largely a reaction to foreign imperialism, it's no surprise that nothing makes the Chinese angrier and more stubborn than the sight of the Dalai Lama and other exiled leaders seeking—and winning—support in America and elsewhere. And yet Tibetan faith in America seems naïve given America's treatment of its own indigenous people, and because historically U.S. policy in Tibet has been hypocritical and counterproductive. For example, the CIA trained and armed Tibetan guerrillas in the 1950s, during a critical period of mostly peaceful (if tenuous) cooperation between the Dalai Lama and the Chinese.

The peace ended when Tibetan uprisings, in which these guerrillas played a part, resulted in brutal Chinese repression and the Dalai Lama's flight to India.

America also represents modernity, and a further complication, beyond the Chinese political agenda, is that the long-isolated Tibetan society must come to grips with the modern world. One college student said, "The more money we Tibetans have, the higher our living standard is, the more we forget our own culture. And with or without the Chinese, I think that would be happening."

Perhaps the most hopeful moment in recent Han-Tibetan relations came shortly after 1980, when the Chinese Party Secretary, Hu Yaobang, went on a fact-finding mission to Tibet and returned with severe criticisms of Chinese policies. He advocated a two-pronged solution: Chinese investment was needed to spur economic growth in Tibet, but at the same time the Han should be more respectful of Tibetan culture. Cadres needed to learn Tibetan; the language should be used in government offices serving the public; and religion should be allowed more freedom.

There's no question that such respect is sorely needed, especially with regard to language. I never met a single government-sent Han worker who was learning Tibetan—not even the volunteers who would be there for eight years. And in Lhasa at the Xinhua bookstore, the largest in the city, I found not one textbook for Chinese students of Tibetan—books for foreign students, yes, but nothing for the Chinese.

Some of the 1980 reforms were implemented, but they were cut short by a series of riots in Lhasa that started in 1987. To Beijing hardliners, the riots indicated that too much freedom is a bad thing, and in 1987 Hu Yaobang was purged, partly for his recommendations regarding Tibet. By the spring of 1989 martial law had been declared in Tibet, and the Chinese concluded that relaxing restrictions on Tibetan culture and religion was tantamount to encouraging unrest. The two-pronged solution was quickly cut in half: Beijing would simply develop the economy, hoping that rising standards of living would defuse political tensions while building closer economic ties with the interior. This policy has been accelerated by the enormous investments of the 1990s.

Development, however, often comes at the cost of culture. Traditional sections of Lhasa are being razed in favor of faceless modern buildings, and the economic boom is attracting hordes of Han and Hui (an Islamic minority) migrants to Tibet.

Outsiders dominate Tibet's economy—indeed, they've essentially built it, inspiring enormous resentment among the Tibetan population. I met some Tibetans who didn't mind that cadres were sent from the interior, but I never met one who wasn't opposed to the influx of migrant workers, especially the huge numbers of Han from nearby Sichuan. Longtime Han residents, too, felt that was a serious problem.

The phenomenon of *liudong renkou*, or "floating population," is affecting urban areas all across China, with some 100 million people seeking work away from home. In the west and south there are particularly large numbers of Sichuanese in the floating population, and during my travels I often heard the same prejudices: the Sichuanese migrants are uncultured, their women loose, their men *jiaohua*, sly. And worst of all, people complained, they keep coming.

Having spent two years in Sichuan, I understand why the Sichuanese so often leave. Their province, roughly the size of France, contains 120 million people, and the economy is so shaky that recent factory closings have led to worker uprisings in some cities. Mostly the Sichuanese leave because they aren't afraid to; they

It is difficult to comprehend the level of corruption that has invaded Alexandra David-Neel's once-described landscape of magic and mystery. The story is that one county level official in Amdo (Qinghai) sold positions to 200 government offices to the highest bidders, including the head position of the Anti-Corruption Unit. And that's just one of the stories we hear. The really spicy ones are never told.
—Tim Norris, "Tibet Journals"

have been toughened by tough conditions, and all across China that is another thing they are famous for: their ability to *chiku*—eat bitter. They work and they survive, and like successful migrants anywhere else in the world, they are resented for their success.

In Tibet the Sichuanese have helped themselves to a large chunk of the economy. This was clear from the moment I arrived at the Lhasa airport, where thirteen of the sixteen restaurants bordering the entrance advertised Sichuan food. One was Tibetan. Virtually all small business in Lhasa follows this pattern; everywhere I saw Sichuan restaurants and shops. Locals told me that 80 percent of Lhasa's Han were Sichuanese, and this may not be much of an exaggeration.

This influx is far more significant and disruptive than the importing of Han cadres, and it's also harder to monitor. One common misperception in Western reports is that these people are sent by the government: the image is of a tremendous Han civilian army arriving to overwhelm Tibetan culture. The truth is that the government has little control over the situation. "How do you cut off the people moving out there?" asked one American who had spent much time in Tibet. "What mechanism are you going to have to prevent that? They don't have any restriction on internal travel—and we always beat them over the head about not having those, because to institute them would be a human-rights issue."

Far from arriving with an ethnic agenda, the independent migrants are for the most part completely apolitical. In Lhasa I often ate at a small Sichuan restaurant run by Fei Xiaoyun, a thirty-one-year-old native of Chengdu who, along with her husband, had been laid off in 1996 by a bankrupt state-owned natural-gas plant. Each of them had been given a two-year severance allowance of thirty dollars a month, and when that was gone, they took their savings and bought plane tickets to Lhasa. They had left their five-year-old son with his grandmother—a common choice for migrants, including cadres. This is partly out of fear of the effects on health of living in Tibet, and also because Tibetan schools are considered worse than those in the interior and children who are registered outside their districts have to pay extra fees.

Fei Xiaoyun never spoke of the growth of the GNP, and she had no interest in developing the motherland. Once, I asked her about Prime Minister Zhu Rongji, whose economic reforms are closing factories like hers, and she didn't even recognize his name. "All of the country's big affairs I can't understand," she said with a shrug. She was simply a poor woman with her back against the wall, and like the rest of the Sichuanese who had made their way to Tibet, she was trying desperately to make a living.

But such migrants have a political effect, as Tibetans watch outsiders develop an economy from which they feel increasingly removed. This also presents a question: If the rules are the same for everybody, why are the Han entrepreneurs so much more successful than the Tibetans? The most common response is that the rules aren't the same: the Chinese have easier access to government *guanxi*, or connections. But even on a level playing field the Han would have more capital and better contacts with sources in the interior. And their migrant communities have a tendency to support recent arrivals. This is especially true of the Sichuanese—one will arrive, and then a few relatives, and before long an extended family is dominating a factory or a block of shops. In front of the Jokhang, the holiest temple in Tibet, rows of stalls sell *khataks*, ceremonial scarves that pilgrims use as offerings. It's a job one would expect to see filled by Tibetans—as one would expect those selling rosaries in front of St. Peter's to be Catholic. But one saleswoman explained that all the stalls were run by Sichuanese from three small cities west of Chengdu. There were more than 200 of them—relatives, friends of relatives, relatives of friends—and they had completely filled that niche.

One day I walked past the *khatak* sellers with a Tibetan friend, and he shook his head. "Those people know how to do business," he said. "We Tibetans don't know how to do it—we're too straight. If something's supposed to be five yuan, we say it's five yuan. But a Sichuanese will say ten." I felt there was some truth to this—the Han are successful in Tibet for some of the same reasons that they are successful in so many places, from Southeast Asia to the United States. They have a stronger business tradition than the Tibetans, and virtually all independent Han settlers in Tibet have failed somewhere else, giving them a single-minded drive to succeed.

Consequently, Tibet feels like a classic frontier region, with typically peculiar demographics. There are disproportionately few Han children, and almost nobody comes to stay: the intention is invariably to return to the interior. The majority of the Han are men, including the government-sent workers. Of the Han women I saw in Tibet, more than a few were prostitutes; locals told me that they had come in a wave in 1994 and 1995, after the investments in the sixty-two major projects. One Han volunteer I spoke with had arrived in a group of thirteen men; one woman had applied but was rejected because the authorities felt that Tibet was no place for a young woman. The young man was resigned to finding a wife during his three paid trips home. "During vacation I'll be able to look for a girlfriend," he said. "I'll have six months. You can meet one then, and after that you can write and call when you come back here."

There were moments when everything—the ethnic tension, the rugged individualism, the hard, bright sun and the high, bare mountains—seemed more like a Jack London story than a real society. One day some American friends and I hired a driver, a twenty-five-year-old Sichuanese named Wei, who was nursing a defeated 1991 Volkswagen Santana. He had a two-year-old son at home, and he hoped to earn enough money by carrying passengers—though he wasn't registered to do so—to buy a new car in six months. We agreed to pay him thirty-six dollars if he drove us to Damxung, five hours north of Lhasa. Drive he did—past the police checkpoint, where he faked his credentials ("It's simpler that way," he explained), and past a Land Rover full of foreigners driven by a Tibetan, who, realizing our driver wasn't registered, swore he'd turn him in at Damxung. "It's because I'm Han," Wei said grimly. "And at Damxung the police will be Tibetan." He drove faster and faster, racing ahead of the Land Rover, until finally he hit a bump and ruptured the fuel line.

The car eased to a stop in the middle of nowhere. To the west rose the snow-topped Nyenchen Tanglha Mountains. The Tibetan driver cruised past, glaring. Wei cut a spare hose and patched the leak, and then he addressed the problem of injecting fuel back into the carburetor. He unhooked the fuel line and sucked out a mouthful of gas. Holding it in his mouth, he plugged the line back in. Then he walked around the front of the car and spit the fuel into the carburetor.

The car started. I could see Wei working the taste of gasoline around his mouth, and then, a few minutes later, he took out a cigarette. Everybody in the car held his breath—everybody but Wei, who lit the cigarette and sucked deeply. He did not explode. He stared ahead at the vast emptiness that stood between him and thirty-six dollars, and he kept driving.

That was the way a Sichuanese did things in Tibet. Gasoline was bitter but he ate it, the same way he ate the altitude and the weather and the resentment of the locals. None of that mattered.

> By compassion I subdue the demons.
> All blame I scatter to the wind.
>
> —Milarepa, Eleventh-century Tibetan saint

All that mattered was the work he did, the money he made, and the promise that if he was successful, he'd go home rich.

Tibet gave rise to exciting stories, but it was indeed *jianku*, and the social problems made a hard place even harder. Near the end of my trip I ate dumplings at Fei Xiaoyun's restaurant, and as I ate, she complained about her situation. Business was bad, and her life was boring; she worked fifteen-hour days and she had no friends in Lhasa. She missed her son, back in Chengdu, and she probably wouldn't see him until the following year. She asked me how long it had been since I'd been home, and I said I hadn't left China in more than two years.

"We're the same," she said. "Both of us are a long way from home." I agreed, and she asked if I missed my family. "Of course I miss them," I said. "But I'll see them next month, when I go home."

It was the wrong thing to say. Her eyes went empty and then filled with tears. We sat alone in the restaurant. It was unusual for a Chinese to show emotion in public, and I didn't know what to say.

Silently I ate my dumplings while she cried, the late-afternoon sun stirring the Lhasa flies that were thick about the table.

Tibet had started to depress me, and I was looking forward to leaving. Strangely, it almost seemed worse for not being as bad as I had always heard. There were definite benefits of Chinese support, and I was impressed by the idealism and dedication of some of the young Han teachers I had met. But at the same time, most efforts to develop the region were badly planned, and it was frustrating to see so much money and work invested in a poor country and so much unhappiness returned. And often I felt that the common people, who knew little of Tibet's complicated historical and cultural issues, were being manipulated by the government in ways they didn't understand. But although I was certain that nobody was truly happy (most of the Han didn't like being there, and most of the Tibetans certainly weren't happy to have them), I wasn't sure who was pulling the strings. One could go straight to the top and probably find the same helplessness, the same strings. It was mostly the irrevocable mistakes of history, but it was also money—simple economic pressure that drove a mother away from her son to a place where the people did not want her.

This was not the first time I'd seen somebody cry in Lhasa. Five days earlier I'd spent the evening in front of the Jokhang temple, where I talked with two Tibetans. The first was a doctor who had done time in prison for writing an article warning Tibetans to protect their culture, and the second was a fifty-three-year-old who described himself as a common worker. Both men were eager to speak with an American, and they had a great deal of faith in America's ability to help solve the Tibet question. That saddened me as well. I wanted to tell them that in America there are many FREE TIBET bumper stickers, but they sit next to license plates that often bear the names of forgotten tribes who succumbed to the same forces of expansion and modernization now threatening Tibet. And the Chinese solution to the Tibet question—throwing money at the problem—also seemed very American. But I held my peace and listened.

"Look at this pillar," the worker said. He was standing next to the temple entrance, and he rested his hand on the worn red wood. "If a house doesn't have pillars, or if the pillars aren't straight, what will happen? It will fall down. It's the same thing here—our pillars are our history and our politics. If we don't have those, our society will collapse, and all of it will be lost—all of our culture."

It was dark, and I could barely make out his face, but I could see there were tears in his eyes. There was no more politically sensitive place in Tibet; virtually every major protest had happened in front of the Jokhang, and I knew it was unwise to speak so openly here. He glanced over his shoulder and continued.

"You need to tell the people of America what it's like here," he said. "You need to tell them what needs to be done." I nodded and shook his hand, but I realized I had no idea what I would recommend, or what the people of America could do. Perhaps we could build casinos.

Peter Hessler went to China as a Peace Corp volunteer and taught English there from 1996 to 1998. His articles have appeared in The New York Times, The Philadelphia Inquirer, The Atlantic Monthly, *and* The Washington Post. *He is the author of* River Town: Two Years on the Yangtze.

PART TWO

Some Things to Do

* * *

Like a Rolling Stone

In Tibet, getting there may sometimes be half the fun,
but usually it's way more than half the trouble.

THE JOURNEY FROM LHASA TO GOLMUD WHERE THE RAILROAD begins takes a full two days. It's about five hundred miles across a desert plateau. A deluxe Mitsubishi bus runs daily over the army-built supply route. Travelers coming the other way told tales of breakdowns and heavy snows in the passes which made them fear for their lives. I was near broke. I couldn't afford to fly, and could ill afford a luxury coach. Following a hot tip from my hotel's manager, I located a local transport company that ran regular buses for less than half the deluxe price.

When Mike found out about the deal he said he too was ready to head back into China, so we decided to travel together. Mike was a Madison Avenue advertising executive in a recent past life. A year earlier, his wife had suggested he take a trip around the world. Or better yet, just go halfway and stay there. So he quit his job and his marriage and had gone native in Lhasa. He bought a floor-length Tibetan coat lined with sheepskin, and a red fox-fur hat. His beard was a short bristly red, his eyes wild blue. He stood over six feet tall, and all suited up looked more intimidating than a Khampa bandit. We met in the dormitory we shared in the Snowlands Hotel.

The discount transport company's vehicle turned out to be a standard city bus, with double electric doors in the center, a low chassis, big glass windows, and hard metal seats covered with thin plastic cushions. Only three passengers boarded with us: a Yunnan native with only half a mouthful of teeth who was transporting five large Tibetan chests to a buyer in Amdo, and two Han Chinese wearing Mao suits. I spoke passable Chinese, so we chatted. One of them was a fortyish Beijing man named Guo who worked as a road supervisor in Lhasa. His companion was a short, timid man who told me, apologetically, that he had four children, which meant he could not have been from Beijing, where the one-child policy was most strictly in force. The two Han Chinese wore only their padded blue Mao suits. No gloves, no hats. The bus had no heating. Dressed like that, I thought the two would freeze to death. It was only mid-March.

Our driver, a young Mongolian named Topo, had brought along with him a buddy named Monzo, who perched on the interior hood of the engine next to the driver's seat. His main function apparently was to keep Topo awake by singing and telling loud jokes in Mongolian. They both wore knee-high leather boots, as if they were moonlighting Mongolian cavalry. Topo wore his fur cap twisted sideways over his long black hair. Monzo's cheeks had a dull blackness about them as if they had suffered frostbite. His eyes held a similar dullness, as if numbed from endless nights driving or drinking or both.

As we headed out of Lhasa, Topo stopped for more passengers, including two families of pilgrims returning to their villages and a hulking great Khampa man with a bicycle. The bicycle caused some difficulty, because the aisle was already crammed full of the man-with-the-half-smile's furniture—as well as a spare tire, a drum full of gasoline, and a blowtorch with an acetylene tank. The road was rough, rutted, and frozen solid, and the bus's shocks apparently had been removed. With each bounce, the furniture crackled with the sound of splintering wood and we caught the occasional whiff of sawdust. Half-Smile clambered back and forth over the top of his load like a four-legged spider, desperately trying to secure his precious chests in place with a bale of wire. The Khampa kept forgetting to hang on to his bike, and every now and then it zipped down the aisle into drums or the chests or the back of Half-Smile's legs.

The road climbed steadily, without a dip, across a broad plateau. All traces of agriculture disappeared except for the occasional herd of yaks or sheep grazing on the dry yellow grass. Snow lay melting in little drifts next to the highway. The few rivers we crossed were frozen solid.

About three hours out of the city, a sudden loud "clunk" came from the undercarriage, followed by a loud scraping screech. Topo jammed on his brakes. The front support bracket of the gas tank had broken off, dragging it along the undercarriage. Luckily, there had been no sparks. I feared the Mongolians would try and weld the tank back in place with the blowtorch. However Topo had a better plan. He simply disconnected the other bracket and the fuel line, then instructed the passengers to lift the tank round to the other side of the bus and we hauled it in through the electric doors. We set it down in the aisle. Topo then reconnected the gas line to the engine through a hole in the floor, and we were off again.

The Tibetan pilgrims got off at small hamlets along the roadside. The Khampa cyclist, however, disembarked in the middle of the barren plateau.

Our road crew spent the morning repairing our vehicle's punctured gas tank, facilitating this miracle with a twist of sheep wool, a twig, and a bar of soap. I received what little satisfaction I could by lending them a sharp knife for the job.

"Do you think that will hold until they can get to a repair shop?" I asked my guide.

"That's as good a repair as you get in these parts," he laughed. "Out here, if you can't fix it, you don't drive it."

—Tom Joyce, "Yeti, Flying Saints, and Boys with Guns"

He said a few words of thanks to the drivers, who had probably saved him three day's riding. He pedaled off over the rocks and small clumps, steering perpendicular to the highway towards a horizon which bore not a trace of smoke that might indicate a tent or a hut somewhere out there.

We stopped at nine P.M. at a small barracks-like compound which seemed little used by anybody. Guo got a room to himself, while Mike and I were given a dank room to share with the little Chinese, whom we named Shorty. With no heat, and temperatures well below zero, it was going to be a cold night. I stumbled over something just inside the threshold. I clicked the light switch. No electricity. I flipped on my flashlight and discovered I had tripped over the remains of some half-eaten animal, as large as a dog. I wished I'd left my flashlight in the bus. I kicked the carcass outside, suddenly grateful for the freezer-room temperatures which kept the room from smelling.

At five in the morning the Mongolians thawed out the engine with the blowtorch. By dawn we had driven forty miles closer to Golmud, making little more than twenty miles per hour. We stopped for breakfast at a small white shack inside a barbed-wire compound. A weak, flickering electric bulb hung over the entrance. Inside, we found three ramshackle tables and a few rickety wooden benches. The cook warmed rice and a chunk of frozen yak noodle soup for us in a wok, heated underneath by a blowtorch. An oil stove would have been next to useless in the cold, and wood was scarce. But *voilà*, our soup was steaming in minutes. On the Tibetan Plateau, there was no household appliance quite so handy and versatile as a blowtorch for warming your soup or starting your engine.

After breakfast, a mangy bitch snarled and barked at Mike, tail between her legs. I suppose she had never seen anything quite so horrifying. Mike's response was to raise his arms out from his sides, maximizing bulk, then growl like a werewolf, and lumber towards the dog Frankenstein-style. All pretense of barking gave way to a pathetic yelp. It scrambled underneath the barbed-wire fence then turned back defiantly on the other side. Undeterred, Mike grabbed the fence in both hands and rattled it violently, howling. The bitch squealed, bolted straight for the hills, not turning back.

Back in the bus, Guo and Shorty eyed Mike with suspicion. Was he as dangerous as he looked?

Throughout the morning and well into the afternoon we traveled in a straight line across the wide plateau. Topo made good speed, not stopping once through the unvarying, hypnotizing terrain. Finally, a little white shack appeared ahead of us, the first building we had seen in several hours. Topo pulled over next to several gas drums and told us he'd need our help refueling. We had to drag a drum of gasoline over to the bus steps, feed the hose through and hand pump it into the tank sitting in the aisle. A flickering electric bulb hung over the entrance of the shack. Inside was a restaurant: three ramshackle wooden tables, rickety benches. We heard the blowtorch flare up in the kitchen, and wondered if Topo had doubled back to our breakfast stop. The cook asked if we wanted yak soup or rice. We looked out the window. No, there was no hill here. It was another restaurant, but identical to the first.

"There must be a whole chain of these," I said to Mike.

"The Bench and Blowtorch..."

"...Franchises from Lhasa to Golmud."

"Just look for the sign of the flickering bulb."

On the wall someone had written something in large, red Chinese characters.

"See that?" said Mike, "It says 'Over 25 served.'"

The food was so good, we licked the grease off the bottom of our bowls.

A Tibetan herdsman and his wife and children came in for a bite of yak as we finished. In a prime location like this, the little franchise seemed well on its way to success.

We drove on, plateau after plateau, up the mountains again to a pass marked 5,165 meters (16,945 feet), and then up again higher. Along the roadside we spotted the occasional dead animal. Shorty told us they had frozen to death. He pointed each one out with a serious nod of his head. Their numbers increased as we climbed higher. Some had been dumped in piles. Many of the carcasses were half eaten, by what we could not guess. Yaks, goats, cows, wild asses, a few dogs. Frightening to think that yaks, with their thick woolly coats, could die of cold. The rough yellow grass grew thinner, then appeared only in sparse patches. Ahead we saw snow on the road. A few old road workers, bundled in Tibetan coats with shovels and brooms stood aside as we negotiated patches of icy snow. We entered a snowfield and stopped for photographs at a 17,126-foot pass in a roaring wind which froze our ears and cut through my coat. The gale shook the thin aluminum walls of the bus. We descended along the banks of a frozen river. White mountain peaks glowed in dull outline against the cloudy afternoon sky. Beside me, Shorty was shivering in his Mao suit. I had given him my blanket, and sometimes shared it with him to keep us both warm. Mike had given Guo his down sleeping bag to bundle in, and let him borrow a second Tibetan fur cap he had bought as a gift to send home. If not for us, we doubted that the two Chinese could avoid hypothermia.

Two hundred miles from Golmud, Topo pulled in at a large army base for the night, in the process entangling the bus in downed power lines. He gingerly backed out without snapping any. We tried to

---

The sleet had not stopped ever since we had arrived at Thango La. There we were stuck amongst 1,400 trucks, and the rain and snow fell harder and harder.

Thango La is the highest point on the road between Golmud and Lhasa. From the 5,220-meter-high pass [17,126 feet], you can see countless lakes which seem like the water-bowl offerings on an altar of a Tibetan temple, and a chain of trucks from the top of the pass to the bottom of the valley.

I saw many trucks washed away in the muddy road, bleeding drivers, dead and injured travelers, and I heard that a couple of drivers had died from hunger. I wondered where my own body would be laid. Many times we had to drive on top of army trucks filled with trunks of trees, or lumber trucks that had fallen down.

—Tenzin Phuntsok, "Diary of a Tibetan Truck Driver"

convince him to press on, to no avail. In two days' driving we had covered a mere 300 miles, with at least another eight hours on the road ahead of us. The last train out of Golmud left at four P.M, so a night stop here would mean we'd probably miss the train and have to spend an extra night at the station. Topo grinned, ignored my pleas in pidgin Chinese, and hopped out to find an officer to ask for permission to stay.

A sudden craziness welled up inside Mike and me, brought on perhaps by the numbing cold and nonstop bouncing of our brains. We paced up and down the clearer portions of the aisle, wondering what to do.

"Call on the gods," Mike suggested.

"Which gods?"

"I dunno. You're the one who knows them. Whichever ones will get us to Golmud. You know, like a rain dance."

We tried mantras and incantations, hymns and promises. Shorty peered at me from under my blanket, as if fearful I might have contracted rabies.

"We're so close, so bloody close to Golmud! But no satisfaction!" I howled, stomping my feet in the bus. "I can't get no—"

"Satisfaction," chimed in Mike.

"I can't get no-o..." We both crooned at the top of our voices.

"...Sat-is-fac-shun."

"And I try, and I try, and I try, and I try...I CAN'T GET NO—"

"SAT-IS-FAC-SHUN!"

By this time we were tromping to the beat, banging the bus seats with our palms, and singing in gasps in the thin, cold air. Our hips twisted, fur hats and earflaps flying, heavy coats open and sweeping as we spun and leapt in the bus. It warmed our frozen feet and gave us considerably more energy. The Chinese had begun to cower against the frozen metal walls.

"...HEAR WHAT I SAY! HEY HEY HEY!"

Topo and Monzo returned to the bus. They watched us with amusement for a few minutes before breaking the news: our prayers had been answered. The army refused us permission to stay. We'd have to push on to Golmud.

Satisfaction!

With 160 miles to go, at ten P.M. at the edge of the frozen Gobi Desert, the bus broke down. Topo and Monzo removed the interior cover of the engine so we could all see the smoke rising and smell the overheated engine parts. They scratched their heads. We held ours in our hands. It seemed something had gone wrong with the cooling system. Monzo got the plastic water jug from the back of the bus. It had frozen solid. He chipped away at the surface with a knife. He rubbed the back of his neck. We had an overheated engine, and only ice to put in it. The drivers conferred in their own language. They picked up the blowtorch and an empty tin can and wandered off down the road into the freezing Gobi, presumably in search of water to melt, for we had not passed a single dwelling for hours. We four passengers huddled together under blankets and sleeping bags and tried to sleep in the sub-zero cold, just hoping the drivers would come back before our carcasses froze like the animals.

The Mongolians returned two hours later, added the little water they had found, and started the bus again. They took the hood off the engine and drove on for another fifteen minutes, until steam filled the windscreen and the motor quit. They stared at the engine again, tinkered with the parts. The metal hissed steam. Mike and I played a game of "do the hokeypokey" to keep our circulation going. Shorty and Guo played a game of "dead frozen yak imitation," and refused our entreaties to shake it all about. I think they were more scared of us than of frostbite.

At 1:30 A.M. another bus pulled up behind us. The Tibetan driver came over to commiserate with Topo and offered to take his passengers the rest of the way to Golmud for extortionate prices. He loaded us all into his heated bus, curtly ordering Guo into his seat with a gruff Tibetan remark. The Chinese official took sudden offense at being spoken to in Tibetan, and shot back an angry rebuke in Mandarin. The new driver began to laugh, his impudence further infuriating the Chinese official who puffed up his chest with self-importance and rage. But the Tibetan pointed a finger at the foxfur hat Guo had borrowed from Mike which was still jammed down over his brow. Guo reached up, touched the fur, and reddened deep. Then he too laughed at the Tibetan's honest mistake. Imagine—a Beijing man mistaken for a Tibetan!

Once he had us on board, our new driver offered the Mongols a large jug of water. They topped up their radiator, and the engine roared back to life. Indignant, we all grabbed our packs, jumped off and raced back to our old bus while the other driver cursed. We were rolling again. The clouds cleared. The moon, near to full, cast a pale light on more snowfields and mountains as we climbed a final pass. Topo put the pedal to the floor on the downhill run, soon overtaking the luxury coach. We flew down the mountainside, all wheels bouncing off the ground. At 5:30 in the morning, Shorty nudged me and pointed to electric lights on the horizon.

Golmud, glorious Golmud, an oasis of dust and concrete in the midst of the Gobi. If you have a fascination with gravel, then Golmud is the place to be. But for us that frigid dawn, Golmud was paradise found. Never has so little meant so much to so few.

Canadian Tim Ward has written three books about his adventures in the remote corners of Asia: What the Buddha Never Taught, The Great Dragon's Fleas, *and* Arousing the Goddess. *His newest book,* The Savage Breast, *details his travels through the Aegean and Southeastern Europe in search of ancient goddesses.*

CHARLES ALLEN

On the Sacred Mountain

A lifetime dissolves on the kora *around Mount Kailash.*

I WANT TO CAMP ON THE RIGHT BANK OF THE RIVER UPSTREAM OF the monastery for no better reason than that the great Swedish explorer Sven Hedin camped there ninety years ago. But Sonam, our guide, seems determined on the other side of the river and when we ignore his advice he goes into an almighty sulk, throwing himself down on the ground with his baseball cap over his face. He lies there while the tents are being put up and he's still lying there when everyone else is having supper. Only when it's dark and freezing does he rouse himself and pitch his tent well away from the rest of us.

Day two of the *kora* should be the easiest: half a day's walk up the valley. The walls of the valley here are quite astonishing in their diversity of form and color. On our left as we walk north are a series of peaks divided by tumbling streams and waterfalls. The central three are like the flying buttresses of some gigantic cathedral and are the abodes of the three Buddhist goddesses of longevity: Drölma, Tsepame, and Nyamgyalma. Opposite them on the right side of the valley, the western flanks of Kangri Rinpoche provide an even more dramatic spectacle. The lower sections appear smooth, warm, and pink-gray like the skin of an elephant and are divided into a series of spurs that also resemble the supports of monster cathedrals. At the top they drop back to form a sort of throne of the gods. Higher still, snow from the summit bubbles over like the froth on an overfilled tankard of beer.

There is no hard climbing here, merely a gentle incline, but I have to keep stopping to recover breath and strength, and I soon get left behind. During one such rest break I watch a herd of blue sheep pick its way cautiously across the lower slopes of the scree, no more than sixty yards away. Just as I'm pondering on why these shy creatures should choose to come down so low and so close to man, I spot what looks like a tail sticking out from behind a small boulder. At the other end of this rock I can see the head of what must be the same animal. If I am not mistaken, what is lurking there, waiting in ambush for the blue sheep, is that rarest of all carnivores, the snow leopard! Very, very slowly I reach across my chest for my binoculars and bring them up to my eyes (or rather, my one good eye). I focus, find the boulder—and there at one end is indeed a short fluffy tail. Then pan right to the other end—and there, instead of the face of *panthera uncia*, I am confronted by the backside of a great fat marmot. What I am seeing is two marmots, both as large as badgers, going about their business of nibbling roots and shoots. Another time, perhaps.

The bird books say that the lammergeier is a scavenger and not a bird of prey. Not so, because I watch one of these magnificent birds come skimming low down the valley like a Tornado GR1 on a low-level reconnaissance run. It passes so close that I can hear its feathers buzzing, with its undercarriage down and the talons outstretched ready to snatch up an unwary marmot or pika.

An hour or so further on the valley divides. The trail crosses the main stream, which has disappeared under several large patches of hardened snow, and turns to the right. The going gets a bit harder and my stops are more frequent and longer. I see a figure hunched beside the path ahead of me: Terry. He has a splitting headache and nausea and doesn't think he can go any further. We sip from our thermos flasks, suck a couple of boiled sweets, and think the unthinkable: perhaps we should turn back. It would be so easy now just to head back down the valley to Darchen and wait there for the others. It would be the unselfish thing to do because we wouldn't be holding them up.

This unholy debate is ended by the arrival of Mel, bouncing like Tigger. How we hate him for being so fit. Then back comes Bagbir, too, waving a thermos flask. He pours us out two mugs of sweet tea and hands round some biscuits. When we've drunk and eaten he hoists up my pack and adds it to his own. He says nothing, only smiles. Impossible to refuse such a man.

The last hour is a daymare. I am only dimly aware of the stupendous sheet of rock and ice which has been coming into view just to our right as we slowly turn the corner of the massif: the sheer north face of the Nine Stacked Swastikas Mountain. Overpowering. Awesome. As dark as the south face is light. Breathtaking, if I had any breath left to take.

We camp tonight in the guest house below the monastery of Drira Phuk, the Cave of the Female Yak, at an altitude of about 16,000 feet. This is the northernmost of

---

We soon came to Bardo Trang, the sin-testing stone. Walking around Kailash is said to wipe out the sins of a lifetime. A serious sin cleansing, however, wiping out all the sins of all your lifetimes, takes a much larger commitment: 108 circuits of the mountain. Nevertheless, even a minor one-life-time scrub up is only possible if you start out with the right attitude, and a sin-testing stone checks your karma quota. The test is simple: you just have to slide through the narrow passage under the stone. Too much sin and you'll get stuck, no matter how skinny you are. And if you have too much sin, a single circuit may simply not be enough to tidy up your life. Fortunately, I slipped through without any difficulty…well, perhaps my hips were just a little wider than I expected.

—Tony Wheeler, "Walking the Mount Kailash Circuit," *Lonely Planet Unpacked*

our four staging posts round the mountain, a simple whitewashed building built over the cave which gives it its name. A Kagyupa lama named Gyalba Gotshangpa is credited with being the first to make a *kora* of the holy mountain in the early thirteenth century. During that pioneering first circuit he stopped here for a brew-up and collected several small stones to form supports for his kettle. To his surprise all were inscribed with mantras. Then it began to sleet and, as he looked for shelter, a *dakini* in the form of a female yak, a *dri*, appeared and led him to a cave.

We were supposed to have had our own yak for this stage of our journey, to carry our baggage. Sonam claims that none are available because so many died in the terrible snowstorms that devastated Tibet's nomadic community in the late autumn. He may well be telling the truth. In their place Sonam has managed to recruit nine young Gelugpa monks, here on pilgrimage. They are fit, strong, and full of high spirits but they have only their maroon togas to keep them warm at night. While we shiver inside the guest house in our thermal underwear and down-filled sleeping bags, they lie outside, huddled up together round a small fire, taking it in turns to keep a flame going all night. It is the wind that chills, not the low temperature.

It's very plain that the three fifty-and-overs—that's myself, Terry, and Dick—aren't up to completing the next stage of the *kora*, from here all the way to Zutrul Phuk Gompa, in one day. So we give ourselves an easy half-day instead and make camp above the moraines at the base of the final snow staircase that leads up to the 18,600-foot Drölma La. On the way we pass through an area that looks like a municipal dump. This is Siwatshal Dutro, regarded by many as the most important power-point on the circuit. Every pilgrim makes an offering here in the form of some personal item, which can be as basic as some drops of blood or a hank of hair. Articles of clothing seem to be the popular choice because the entire area is strewn with ragged bits of cloth, including numerous hats. The site takes its name after a famous cremation ground near Bodh Gaya in India and the act of leaving some personal items symbolizes a renunciation of all worldly goods. What takes place here is a ritual death in preparation for the rebirth which follows once the pilgrim has attained the high point of the circuit at the Drölma La. We are rather spoiling the process by camping overnight midway between these two stages, a night in a state of purgatory, as it were.

My left eye is now pain-free. For the first time since crossing into Tibet I can take full bifocal account of our surroundings. An almost unbroken stream of pilgrims passes our tent for much of the afternoon: pilgrims of all ages and from every social level, from sun-blackened shepherds in animal skins to the privileged few who sport Western trophies such as shades and parkas. A few stop to stare at our outlandish bulbous tents but for the most part they are preoccupied in their own thoughts. They trudge forward in silence or murmuring prayers, left hands working prayer beads, right hands turning prayer wheels. A mile ahead of us the trail cuts a steep diagonal across the mountainside, the pilgrims silhouetted against the snow like a line of pinpricks on white paper.

This route leading up and over the shoulder of the holy mountain was revealed to Lama Gotshangpa by twenty-one Taras (in Tibetan, Drölma), who appeared in the form of wolves: "He followed them and so walked to the summit of the pass where he saw them merge one into

---

As we waited on tiny stools for dinner we could see into the kitchen, like the stage set for a Grimm's fairy tale. A waist-high cauldron seethed with cooking rice. The chef, in black rags, moved like a frantic spider between two woks over burners on the dirt floor. His gangling assistant applied a bellows to the fire, raising a cloud of ash. Everything in the kitchen was blackened. An elderly Englishwoman who had the fortitude to make it this far stood on the sidelines exclaiming "simply appalling" over and over. We shared a platter of gray fat and wood fungus with a French couple and two Tibetan monks. The monks carefully ate all the gobs of fat we were avoiding.

—Valerie Brewster,
"Postcard from Tibet"

another until only one remained, which then vanished into a boulder. Ever since then the name of that pass has been famous as the Drölma La."

At something over 17,500 feet, this camp is the highest that the three oldies of our party are ever likely to experience. I earnestly hope so. Five of us bed down early in the afternoon to keep warm but Mel and Binod scamper up the nearest peak and return full of sickening *joie de vivre*. Early supper at six P.M. and all tucked up in our sleeping bags by seven P.M.

The first note in my diary for the following day reads: "Night too frightful to recall." Not so. I can vividly remember a night of fitful sleep racked by short, sharp nightmares dreamed up by a brain starved of oxygen. Double doses of Panadol do nothing to alleviate the headache. The wind tugs and bangs on the tent in sudden, irregular bursts. At midnight Dick decides that he has to have more air and unzips the opening. The temperature plummets. I am already wearing every available stitch of clothing; even so, my feet and my buttocks slowly harden into blocks of ice, as does that tiny part of my nose which is still directly exposed to the open air. Sleep is out of the question. I lie shaking, trying to think of things to think about—not easy when one's brain is only just ticking over—and listening to Dick's irregular breathing. This is alarming. His lungs attempt to draw in more air by taking deeper and quicker breaths that build up over two minutes or so into a crescendo of snorts culminating in one great gurgling gasp. At last the lungs have enough air, so they switch off and Dick stops breathing all together. There is medical name for this condition which I know perfectly well but I cannot for the life of me remember what it is, nor how life-threatening it is or is not. For what seems like an eternity I wait anxiously for signs of continued life. Then his lungs splutter into action again, and the cycle is renewed. Even so, there are a number of times when I have to sit up, lean over him and expose an ear to check that he really is still alive. This is not as easy as it sounds because the simple act of raising oneself on to one's elbows and twisting the upper part of the trunk leaves one panting.

By about four o'clock in the morning I've had enough. I wrig-

gle over to the flap of the tent and very, very slowly, inch by inch,
zip it up again. I defrost and fall asleep. Thirty seconds later Muhun
is unzipping the tent with a cup of tea in his hand.

Up and dressed at six, stamping about in my boots to get the
circulation going again. The monks are still sleeping. Again they
have slept out in the open air, but this time without a fire. They
have piled themselves together into a heap like puppy dogs and lie
completely covered by their red togas. However, it has snowed during the night so now they are half-hidden under a thin film of
snow. It's hard to believe that they could survive under such conditions and, indeed, when they start to emerge, they look pretty
rough. They hadn't expected this extra night on the bare mountain
and their smiles are a little strained.

The blessed sun reaches us at seven and by eight we've joined the
pilgrims who are already on the trail. The snow is crisp underfoot.
Despite the stiff climb an overwhelming sense of happiness affects
us all. Whatever our motives, every one of us climbing this staircase
has had to work hard to get here. This is the culmination of days
and weeks and even years. And now, for all the physical pain that
we're still going through, we *know* we're going to make it. Our worries are behind us. I stop frequently to regain my breath, to ease the
frantic pumping of my heart, and these moments are often shared
with elderly Tibetans. We laugh at each other as we ease our loads
off our backs. We mop our brows and shake our heads in shared
discomfort. Then we pull on our loads, look up at the dazzling snow
above us and push on. This is a shared communion, this last thousand feet.

About two-thirds of the way up the strangest thing happens. I've
heard of climbers becoming aware of invisible companions at their
side and now it happens to me. I have the strongest sense of someone at my left shoulder, just out of sight, walking slightly behind and
above me, higher on the slope. I can even hear his boots crunching
in the snow. Several times I stop and turn, expecting to see someone overhauling me on my left, but there's no one there. The con-
viction grows in me that it is my father. He and I had been planning
a last great adventure in the mountains together shortly before his

death. As a political officer in the Indian Political Service in the late 1940s and early 1950s he had spent months touring in the foothills of the eastern Himalayas as part of his job, but had never achieved his ambition of entering Tibet. Now I feel his presence at my side, silently urging me on. This is so very real that I turn and smile and lift my ice-axe in salute to him, because I want him to know that I know he's with me.

Then from far above, faintly at first, the shouts of those who have already reached the top. Now our turn approaches. The blue sky grows above the snow. A first glimpse of brightly colored prayer flags flapping in the wind. Then more blue sky and more prayer flags, long strings of them stretching out to left and right. Another dozen steps and a big flag-covered boulder rises in front of us. The tiredness is gone. We run forward and duck under a tangled mass of flags, emerging on the other side with shouts of "Lha-so-so! Lha-so-so!" We have left behind our old lives and are reborn. We are starting again with clean slates. Laughter fills the sky. We have come through. Our perspectives have changed: we are no longer looking up, but down on the world. Hugs all round.

This is where I promised to leave Sandra's rosary, which I have carried wrapped around my ice-axe. I know now that I must leave something for my father, too, so the rosary and ice-axe stay together and are buried under a small cairn of stones. This, too, is a great place for leaving personal objects, and all of us leave something behind here: Dick leaves a photo of his wife and another one of his recently deceased cat. It is also the custom to take something as a personal memento. I choose a string of prayer flags and leave behind some new ones, which Mel helps me erect on the highest point I can reach.

Within ten minutes of our arriving at Drölma La the weather has changed dramatically for the worse. Clouds descend, hiding the summit and the surrounding peaks from view, and it begins to snow. The wind begins to bite.

We start the descent in a hurry, knowing we have miles to go before we sleep. We scurry past the famous frozen lake just below the pass, said to be one of the highest in the world, scarcely giving

it a glance. My elation at having reached the p La is replaced by an
overwhelming melancholy. I know this is physically induced: the
effort of keeping myself going over the last two days is taking
its toll.

Warm soup, shelter from the wind, and kind words are waiting
for me when I reach the floor of the Lham Chhu valley. After lunch
we push on again. The high spot of the afternoon is the singing of
a party of young Tibetan women who overtake our party and keep
pace with us for a short time. They exchange plaintive songs and
occasionally join together in delightful harmony as they walk. I
spoil it all with my rendering of "Viktor's Farewell from the White
Horse Inn." This reduces them to shocked silence and they quickly
scamper ahead.

*Charles Allen was born in India, where six generations of his family served
under the British Raj. After being educated in England he returned to the
Indian subcontinent in 1966 to work with Voluntary Service Overseas in
Nepal. He ended his service with a long walk through the Himalayas that
won him the Sunday Telegraph Traveler of the Year trophy in 1967. A writer
and oral historian specializing in colonial and military subjects, he is the author
of several books including* Tales from the Dark Continent, Tales from
the South China Seas, Plain Tales from the Raj, *and* The Search for
Shangri-La: A Journey into Tibetan History, *from which this story was
excerpted. He lives in North London.*

KEVIN ENGLISH

A Meeting with a Monk

The unexpected encounters are best.

STILL STRUGGLING TO CATCH MY BREATH AS I SCALED THE SEEM-
ingly insurmountable fourth flight of stairs to my guest-house cubi-
cle, I knew I was overexerting myself. However, after spending
nearly a week acclimatizing in Lhasa, I was restless to venture out
beyond the confines of the city into the mysteriously stunning
Tibetan countryside. I had briefly glanced upon the vast bronze
frontier through my cracked airline window, and was awestruck by
the raw beauty, which appeared to sprawl out in every direction.
Unfortunately, the high altitude of this kingdom virtually paralyzes
the visitor upon arrival, forcing one to succumb to a slothful
existence. I was certainly no exception to this phenomenon.
Thankfully, the exotic sights and sounds of Lhasa provide a stimu-
lating diversion to allow your ill-prepared lungs to catch up to your
uninhibited spirit. Nevertheless, by the sixth day, my need to press
on began to take precedence. As an avid backpacker, I was eager to
explore the remote villages and ancient monasteries which lured me
to this special place.

To test my altitude preparedness, I proceeded to the nearest bicycle rental outfit, where for little more than a dollar and a careless
signature on a Chinese form, I acquired transportation for the day.

I had read about the nearby Drepung monastery complex, the original home of the Dalai Lama before the construction of the Potala Palace, and determined that it would serve as the perfect day trip. With tremendous jubilation, I placed my feet on the pedals and raced off into the colorful Tibetan traffic. Buses, trucks, wagons, tractors, rickshaws, and fellow cyclists all shared the broad, unmarked streets of the city. Using the Potala and the position of the sun as chief landmarks, I plowed through the bustling lanes toward my destination. A sweet rush passed though me as the winds and the smells of the city enveloped my body. Mesmerized by this wondrous sensation, it took a great while before I realized that the bike I was riding was truly of local variety—loose handlebars, no gears, and a misaligned front wheel. I passed the remainder of the day riding on the simple faith that somehow every piece would hold in place.

Before long, the impressive Potala faded into the distance, and fields of brilliant yellow mustard plants, swaying playfully in the brisk wind, surrounded me. Steep brown hills rambled on endlessly in every direction. A multitude of Tibetan farmers dotted the landscape and faint hints of their songs and chatter were carried to my ear by the breeze. The faces of these remarkable individuals will never leave me, their pervading smiles and windswept features meshing to form simple yet striking countenances. After a few miles of fairly level cycling through this splendid slice of countryside, I reached my turnoff. Up to this point, biking at 12,000 feet had been surprisingly painless, yet it was apparent that an immense challenge lay ahead. Drepung, my destination for the day, sat atop a steep hillside, with only a rough dirt road leading the way.

Attempting to climb forward on my gearless wonder, I began to gasp for air. The deep, sand-like path added an insurmountable degree of difficulty to the steep grade. Consequently, after a few more labored huffs, I found myself walking along the track, bicycle in tow. However, this unexpected setback afforded me the opportunity to become introspective, a trait this landscape effortlessly manifests in all of its travelers. Unfortunately, my mind repeatedly dwelled on a worry that my trusted guidebook had engendered.

The author had described in great detail the monastery's savage resident dogs! Furthermore, the text made a special effort to highlight that despite the great potential for dog bites, treatment for rabies was unavailable in Tibet. I had not previously concerned myself with this information, as I have always considered myself an animal lover, and felt quite comfortable around dogs. Nevertheless, as I climbed further and further up the dusty trail, the image of vicious hounds consumed my thoughts.

To quell my burgeoning apprehension, I decided to look through the woods along the corridor for a walking stick for security. However, within moments of stepping off the path, a decrepit minibus loaded with pilgrims passed by, which led me to reconsider my actions. I was aware that in Buddhist philosophy, all living things are sacred. Therefore, I wondered if my tramping through these woodlands was taboo. Fearful of offending the locals by tearing a branch from a tree, I instead scoured the ground for a dead limb. Unfortunately, the pickings were sparse, and I managed to find only a pathetic twig for my defense.

Perhaps the most vivid image I still have of Tibet is the overwhelming contrast between the bleached white monastery complexes and the jagged brown peaks that surround them. Drepung was no exception. The austere beauty of this sacred place was astonishing and quickly put my dog-infested imagination to rest. Thus, once I reached the complex, I parted with my worthless limb and mocked myself for my lapse into paranoia. Despite the midday heat, I decided to first explore the pilgrimage trail, or *kora*, encircling the entire structure of the complex to gain a better sense of the setting's enormity. The rugged path was dotted with numerous patches of prayer flags and stones as well as a multitude of sacred paintings, carvings, and stupas. After a few minutes, I passed an older pilgrim who was shuffling along peacefully while spinning his prayer wheel and chanting a mantra. I nodded hello, but intent on not disturbing him, I continued forward. As I wandered on, the trail became quite removed from the monastery, but the view intensified. The distant image of monks, pilgrims, and livestock harmoniously performing their daily rituals was truly inspiring.

As I continued forward, spooking the occasional sunbathing lizard, I happened upon a mangy dog lying on its side, virtually lifeless under the intense sun. I laughed at my earlier antics to acquire protection from such a debilitated beast. However, as I continued to walk, I noticed more dogs in similar sedentary states. Many appeared to have secured havens underneath rock outcroppings, while others opted to lie haphazardly across the trail. Fortunately, each dog appeared to be wholly uninterested in my presence. Nevertheless, as I tiptoed through the makeshift canine obstacle course, I grew more conscious of the distance I had traveled from the monastery. Consequently, despite clearing the area, I decided to glance backward. To my utter disbelief, at least four or five dogs had slowly begun to track me! My heart immediately awakened with a loud beat and I began scurrying for another stick to avert an attack. Unfortunately, the barren landscape offered little vegetation beyond scrub brush. I promptly changed course, and set my sights on a few decent sized rocks. To my horror, every accessible stone had some form of sacred carving upon it, which forced me to leave them in place out of respect. Peering back again, the once non-intimidating dogs appeared reenergized and were climbing closer. Many of these dogs are hypothesized to be the reincarnations of monks who had not studied their lessons properly or had betrayed their duties altogether. As a result, they did not transcend into their next life in the typical "upward" fashion. Of course this information, although interesting, offered little solace or guidance in the midst of this unexpected pursuit. With no clear escape in sight, I opted to sprint ahead and hide behind a high rock outcrop beside the trail. I did so, and with profuse sweat dripping from every pore of my body, I cowered nervously and studied the beasts as they circled about in search of me. To my astonishment, they retreated!

After allowing my heart to regain its natural rhythm, I veered away from the *kora*, to avoid a repeat encounter. Unfortunately, my only partially acclimatized body suffered greatly as I attempted to scale the sheer hillside. To compensate, I searched the area for a shady resting spot. Upon locating a flat rock largely tucked into the shadow, my spirits lifted. The serene view from my pleasing outpost was most welcome after my ordeal. Drepung now appeared incred-

ibly tiny against this seemingly infinite landscape. However, before
I had the opportunity to fully
settle down, an elderly monk
in a maroon robe appeared on
the horizon walking in my
direction. He was skillfully
carrying an enormous metal
container of water on his
back, which was adjoined to
his forehead by a worn leather
strap. As he approached, glis-
tening with sweat, yet still
smiling, I greeted him with
hand gestures and inquired
about his destination. He
pointed to the crest of a distant ridge. Glancing further
up the slope, the landscape
appeared absolutely barren
and uninhabited. However,
upon closer inspection, I
noticed a figure in pink
perched alongside a large rock
face, far in the distance.
Somehow, at that moment,
the scene before me began to
unfold. As unfathomable as it
seemed, I was fairly certain
that the image was a distant
cave and its resident monk! I
had heard of such existences
within the Buddhist faith, but
I imagined them to be largely
confined to the past. Despite
my exhaustion, I could not
contain myself from trekking

Tibetans are fond of dogs:
these hounds perform guard
duties in many villages around
Tibet. Dogs are believed to be
reincarnates of renegade monks
who didn't quite make the grade,
and hence are accepted at monasteries. Sometimes dogs operate
in packs around monasteries, and
on occasion can be extremely
dangerous. Travelers have been
attacked and dragged to the
ground in some places, and then
rescued by monks. Dogs are
known to carry rabies in Tibet:
to be on the safe side, if a dog
draws blood, you should get a
course of rabies shots (at the
People's Hospital in Lhasa or
clinics in Kathmandu in Nepal).
The best strategy is not to get
bitten in the first place. Treat dogs
with extreme caution: carry a
stick, or an umbrella, or pick up
a stone if a dog approaches. If a
dog attacks, clobber it on the
sensitive snout area. You might
also consider squirting a water
bottle or using pepper spray.

—Michael Buckley, *Tibet:
The Bradt Travel Guide*

onward for a better look. I exchanged a bow of respect with the
elder monk and carried on.

As I scurried nearer and nearer, it was clear that I was approaching a young man in a pink robe. He was focusing on me as intently
as I was watching him. Once we were finally in close proximity to
one another, I made a gesture to ensure that it was acceptable to
proceed. A broad smile appeared across this younger monk's face
and he promptly received me into his cave. Although it was no
more than six feet long in any direction, he offered me an
impromptu tour of his cozy abode. It centered on a beautiful shrine
with many Buddha sculptures and pictures (including forbidden
photos of the Dalai Lama). Other notable possessions included a
rock shelf holding all of the scriptures and teachings he was studying, canisters of tea and yak butter, a small table, and two cushions.
After touring the residence with just a whirl of my head in each
direction, he swiftly poured us two bowls of yak-butter tea. An
acquired taste, this traditional concoction consists of exceptionally
salty lard blended with hot water and bits of tea. Although it had
already rated as my least favorite Tibetan custom, I was delighted to
partake under these extraordinary circumstances.

We proceeded to sip our tea and stare at one another for an
incredibly long period of time until I decided to share a few items
from my backpack. He most enjoyed leafing through the pages of
my guidebook, especially those with pictures of various Tibetan
landmarks. When he uncovered a page containing a sketch of the
Dalai Lama, he thrust the entire book to his chest and then lifted it
above his head. Based on his expression, I was certain that this image
had conjured up intense emotions within him, which an outsider
such as myself could never fully comprehend.

Perhaps due to my initial nervousness, I finished my bowl of tea
in record time, which only led to a prompt refill. It was at this time
that I finally realized that I had forgotten all about my tiny Tibetan
phrasebook. As I grabbed hold of it, he too rejoiced at the sight of
recognizable script and the potential for dialogue it held. Over the
next few hours we exchanged such broken phrases as "this is a cave"
and "I drink tea." However, even with our impaired dialogue, I

learned that he was studying in this cave, and would not return to the monastery for months. He showed me how the two cushions we were sitting upon also served as his mattress when placed together. Although a stack of thick blankets was heaped in the corner, I shuddered at the thought of the frigid night temperatures at this altitude come autumn. Nevertheless, in spite of these spartan conditions, his pleasant demeanor reflected a state of contentment which permeated the cave.

The entire experience of this meeting was magical. Our ages must have been quite similar, but I marveled at the extreme differences between our existences. I asked my new friend to sign his name in Tibetan into my journal. He did so, carefully depicting each character as he went along. With seemingly nothing to leave him, I remembered that I was still wearing my hand carved Buddhist good luck charm made of yak bone. Removing it from my neck, I placed it in his hand. He clearly recognized the characters, and he clutched the piece to his chest. I wish I could have explained that a Tibetan man, living in exile in Nepal, gave it to me as a good luck charm to trek over the high passes of the Annapurna in the Nepalese Himalayas. Instead I opted

Down a lane from the Barkhor bazaar, past a long row of prayer wheels, we found a crowd of pilgrims squatting around huge, steaming caldrons of yak-butter tea. Old people in traditional woolens and animal skins twirled prayer wheels, chanted, and cooked *tsampa* over smoky fires. They were gathered before a temple of the protector, Guru Rinpoche, enjoying each other's company and their shared devotion in a setting straight out of the Middle Ages. After we'd paid our respects inside, they insisted we join them for tea, showing a touching generosity with their meager possessions even though, by comparison, we were unspeakably wealthy and from appearances could have been visitors from another planet.

—Larry Habegger,
"Glimpses of Tibet"

for the translation of "you and your cave are beautiful." Shortly thereafter, I began my descent back to the monastery. To my surprise, throughout the entire journey back to Lhasa, I never once thought about those dogs.

Kevin English is a freelance writer currently living in New Mexico. In addition to traveling and writing, he is a public health specialist working collaboratively with Native American tribes on reservations throughout the Southwest. Traveling has reaffirmed his belief that exotic adventures can be had anywhere, from the Tibetan Himalayas to one's own backyard, but are only possible with an open mind and spirit.

SVEN HEDIN

The Holy Lake

In 1907, the famous Swedish explorer
tests the goodwill of the Gods.

HOLY, HOLY, HOLY, IS THE TIBETANS' TSO MAVANG, OR TSO
Rinpoche, the Manasarovar of the Hindus, Brahma's soul. A garland
of mountains rises on its banks; and golden eagles, from their nests
below the permanent snowfields on Kailash in the north and the
Gurla Mandata in the south, contemplate its turquoise-blue surface,
upon which the faithful from India see Siva, descended from this
paradise, circling about in the form of a white swan. This lake has
been celebrated for thousands of years in ancient religious hymns.
In the part of the *Skandha Purana* entitled "Manasa-khanda" it says:

> When the earth of Manasarovar touches anyone's body, or
> when anyone bathes therein, he shall go to the paradise of
> Brahma; and he who drinks its waters shall go to the heaven
> of Siva, and shall be released from the sins of a hundred births;
> and even the beast who bears the name of Manasarovar shall
> go to the paradise of Brahma. Its waters are like pearls. There
> is no mountain like Himachala (Himalaya), for in it are Kailash
> and Manasarovar; as the dew is dried up by the morning sun,
> so are the sins of mankind dried up at the sight of Himachala.

★

Not without a sense of reverence did I encamp on its shores. I wanted to examine this lake; investigate its hydrographic relations to the Satlej (that being an old, moot question); measure its depth, which had not hitherto been done; and thus, by deeds, celebrate its blue-green waves. On its waters, we were 15,200 feet above sea level.

The lake is oval-shaped, its northern part swollen out. Its diameter is about fifteen miles.

And now we were to venture on the Holy Lake. We waited over July twenty-sixth and twenty-seventh, but the wind was too strong. Our Tibetans cautioned us. We would be sucked into its depths and perish. On the evening of the twenty-seventh, the wind subsided, and I decided to row across the lake during the night. I took a compass bearing on the opposite (western) shore, and directed my course toward S 59° W. Shukur Ali and Rehim Ali were at the oars. We took along a lead line, speedometer, lantern, and food for two days. The smoke from the campfire rose perpendicularly toward the stars as we pushed off. "They will never reach the other shore of the lake, the lake god will pull them down," said our Tibetans. And Tsering shared their fears. It was nine o'clock. The dying swell sounded melodiously against the shore. After only twenty minutes of steady rowing, the light from the campfire vanished; but the swell on the shore was still faintly audible, far away.

Even if you don't have time to hike the four- to six-day pilgrimage circuit around the sacred Manasarovar, set aside at least a few days to walk or camp along the shores of this magnificent lake. The trail is almost flat for the entire journey, the water is crystal clear, and the views are befitting the most famous lake in Tibet. From the southern shores sweep in the icy flanks of Gurla Mandata, the highest peak in Western Tibet. Visible to the north from many points on the lake is the white, rounded pyramid of Mount Kailash, and around the shores are six active temples.

—Gary McCue, *Trekking in Tibet: A Traveler's Guide*

Otherwise, only the splashing of the oars and the singing of the oarsmen disturbed the silence.

Midnight was approaching. The whole sky flamed up blue-white, from sheet lightning behind the mountains in the south. For a fraction of a second it was as bright as at noon. The reflection of the moon swung silver-white on the sheeny water. The depth was already 210 feet. My oarsmen were awestruck. They sang no more.

In the light of the lantern, I read off the soundings and the instruments, and made my notes. A fairylike atmosphere surround-ed us. In the middle of the night, in the middle of a lake as sacred to hundreds of millions of Asiatics as the Sea of Gennesaret to the Christians! Though the holiness of the Manasarovar is thousands of years older than the veneration accorded to the lake of Tiberias, Capernaum, and the Savior.

The hours of the night passed slowly. Dawn showed faintly in the east. The heralds of the new day peeped out above the moun-tains. Feather-light clouds took on rose tints; and their counterparts in the lake seemed to be gliding over rose gardens. The sun rays struck the peak of the Gurla Mandata, and it shimmered in purple and gold. Like a cloak of light, the reflection clothed the eastern mountain slope. A girdle of clouds, halfway up the Gurla, cast its shadow on the slope.

The sun rose, sparkling like a diamond; and life and color were imparted to the entire incomparable landscape. Millions of pilgrims had seen the morning proceed victoriously over the Holy Lake; but no mortal before us had witnessed this spectacle from the center of Manasarovar.

Geese, sea gulls, and sea swallows flew shrieking across the water. The oarsmen were sleepy; sometimes they fell asleep on their oars. The morning hours passed, and still we continued to be the center of the landscape. I, too, felt sleepy. I closed my eyes, imagining the sound of harps in the air, and seeing whole herds of red wild asses, chasing one another across the lake.

"No, this won't do!"

To energize my men, I gave them a shower with my hand. At the next sounding place, where we found the greatest depth of the lake,

286 feet, we had our breakfast of goose eggs, bread, and milk. The lake water was as sweet as that of a well. It was noon. Now it was evident that we were approaching the western shore, for its details became visible. After eighteen hours' rowing, we finally landed.

We gathered fuel, made tea, fried mutton, smoked our pipes, chatted, changed the boat and sail into a tent, and turned in as early as seven o'clock. The next day, we sailed north, not far from the shore, passing the monastery of Gossul Gompa, on its high terrace, and spent a new night on the western shore. Long before sunrise, the west wind set in with noise and bluster. At half-past four we pushed off. We had not gone many cable-lengths from the shore, when the wave crests rose to an appreciable height; and with the wind right from behind, we flew across the lake, back to the camp, where our people received us on the shore, happy and amazed, having waited ever since they saw our sail, like a white spot, in the distance.

On August the first, we moved the camp southward, the caravan walking on the eastern shore, while I rowed. In the south rose the Gang Lung mountains, at the foot of which, as I had proved, was the source of the Satlej. At Yangönpa, where we pitched our tents outside the walls, thirteen monks received us with great friendliness. They were amazed to see a boat on the Holy Lake, and could find no other explanation of my fortunate journey than my friendship with the Tashi Lama. In the dark temple hall of the lake deity, Hlabsen Dorje Barvas, there was a picture of the god rising from the waves, the dome of Kang Rinpoche, the holy mountain of Kailash, towering above his head.

August 7, 1907 belongs to the days distinguished by three stars in the record of my life. At sunrise, a lama stood blowing his shell-horn on the temple roof of Tugu Gompa. A group of Hindu pilgrims were bathing at the shore, pouring water over their heads, like the Brahmins when they worship the holy Ganges on the quays of Benares. The Kang Rinpoche was obscured by clouds.

With Shukur Ali and Tundup Sonam, I entered the boat. We had with us furs, food, sail, and spare oars. But this time the lake was absolutely calm, and we had not stepped the mast. Our direction was N 27° W. After several hours of rowing, the Gossul Gompa appeared, like a speck, in the distance, on the port side. It was one o'clock. Yellow clouds of dust whirled round on the shore in the northwest, and the wind blew from that direction. Dark fringes of rain hung along the mountain slopes. A heavy rain poured down upon us. It turned into hail. I had never seen the likes of it! The stones were as big as hazelnuts; they beat the water like projectiles, in billions; the water splashed and squirted as they fell; it boiled and seethed, and the spray whirled along the lake. Only the waves close by were visible. Great darkness surrounded us, but the interior of the boat was white with hail. The hail changed into pelting rain, which descended madly. I had pulled the fur over my knees, but pools formed in the folds.

It was quiet for an instant; but the very next moment a new storm set in, this time from the northeast. We heard it roar in the distance like heavy artillery. For a little while longer, we attempted to steer our course northwestward, to the point set by the compass; but the waves grew larger, and their foamy crests dashed in over the starboard rail. The water in the boat rose, clucking and gurgling with our rolling. We had to steer southwestward, in the direction of the wind. A dangerous maneuver! But it was successful. And now a journey began that I shall never forget!

Gale! We were three men in a nutshell, in the midst of waves as high as on a stormy sea of my home country. I did not notice how I froze as the water washed over me and in under my leather waistcoat. We sank in troughs of malachite-green water, seeing, through wave crests as clear as glass, the sun shining in the distant south. We were lifted, amid foam, on raging crests of waves, where the boat trembled for a second, before plunging again into a dark grave of water, that seethed menacingly. Slowly the boat filled. Could we stay afloat until we reached land? If only we could have got the sail up, it would have been easier to keep our craft steady in the wind. Now it wanted to go up in the wind, and lie with starboard rail to windward. I leaned on the tiller with all my strength, and Tundup exerted all the pressure he could bring to bear on his oar.

"Pull away, pull away!" I called out.

He *did* pull away, and his oar broke with a loud report. Lost, I thought. Now we were *bound* to capsize. But Tundup was a capable fellow. Without thinking, he went for the spare oar, pulled it out of its loops, fitted it in the rowlock, and pulled away before the boat had had time to turn. The more water we shipped, the deeper we lay, and the easier it was for the waves to enter.

"Ya, Allah!" Shukur Ali called out, in a dull, grave voice.

We had been struggling for our lives for an hour and a quarter, when it cleared; and we perceived the Gossul Gompa far away, straight ahead of us. It grew rapidly in size, and the monks stood looking at us from the balconies of the monastery. We were hurled into the surf at the shore, and the boat was drawn out again by suction. Tundup Sonam jumped overboard. Had the fellow gone mad? The water was higher than his breast, but he grasped the boat firmly and pulled us in. We followed his example in shallow water, and dragged our nutshell ashore.

We were all in, after our hard struggle; and we threw ourselves headlong on the sand, without saying a word. After a while, some monks and youthful novices came down to us.

"Do you need any help? It looked nasty when you were tossed about on the lake, which is angry today. Come up to us, we have warm rooms."

"No, thank you! We will stay here. But give us some fuel and food."

They soon returned with sweet and sour milk and *tsampa*. Of all our food, only the tea could be used. They made a welcome fire of twigs and dung; and we undressed by it and dried our clothes, as we had so often done after shipwrecks on the Tibetan lakes.

In the morning Robsang rode up with fresh supplies, though everybody believed we had perished. The Tugu Gompa monks had burnt incense before the image of the lake god, and had asked him to spare us. That was considerate of them! God bless them for that!

I stayed in the Gossul Gompa twelve hours. Now I sat, sketching, between the eight pillars in the chamber of the gods; now I observed the image of the mysterious son of Sakia, on which the monks sprinkle holy water, with peacock feathers, from a silver bowl, all the while mumbling, "*Om a hum*." Here, too, the lake deity, in his own hall, reigned in mysterious twilight.

I walked out on the terraced roof. The Holy Lake, which yesterday had done everything to drown us, was now smooth as a mirror. The air was slightly hazy. One could not see whether the eastern shore was mountains or sky. The lake and sky had the same values. Objects swam before my eyes. After the rough lake of the previous day, the whole temple swayed under me, and I felt as if hurled into infinite space. But beneath lay the Holy Lake, along the shores of which innumerable pilgrims had walked themselves weary, to secure peace for their souls. The Manasarovar, the hub of the wheel which is a symbol of life! I could have stayed there for years, watching the ice extend its roof across the depths, the winter storms driving whirling snow across land and water, the approaching spring breaking up the cover, in its turn being succeeded by the temperate summer winds, heralded by the dependable flocks of geese. I should have liked to sit there, seeing new days swept forth on the wings of the morning, and becoming one with the changing and ever equally fascinating prospects over the Holy Lake which unfold before the eyes of mortal man every day and night of the year.

Sven Hedin, an author and artist, became best known in the late 1800s as the Swedish explorer who found long-lost treasures along the Silk Road. His discoveries over the next forty years in Central Asia and Tibet brought him worldwide acclaim, as well as a British knighthood, honorary doctorates, and two gold medals from the Royal Geographical Society. He published more than fifty books, including My Life as an Explorer, *from which this story was excerpted. He died in 1952.*

Bicycles to Burang

*They explore the immensity of the Tibetan
Plateau on two wheels.*

"TOO MUCH GEAR," PAT WAS SAYING SURROUNDED BY ALL THE
things we had thought essential.

We were trying to pack the bicycles. Friends with expertise in
cycling had warned us that forty pounds was an excessive weight.

"How much do you think you have?" I asked.

"With the bike I'll bet it's a hundred pounds."

We all had as much. Discarded food, clothing, and other gear
gradually grew into a sizable heap as we tried to reduce our loads.

"What do we do with all this, just leave it here?"

"How about these guys?" Pat meant the Tibetan herders who
had come past our camp many times during our stay, occasionally
going home with small gifts from us. Three of them now stood
watching our amazing display of stuff.

We piled the surplus neatly, zipping most of it into several large
burlap duffels. I made gestures to the Tibetans: "Wait a few minutes, and you can have what you want." They showed keen interest,
I thought.

As for trash, we dug a hole three feet deep. Everything went in
there. Topping it off with a sprinkle of stove fuel, I set it afire. Ant
and I stirred the blaze to get a thorough burn before refilling the

hole with dirt. The Tibetans had moved back a hundred yards.

"What do you suppose they think we're doing?" asked Ant. The Tibetan method of dealing with trash was tossing it to the wind.

"Some strange foreign rite, I suppose."

"Like this?" Ant began dancing around the flames. I joined him. We spun our sticks, leaped over the fire, and made gibberish noises. Ant suddenly stopped. "Look at that!"

The three Tibetans were running through the thorn-bush away from us. I had never seen them run before, and more than two weeks later, on our way back past Kailash, we saw that our neat discard pile had not been touched. In my mind's eye, it is there still. People are piling stones on it now. Gradually, it is becoming a *mani* wall, a monument to join the other revered sites on the Kailash trail.

We left that afternoon, headed toward Lake Manasarovar and Burang, a trading community on the Nepalese border. Knowing the border was closed to us, we nonetheless wanted to see the snowy crest of the Himalaya at closer range before heading on west.

It gave me a great feeling of freedom, to be on the bicycle at last, pushed eastward by a strong wind across the plains.

I was having a contemplative moment on top of a mountain when out of nowhere a horse and cart pulled up. A stunningly attractive young girl jumped off the huge pile of stuff on which she had been sitting in the back of the cart, ran up to where I was sitting (it had taken me about half an hour to climb up, she took a few minutes), draped her bundle of prayer flags on the collection beside me, curtsied to me like it was perfectly normal to see an Englishman sitting alone deep in thought on top of a mountain, and sped off. I couldn't help but notice that her clothes looked immaculate, which confused me, because every time I put on a clean t-shirt twenty seconds later it looked like I had been wearing it for six months.

—Philip Blazdell,
"Travel in Tibet"

The road was smooth, and despite continual adjustments to our loads, we covered about twelve miles in three hours, making camp under a windy, spectacular sky beside a nearly dry slough. I collected cooking water from a yak's hoofprint, the only place deep enough to accept my cup.

Later, as we sat eating supper from a communal pot, Naomi made an announcement. "I figured out why I've been feeling rotten," she said.

"You have?" I said.

"High-altitude morning sickness."

"No kidding? Is this a surprise?"

"Not entirely."

"Well, congratulations, I guess. Are you worried about the altitude?"

"Tibetan women do it all the time."

"Yeah, but on a bicycle?"

I was impressed. After a month in Tibet, and lots of physical activity, I was still not fully acclimated. It was all I could do to manage basic tasks.

That became obvious the next day. It began with two hours of easy pedaling to a place called Barga. The road, on smooth, packed earth, followed a telephone line. I was surprised to see how common phone lines were in Tibet, considering how rarely we came across an actual telephone outside of Lhasa, and of those, I never did hear one ring, or see anyone using one. Nonetheless, the poles marched across the landscape like picket fences and symbols of national unity: every one in line, linked by common purpose, attached ultimately to Beijing and the source of power.

The place called Barga was an old mud fort with clay gun turrets on its flat roof, standing guard over a fork in the road. Uncertain about which way to go, we stopped outside the compound. I was just laying my bike on the ground, intending to knock on a wooden door when a huge mastiff rocketed out from a hole in the wall. He flipped over on his back when he hit the end of his rope, got up, and came at me again. Purely by luck, I had stopped about three feet short of where his rope would reach, but that didn't stop him. He was determined to stretch it or break it and turn me into a suitable offering to the vultures. We all backed up.

A woman came out to see what the racket was about, kicked the dog into silence, and said hello to us as if we were just the most normal sight in western Tibet.

"Burang?" I said, pointing to the southern road.

"Burang!" she said, nodding and laughing. Burang seemed to be a great joke.

Maybe she had tried bicycling that road. For starters, it led up a slope the scale of which was impossible to judge without trees or buildings. It looked to be 200 or 300 feet high but turned out to more like 1,000. Getting to the top took us until noon. I could barely manage to pedal about 100 feet before stopping to pant for a few minutes. When I finally reached the pass, I lay down on the gravel and fell asleep for half an hour. Having overexerted, I couldn't eat. Then it was down a long slope toward the shore of Lake Manasarovar.

By the time we dumped our bikes on the smooth cobblestone beach at the base of a spectacular little gompa, all I wanted was to close my eyes and lie on the shingle. I was doing that when Wendy announced other plans.

"Let's get this tent up."

"Are you being crabby?"

She looked fierce. "I want to get the tent up so I can go to the *gompa*." I didn't see the connection. "Go to the *gompa*. I'll put up the tent." What I really meant was "Go while I pass out here on the beach." But we put up the tent, and her gomping plans proved to be the reflex of a diligent traveler, because we both fell into the tent, feet sticking out the door, and were asleep in the afternoon sun.

Later, I sat watching fish jump in the sacred water and thought I wanted to catch one. Our diet of unmitigated starch had made me think that a stiff dose of protein might improve my energy. So I rigged a line using dental floss and a hook fashioned from a spare bicycle spoke and baited it with Italian sausage (which I pilfered from a tiny stash Lee had been carefully husbanding), all the time worrying that it must be a sacrilege to kill a fish from a holy lake. I had read that Tibetan Buddhists considered fishermen to be among the lowest levels of humanity, lower even than butchers, who were certainly down there. So I watched, waiting until I thought none of the Tibetan pilgrims who were also camped on the beach was on the lookout, and heaved my equipment into the water. Still, my conscience bothered me. I felt as if I was casting in the baptismal font at a church. Finally, seeing two pilgrims headed my way, performing their lakeside devotions, I ran to the water, pulled in the line, and gave up on the idea.

Four months later I learned that Tibetans give pregnant women dried fish from Manasarovar to ease the pain of labor, so I suppose they do catch them.

Neither Manasarovar nor its near twin, Rakshas Tal, has a surface outlet. They are both tarns, fed by numerous permanent and seasonal streams flowing from the surrounding mountains. According to religious belief, Raksas Tal is a black lake, allied with the darker forces of life (*rakshas* being a class of demons). As such it balances the sacred vessel of Manasarovar, recipient of water emanating directly from heaven via Mount Kailash. Having gathered itself in the lake, the same water, moving through underground channels, reappears as the four sources of the Ganges River in India.

In Manasarovar, the springs of heaven are so powerful that they raise the middle of the lake. When he launched his portable boat on a survey expedition in 1907, explorer Sven Hedin was told that he would never reach the center of the lake because it was uphill all the way, but if by some unlikely happenstance he managed to get there, he need not worry about storms. The peaceful center of heaven's lake is said to remain calm on the windiest of days, when breakers beat against the rocky shores.

Finally, in the evening, Wendy and I climbed the hill to the *gompa*. Its name was Chiu, which means bird, and like so many spectacular Tibetan buildings, it occupied a place more suitable for birds than people—a sharp pinnacle of red rock high enough for a fine view of Kailash.

Like the *gompas* at Kailash, Chiu had been destroyed and partially rebuilt, beginning in 1983. Even so, it looked ancient, its architecture timeless.

We called hello at the entrance. Hearing us, a young monk emerged and cordially showed us to the main prayer hall, a small but well-equipped room. *Thankas* hung around the walls, some new and some so old that no discernible picture remained. There were two drums painted blue, a wooden frame filled with Dalai Lama pictures, posters of holy places in Tibet, *katas* (white ceremonial scarves) hanging from a wire, and various statues.

It was a neatly kept room with a bright view of the lake, and I liked being there. In the warm evening light, the atmosphere was almost Mediterranean—blue water, white walls, the sound of shore birds heard through an open window.

Leaving that room, following a winding stone stairway, we came to a heavy wooden door. It had to be lifted by a steel ring like a trap door. "Guru Rinpoche," said the young monk; he was referring to Padmasambhava, the saint who brought Buddhism to Tibet in the eighth century. He is said to have spent the last seven days of his life in this place. Peering in, I could discern stone slabs leading into blackness. Wendy sparked a propane lighter, in the glow of which we entered a cave the size of a closet, its walls lined with cloth, three statues at one end, brass bowls of water on a shelf in front of them.

Wendy put out the flame. We were both so tired that we sat on the bottom step for a while, in total darkness. Somewhere, in some other room, a drum began beating, low and steady and hypnotic, sounding through the living rock. *Droong, droong, droong*—it could have been the heartbeat of the mountain.

By the time we came out, the sun was setting. The hills were orange. A pretty young woman with only three front teeth and her daughter in her arms came out to see us off and to give us a gift— a handful of puffed barley still hot from her pan. We smiled and bowed to each other. The baby wore a hand-knitted cap, which Wendy admired; then she brought out her own knitting, a mitten in progress, which was in turn admired. The woman then pointed to my camera with a questioning look, so I lifted it as if to make a picture, and she ran back inside calling to her husband. A moment later he came out behind her to pose for a family picture, on the terrace of their *gompa*, with Manasarovar and Gurla Mandata in the background. Finally, beneath the rose-tinted sky, we left with feelings that had become all too familiar: I loved this place and its people. I was moved by the beauty of their chosen setting. And I felt like an oaf, not being able to talk with them.

Before dawn the next morning, I climbed a hill from which I could see Kailash, Manasarovar, and Chiu *gompa* all in one view. Sunrise was a pale golden shiver in the east. It colored the lake and gave the white-painted *gompa* a warm glow. Ducks flew in shoals, landing on the calm water and taking off again in a shimmer of wavelets and a clatter of feathers. A dog came up the hill to sit beside me. We waited together as the sky intensified. Suddenly Kailash ignited—first red, then yellow, then white—and then the sun spilled over the black rim of Manasarovar. At that instant, just as the first rays touched the prayer flags, someone inside the *gompa* released a puff of white juniper smoke into the air. A salute. An acknowledgment of the surrounding world and its ancient rhythms. I needed no common language to understand that sentiment.

When reading the old books recounting European explorations of Tibet, you begin to notice a certain similarity among them. After ambitious beginnings filled with details and sharp observation, their writers often lapse into dull recitation of itineraries. For example, in his *Diary of a Journey Across Tibet*, Hamilton Bower wrote:

> Camp 77—After the march the Tibetans made out that we would have to do another five marches before beginning to descend.
>
> Camp 78—About five miles of the march lay along a road that comes from Tuman Chaka; after leaving it we went about six miles to a place where there was a pool of water not quite frozen to the bottom, and camped.
>
> Camp 79—After leaving the last camp we ascended a small and easy pass, and descended into a wide open valley in which some yak were grazing. To the northeast a range of mountains with some fine snowy peaks, evidently the Dang La range, was

seen, and in the valley a stream was flowing in an east-south-east direction.

In Tibet, in this wonderful landscape that has the power to grab your heart and hold it hard, this place of great, empty, reverberating silence where the land lies open to the sky and you really could imagine God wanting to live there—in this huge powerful place, you nonetheless find yourself plodding along from stage to stage in a dizzy sort of dream, too small for the surroundings and too tired to ponder the improbability of being there. The sun shines bright and hot. The air is thin. Shadows stab the ground like black ice. But it's hard to pay attention.

It's hard to think of anything beyond getting down the road. And then a sacrilegious thought pops uninvited into your mind. You begin to consider if Tibet isn't best appreciated as a memory, something to polish up and keep in the nostalgia kit for the graying years. That rocky road past Gurla Mandata: how will it play in old age? That's the important thing.

I thought about that over the next four days, bicycling to Burang past Raksas Tal (not black at all but lambent turquoise, ringed by glowing pastel hills) and around the shoulder of Gurla Mandata. I told myself to appreciate what I was seeing then, to pay attention, because I might never return. The glaciers

English traveler Robert Byron, who referred to Tibet as Asia Magna, was perhaps the first writer, and the first real "tourist," to travel to Tibet after the Younghusband expedition (although numerous military and political officials preceded him). The adventurous Byron, who wrote of the trip in *First Russia, Then Tibet,* came in the early 1930s, when it took him eight days to fly from London to India on Imperial Airways' new Air Mail service. His mother's only advice was to plead with him not to bring back a Buddha.

—Garry Marchant, "The Road to Gyantse"

were magnificent, the lake glittered in the sun, icy torrents poured down each ravine, and Kailash, visible much of the time, raised its perfect summit above the whole scene.

For centuries, southern pilgrims have come this way, up from India, through ranks of mountains to the high plains, and suddenly, standing alone and formidable across the waters of Raksas Tal, there is Kailash, touching the sapphire sky. Seen from here, who could doubt its holy nature? There are many higher mountains, but none so singular.

Frequently I would stop my bicycle just to stare, fixing the view in my memory, before turning reluctantly back to the road.

Travel, according to some, is not genuine without travail; as if hardship is the only means of knowing a place. I disagree with the premise, but I understand the basis of the idea, especially in reference to somewhere like Tibet. If travel is too easy, you miss something important, something intrinsic to life in a hard land. If you wish to understand a place, you should move through it the way local people do, not in the isolated artificiality of a tourist coach.

On the other hand, difficulty for its own sake is meaningless. It's also boring, unless it occurs on an epic scale, like Shackleton's experience in the Antarctic. By and large, when the road is rough, everyone finds it rough—and dusty and tedious. The sun shines equally hot on all heads, and it isn't worth much that I thought bicycling was an inappropriate way to travel between Kailash and Burang.

Even so, bicycling in Tibet is worth describing one time, if only to serve as a warning. Local people walk, and I don't wonder why. First of all, there's the ungraded track that passes for a road. Glacial cobblestones the size of melons go for miles at a time. They jolt you, throw you off balance, and roll under your tires. You take it in the arms, shoulders, and eventually in the stomach. The pace is slower than walking.

Where cobbles leave off, you get corrugations. The pace remains slow, but the jolting is rhythmic now, predictable, punishing like a Chinese water torture—bump, bump, bump, bump—until you have to stop and recollect your wits.

Sand stops you dead. Hit a small patch, and it wrenches the front wheel sideways, throws you over the handlebars, lands you on your face. If you're lucky, you avoid smashing your groin on the handlebars as you plunge forward.

Where glacial dust as fine as talc lies six inches deep over cobbles or loose gravel, it is impossible to ride, even downhill. You walk and cough, dragging the bicycle's dead weight.

Distances in Tibet are enormous. Pedal all day across a flat plain and you still might camp in a place that seems no different from your starting point. The lack of scale plays tricks with your vision. Coming over a rise, I once saw a truck ahead, lying on its side, debris spilled beside it. An accident, I thought. Then astonishingly, the debris collected itself and stood up. It was Jeff. He had been resting beside his tipped-over bike — not a truck at all.

It works the other way. You look ahead at a low pass. It seems close. You start grinding uphill and realize, as minutes turn to hours, that the summit is actually a long way ahead.

The Tibetan sun is unreasonably hot but so intense that you have to wear full clothing;

In general, the roads in Tibet have improved dramatically since the 1980s, particularly from Lhasa to the airport, which has been widened and paved, and from Lhasa to the Nepal border, which now goes via Shigatse and can be completed in a day and a half (except during the summer monsoon months of July and August, when washouts can block the road for days at a time). Previously it took a minimum of three days to reach the border, and at least one more day to get to Kathmandu. The drive from Lhasa to the holy mountain of Mt. Kailash in far West Tibet, however, is still one of the roughest roads in the world. Plan on five bone-jarring, dust-eating days via the south road from Lhasa, and at least seven days along the more beautiful but longer northern route via the prefectural capital of Ali.

—Gary McCue,
"Tibetan Roads"

even drenched with sunblock, exposed skin burns bright red, then blisters. Worst of all, the road surface is so demanding you can't look at the scenery. Glance up for a moment, and the bike goes off the road. It does that often enough without your glancing up.

Although I wrote daily in my diary, the entries were rather stunted—a bit like those of Hamilton Bower. I might as well have written: We went past Gurla Mandata for four days and arrived at Burang.

Jeremy Schmidt, a writer and photographer, has credits in magazines including Audubon, Outside, Sierra, *and* National Geographic Traveler, *and is the author or co-author of numerous books, including* The Rockies: Backbone of the Continent, The Saga of Lewis and Clark, *and* Himalayan Passage, *from which this story was excerpted. He lives in Jackson Hole, Wyoming.*

MICHAEL BUCKLEY

The Lost Kingdom
of Guge

The author enjoys an indelible experience
in the back of beyond.

IN THAILAND, I ONCE WENT TO RIPLEY'S MOTION MASTER
Theater—an innovative kind of theater that utilizes, apart from big-
screen Cinemascope, the added sense of motion. Your seat is rigged
up with high-tech hydraulic gear: you're strapped in with a full lap-
and-shoulder seatbelt. You watch a RoboCop motorcycle chase or
a high-speed spaceship pursuit: synchronized with the action, you
are hurled to the left, right, upward, downward, sideways—
hydraulically, of course—as you hang on for dear life with hand
grips. The show lasted seven minutes—the expensive technology
couldn't be sustained any longer.

The Land Cruiser to west Tibet was just like that except there
were no handgrips, no seatbelts—and the show went on for five
days. Five days of being banged around from teakettle to breakfast
time to get to a town called Zanda. Our target was the site of the
ancient kingdom of Guge (pronounced Goo-gay)—with ruins
scattered in valleys around Zanda. It required a stack of permits—
town permits, military permits, cultural relics bureau permits, you
name it. We had enough paperwork to open an origami salon. But
eventually we edged closer to our target.

Perhaps "edged" is not the word I'm looking for here. There

was virtually no suspension in our Land Cruiser—the shocks were shot. If you were in the back seat and the driver hit a rut, you would fly up and bang your head on the roof—and then be thumped down hard on your ass and get the stuffing knocked out of you. There were hardly any springs left in the seats, either, and you'd get showered in dust. At times it got so bad you had to wear a silk scarf or something over your face to filter the dust out of your breathing apparatus. And you might, as I did, take to wearing a wool hat to soften the blow on the interior roof.

Actually, it was more comfortable in the front cabin of the truck. We'd hired two vehicles, a Land Cruiser and a Dongfeng truck. The latter acted as a tow truck should the Land Cruiser ride too deep on a stream crossing—which at one point ours did. Coming round a bend in the truck, I got to witness the spectacle of four bedraggled foreigners struggling to get out of a river, away from the Land Cruiser, which had water swirling over the tires. The driver, Speedy, had seriously misjudged the depth of a stream crossing. Fortunately, the Land Cruiser started up first time after being hauled out.

Our team of backpackers had clubbed together in Lhasa to split expenses on this epic 4WD tour of far western Tibet, a round trip of some 2,000 miles, taking twenty-five days to complete. Our main targets were the ruins of the Guge Kingdom and the hike around sacred Mount Kailash.

It was a motley crew of riders. Pema was only twenty-one. She was given her Tibetan name by her Swiss father, who used to work in Nepal—and who encouraged her to come back and see the Himalayas. At the other end of the spectrum was Diane, from Belgium, in her forties—a latecomer to trekking. Her role model was Alexandra David-Neel—the famed French explorer who traveled extensively in her fifties, carrying a revolver to protect herself. Like her mentor, Diane was obstinate, moody, and cantankerous by turns, and bossy. Others in the group were Verena, from Austria; Kozo, a young Japanese; and Barbara, a Filipino photographer based in Hong Kong.

The Tibetan crew consisted of Doko, the young guide; "Speedy," the Land Cruiser driver; and Tenzin, the Khampa truck driver who seemed to have a woman in every major town along the route. Speedy was inseparable from his Chicago Bulls cap: the NBA is big in Amdo, where Speedy was from. Speedy was so nick-named because of his terrify-ing shortcuts—he liked dri-ving straight down sand dunes, instead of using the switchbacks provided. Moody Doko would cheer him on, while the rest of us gritted our teeth. It was much more relaxing in the cabin of the truck—if only because Tenzin loved to sing, and had a great voice, and an endless reper-toire of nomad folk songs. Which he was keen to expand on: this Tibetan bard hounded us to sing in English or in French.

The hardship of the trip was counterbalanced by the stunning scenery en route. We planned to take the northern route to Ali, and from there dip south to Guge and Kailash, and return to Lhasa on the southern route. The initial route took us on a great loop through Chang Thang, the vast desert and grassland region of northern Tibet. We passed nights in no-name inns

A t times, what smattering of a road there is disappears. We are in absolute no-man's land and our driver is simply eyeballing the way. We reach a plateau area and come up against a frozen river. The driver slowly follows the river's edge for some distance and speeds up when he sees a small bridge up ahead. The bridge, it turns out, is caved in as if a large vehicle has crashed through it. The bus stops and we all follow the driver as he gets out and surveys the thickness of the ice. We line up along the shore and watch him make a run for it. He gets about a third of the way across and what do you know, he crashes through. The rear wheels hang up on the edge and prevent the whole bus from sliding down to the bot-tom. We scramble to the end of the thick ice and pull the driver out of one of the back windows.

—William Eigen, "At Large in the Common World"

at horrible, polluted truck-stop towns en route—Tsochen, Dongco, Gertse, and Tsaka. But otherwise, it was pristine terrain and we spotted Tibet's rare wildlife—*kiang* (wild asses), black-necked cranes, the odd antelope. We'd see groups of four or five—not exactly the great herds that used to roam these high grasslands. The once-abundant wildlife has been machine-gunned into oblivion by Chinese settlers and military, for food and for sport.

Speaking of food: the back of the truck was stacked with barrels of gasoline. Gasoline depots are few and far between out this way, and more designed for the Chinese military. Besides, any gas out west is way more expensive than it is in Lhasa. Over and around the gas barrels were burlap bags and cardboard boxes packed with food—potatoes, carrots, bottled water, 761 army-ration biscuits, and other essentials that we'd salvaged at Lhasa's main market. Trouble was, the two elements—food and gasoline—got mixed together a few days' ride out of Lhasa. A gas barrel sprang a leak somewhere, but the driver couldn't determine which barrel it was, and didn't care to empty the entire cargo to find out.

So we had potatoes that reeked of gas. Which was quite danger-ous because the method of cooking was a miniature flame-thrower—the same device used to heat up the engine when frozen (the Tibetan version of antifreeze). You'd aim this gadget side-on at an elevated pot, and a great flame would shoot out and nuke the food.

The tough-as-nails Tibetan crew turned their nose up at our gas-scented food. They had their own Hessian bags, filled with dried carcass of goat, or rock-hard yak-cheese—things like that. At picnic stops, they'd exhume the carcass of the day, and resume work on it, carving off great hunks of dried meat with their knives. A bit like beef jerky in texture.

When we got to Ali, Doko became bored with permit proce-dures at the PSB office, which were taking forever. I was scribbling some notes, and he looked over my shoulder.

"So how's the book?" he asked.

I could've strangled Doko right then and there, but fortunately the PSB woman didn't tune into the conversation. She was too pre-occupied with the problem of Belgium. Belgium was one of the nations listed for our permit. But what exactly was Belgium? She'd never heard of Belgium. We sorted this one out by indicating Belgium was sandwiched between England and France.

"How many books have you written?" piped up Doko again.

"Listen Doko, I don't write any fucking books, okay?" I shot back.

"Okay!" he laughed. It was a knowing laugh because he had recognized my face in the author credit page of the Lonely Planet guide to China.

We had no desire to stay in Ali, but permits had to be checked, validated, re-checked, and stamped again. Ali is an architect's nightmare of concrete blockhouses, kiosks, and garbage strewn all over. And at night, tuneless wailing from karaoke bars. This is Karaokeville—full of Chinese army officers, and girls in private karaoke booths—in the middle of the desert, in the middle of nowhere, in west Tibet.

So you're driving along one day—and suddenly you forget where you are, or where you are going, or what you're doing, or why. Ever experienced that feeling? It happened to me in the cabin of the truck—I'd been dozing off, in some distant dream world, and woke up when the engine started wheezing and spluttering. I wearily opened my eyes—and my jaw dropped. There was snow everywhere. There were great peaks all around, with yaks cavorting in the background. I thought I must be hallucinating from the altitude: my eyes grew wider as we crested a pass that registered 17,400 feet on my altimeter. How high? asked my fellow trucker. Um, fairly high, I hedged, gasping from the thin air. We were driving over an entire mountain range! And if my sources were correct (putting Zanda at 12,000 feet), that meant an astonishing drop of 5,400 feet on the other side of the pass.

It was indeed a long drop down. At dusk, we leveled out. We came to a canyon, followed a riverbed. This turned out to be a phantasmagoric canyon, a sorcerer's creation of mud and clay, sculpted into surreal shapes. And it went on and on…for over an hour. It was thoroughly entrancing. "It is very shapeful," said Doko. "The rocks have shapes like *chortens* or castles." He pointed out a huge rock resembling a seated Buddha, and another that looked like an old man with a wispy beard. The imagination could run riot here. Phantoms appeared everywhere—warriors, kings, queens, monks. They all seemed to jump out of the clay—silent sentinels guarding the approach route.

In one day I'd absorbed enough new landscape to last the brain several months to process. Finally, in the distance, rays of light lit up Zanda, on an outcrop. Set in barren desert terrain, Zanda is unmistakable—it is an oasis with poplar trees. The Sutlej River lay in our path: it required another six miles of detouring to gain a bridge across the river, and at one corner Speedy almost lost it on a piece of loose gravel. He could have sent us plunging into an abyss, but at the last minute, the Land Cruiser corrected itself, and we all breathed easier. Speedy, of course, would not acknowledge that he'd almost killed us all. He laughed it all off. But you could tell it was a nervous laugh.

That said, the trip to Guge was a hell of a lot easier than it used to be. The earliest Western accounts of this hidden valley—the Guge Kingdom—were by Jesuits, who'd heard rumors of a lost Christian-like sect. In March 1624, two Portuguese Jesuits—Father Marques and Father Andrade—set out from India disguised as Hindu pilgrims. They were on foot, with pack animals, crossing passes that were probably 18,000 feet or more. At times, they sank into snow up to their chests. They complained of frozen feet, of blindness, and of suffocating "poisonous vapors"—probably the first Western accounts of altitude sickness, by the first Europeans known to enter Tibet. Their round trip from India took over eight months.

Arriving in Tsaparang, the center of the Guge Kingdom, the Jesuits were surprised to be warmly received. They puzzled over how people in such a barren wasteland could survive—all the food had to be imported from fertile valleys that were two weeks away on foot. But part of the jigsaw fell into place when they witnessed a caravan of 200 Chinese traders passing through, carrying silk and porcelain—Tsaparang was an important trading center. And flocks of goats and sheep kept the royal court supplied for basics.

Father Andrade wrote of being invited by the king to Toling Gompa, to celebrate a special occasion. There were over 2,000 monks in attendance. The Jesuits found that temple rituals bore superficial similarities to Christian—monks in robes spent hours chanting—but drinking from human skullcap vessels and playing trumpets fashioned from human thigh bones were definitely a little different. Andrade was the first to publish to the world the sacred chanting mantra "*Om mani padme hum,*" but could not determine its meaning (which experts still debate today). Andrade returned to Tsaparang in 1625 with fellow missionaries; the Jesuits eventually built a small church in Tsaparang. Andrade died in India in 1634—poisoned by a colleague who evidently didn't share his enthusiasm for the Inquisition.

But back to the religion of Guge. It was actually quite special. In the ninth century, Buddhism was snuffed out in central Tibet by King Langdarma, a staunch supporter of the rival Bon faith. Upon the assassination of Langdarma, Tibet was broken up into lay and monastic pockets of influence. The Guge Kingdom became an enclave that was vital for the

What Portuguese explorers, Andrade and Marques saw in far western Tibet in 1624 was an ancient civilization in final decline. It was the Buddhist kingdom of Guge, centered on the rock fortress of Tsaparang, at the southern end of the gorge of the Garuda valley. Within forty years the kingdom would be overthrown, the fortress-city and its surrounding monasteries abandoned. Three centuries later a German Buddhist by the name of Lama Govinda came to the spot where the two Jesuits had stood and set down a graphic description of the "paradise" spread out before him: "The greatest surprise…was to find the main temple not only intact but actually covered with a golden roof that gleamed in the wilderness of rocks and ruins like a forgotten jewel—a reminder and symbol of the splendor and the faith of a past age, in which this valley was inhabited by thousands of people and ruled by wise and pious kings…"

—Charles Allen, *The Search for Shangri-La*

survival of Buddhism. The King of Guge at that time promoted cultural exchanges with Indian Buddhists: Guge became an important center of Buddhist studies, a reputation that grew with the arrival of eleventh-century scholar Atisha, from India.

The Guge Kingdom probably lasted more than 500 years. In several sources, it has been described as a cultural Mecca—a citadel greater than Lhasa at the time. But around 1650 (some sources give 1630), Tsaparang was suddenly abandoned. It is said that the King of Guge angered his lamas by favoring Father Andrade and that factional fighting ensued—and that the kingdom tore itself apart.

Other sources claim that a two-year siege by Ladakhis led to the fall of Guge. The reason: the king rejected a bride who happened to be the sister of the King of Ladakh, who was supremely insulted. Although well-entrenched in his citadel, the King of Guge decided to cut a deal and surrender, according to one source, but this backfired because the treacherous Ladakhis had no intention of honoring the deal. The king and the royal family were carried off into exile, and his followers were reduced to slavery (another source claims the king and his courtiers were killed on the spot). Whatever the case, Guge fell into obscurity and ruin. Not only that: successive waves of invaders went to great lengths to wipe out all traces of the kings of Guge, making it nearly impossible to recount the history of the place.

As I trace a mandalic mural in the Red Temple at Tsaparang with my flashlight, I am convinced of one thing. This must have been a brilliant culture. We'd arrived by Land Cruiser, on the short commute from Zanda—only sixteen miles distant, but it seemed to be light years away. To enter the temples at Tsaparang is to venture into a different world, to be in the presence of master artisans. The murals resonate their power and that of their patrons: they are mute testimony to the brilliance of the Guge Kingdom. They speak of a culture that is at once alien yet highly imaginative, with bold design and vibrant use of color.

Eerily illuminated by flashlight are huge, beautiful Tara frescoes—white, green, wrathful manifestations—and other icons from the Tibetan Buddhist pantheon painted on the walls. And fantastic creatures—half-beast, half-human. And then the flashlight picks up some detail that turns out to be a stunning miniature, an entire work of art in itself. The murals are breathtaking, and also offer some clues about dress and customs in the long-lost kingdom of Guge. Not everything portrayed is mythical. Really bringing Guge to life are frescoes of courtiers welcoming an important envoy, arriving by donkey. Another fresco shows a high lama giving teachings. Moving along to the Yamantaka Chapel (named after resident tantric deity, Dorje Jigje), the walls bear a quite different kind of ancient mural: sumptuous paintings of Tibetan tantric deities tangled in *yabyum* embraces with their consorts.

The murals date from the sixteenth and seventeenth centuries, before the fall of Guge. We will probably never know the identity of the artists at Guge; in the tradition of Tibetan Buddhism, this kind of art springs from an anonymous well. We do know that the king of Guge was wealthy enough to be able to import artisans from regions like Kashmir. But while the style may be Kashmiri, it is also distinctly Tibetan. Visiting in 1933, Italian scholar Guiseppe Tucci noted "an art peculiar to Guge, distinctive in itself and independent of the art movements in other parts of Tibet."

Tucci was among the handful of privileged Westerners to see the site in its pre-Chinese days. He left a detailed description of the artwork in its more intact state, particularly the statuary. Guge seems to have escaped plundering by Western treasure seekers and museum collectors, but not so the Chinese. In the mid-1960s, Red Guards ran amok and trashed the temples of Guge—smashing precious statuary in their wake—but miraculously, the murals were left largely unscathed. The temples suffered some water damage, but since this is a desert area, things are kept freeze-dried naturally. It's an odd juxtaposition of clay ruins, destroyed statuary, but intact murals on the temple walls.

Having nearly destroyed the place, the Chinese now see fit to be overly protective of it. The Chinese appear to have a monopoly on Guge Kingdom photography. In addition to the reams of paperwork we have already acquired, we discover that if you want to photograph interiors at Guge, you need a special permit from Beijing. A little inconvenient, at this point, to arrange that—and it is most likely exorbitant and time-consuming to procure.

So we employ a shortcut: Doko and Tenzin will keep the Tibetan caretaker busy with a flask of *chang*, while Speedy brings along all the keys to the chapels. There is nobody around except us—nobody to notice the odd camera-taking episode. A second photography problem: there is hardly any light to work with. The chapels are dim, and even when electric light switches are found, the murals are dim. Fortunately for me, Barbara has a whole bag full of photo gear, and I borrow a flash unit from her, hoping it will communicate with my camera and synchronize to take the right exposures.

> We demonstrate with our bare hands as we are fighting for the truth. If we have truth on our side, we don't need any weapon. The Chinese are suppressing us with force because they have no truth on their side. We don't have to do that.
>
> —A Tibetan Nun

We are still at the lower extremities of Tsaparang: the site is a great peak made of clay. Winding upward from the lower temples, we walk past a series of "cave-condos" fashioned from clay, and small fort-like structures with watchtowers poking up. To withstand siege, Tsaparang citadel developed an ingenious system of tunneling to internal springs deep in the mountain. Other tunnels serve as escape routes. We could not see these, but to reach the top of Tsaparang citadel, you must scramble through a long spiraling tunnel that is bored out of clay, with steps cut out. This tunnel could be completely sealed in times of siege.

At the uppermost reaches, crowning this mountain of clay, is Tsaparang Dzong, with various structures thought to serve as palaces for the king, queen, and high officials. The finest artwork at Tsaparang is to be found in a tiny building here, thought to be the *gonkhang*, and probably the site of initiation rites. Centerpiece of the *gonkhang* is a large 3-D mandala that now lies in ruins—smashed to pieces by Red Guards. However, exquisite miniature murals still grace the walls: depicted are rows of voluptuous dancing *dakinis*, who personify the wisdom of enlightenment. Apart from their elaborate jewelry, they are naked, representing the uninhibited dance of awareness. In Tibetan lore, *dakinis* live in hidden heavenly paradises and, like personal guardian angels, appear mysteriously to practitioners when they face great trouble, to provide motivation when the chips are down. Below the *dakinis* are gory scenes of disembodiment from hell realms. The chapel is dedicated to protector deity Demchok, shown in murals with his consort Dorje Phagmo. Together they symbolize the union of bliss and emptiness.

The view from the top of the citadel is phenomenal. On this crystal-clear day, dramatic desert landscapes stretch to the far horizon. "Desolate" and "barren" are two adjectives that spring to mind, but somehow seem sadly inadequate to convey the immensity of space, and the stillness that envelops it. Standing there, some lines from poet Percy Shelley popped into my head—lines I'd learned by heart long ago, about an Egyptian king:

My name is Ozymandias, king of kings:
Look upon my works, ye mighty, and despair!
Nothing beside remains: round the decay
Of that colossal wreck, boundless and bare,
The lone and level sands stretch far away.

Back in our base in Zanda, there were more glorious murals to be viewed at Toling Gompa, but at a price. The monk-caretaker who held the keys to the different chapels was a highly skilled extortionist. Every step of the way, every new door, required more cash donations, and it got to the point where some among us just said no (or used stronger language). But I persisted, because at this point the money wasn't going to stymie my thirst for such original artwork.

Scattered through the valleys around Zanda are numerous meditation caves, some lined with murals. More are waiting to be discovered. Incredibly, I found that the concept of a citadel topping a mountain of clay was not limited to Tsaparang. Just outside Zanda is a similarly sited citadel, with access through a huge tunnel carved into the side of the clay mountain. This is the weirdest hiking I've ever done—once through the tunnel, you reach an upper plateau, with scores of former cave dwellings, and dangerous crevasses of clay. And majestic views of the valley where Zanda lies.

From this aerial perch, Zanda seems like a fantastic, mythical place. It has that touch of Shangri-La: a remote valley, an oasis of poplar trees, an ancient ruined temple, and snowy peaks in the distance. But my idea of Shangri-La is not a Chinese army base and Chinese restaurants—which, essentially, is what Zanda is. Although there is a Tibetan quarter near the monastery, Zanda is not a Tibetan town anymore. It's a Chinese garrison town, little more than a main drag lined with concrete blockhouses. Most large towns in Tibet have an obvious military presence, but it is more pronounced here because of an ongoing territorial dispute between India and China. Zanda lies close to the border with Ladakh.

In the final hours in Zanda, before our Land Cruiser headed south, I went about some mundane chores. One of these was to visit the tiny post office. I had bought some postcards of the Guge ruins in Lhasa and wanted to post them from Zanda (where no postcards were on sale, naturally). I always do this from really remote places, just to see if the post actually works.

"*Feiji!*" I said to the woman at the post office hopefully, slapping my right hand off the palm of my left—imitating a plane taking off. At this, she let out a high-pitched cackle. Airmail! Airmail from Zanda! She rushed to tell her co-workers. Pretty soon there were guffaws coming from all directions. Airmail!

Michael Buckley is the author of Heartlands, *a book about travels in the Tibetan world, from Bhutan to Ladakh and beyond. He is also the author of* Tibet: the Bradt Travel Guide, *and in addition to having cycled all over Asia and the Himalayas, he has been a long-time contributor to Travelers' Tales.*

At the Norbulingka

When in Lhasa, take a stroll this way.

THE WALK OUT TO NORBULINGKA IS ALONG A DUSTY STRETCH OF tarmac edged by knobby willows and a variety of repair shops full of motors, tires, axels, pots, and pans. There are a few tea shops along the way with narrow benches in front of them on which you can sit and watch the minimal traffic pass by. Norbulingka is usually called the "summer palace of the Dalai Lama." In actuality it is a park which contains a number of palaces of a number of Dalai Lamas, all in ill repair.

I crossed the road which leads to the Holiday Inn and entered a small enclave of arts and crafts shops before the gate of Norbulingka, which has grinning green and white monsters, snow lions I think, painted on its doorknobs. I browsed among their Chinese silk rugs, rumor has it woven in prisons. I was there well before opening time, which meant the ticket booth was closed and I walked in free. Wandering about looking at other shops inside the gates, I tried to remember through which of the red and yellow painted doors I would enter the fourteenth Dalai Lama's palace, as it had been five years since I had last been here.

In front of the doors were large squares of granite set about trees neatly enclosed in stone fences. There, sitting on the fences, were

Tibetan nomad women with brilliant strands of fuchsia and turquoise yarn braided into their hair. Their voluminous gowns were cinched at the waist by hand-woven aprons in stripes of green and pink or blue and brown. They were all draped with beads at wrist and neck, bells at their waists, and turquoise-and-silver amulet boxes on their bosoms. We gazed at each other in delight attempting to talk a little but my Tibetan was hardly better than their English. One offered me some snuff which she kept in a silver box secreted in the depths of her gown. Then their men called them away from such frivolous activities so they could walk around the palace, an act of Buddhist worship as well as sightseeing.

The park was empty except for me and a few snack bars set up under the trees where women sat knitting behind wooden tables where they sold candy, Chinese chewing gum, which in taste and texture arches the spectrum between very peculiar and truly awful, and peanuts. I meandered some more and hearing the tinkle of bells walked around the corner and saw people going into an entrance on the left side of the wall of the fourteenth Dalai Lama's palace. I ambled up and said, *"Tashi delai"* and with gestures asked if I might enter. "Of course," said the young man who was hanging about at the gate watching the proceedings. Later, I was able to figure out on my map that I had been in a part of a building called Kelsang Potrang.

There was a ceremony taking place for two purposes, as I later discovered. An ancient tree in the temple court had recently fallen and was now lying at full length on its stones. The tree's spirit was being honored. I sat on one of its knobs among a group of elderly women who were leaning against it. But the ceremony was also for the spirits of the dead who were having difficulty finding their next reincarnations. I assumed that these were troublesome spirits who would cause mischief in their roamings. In the center of the courtyard there was an elevated throne on which the chief monk sat. The front of it served as a firewall since there was, at its base, a small but very briskly burning fire. He was in splendid robes of heavy, vivid brocades and over them a poncho of brocade shot with silver and gold. He was such a mound of draperies and cloaks shimmering in the sun that he looked as though he wouldn't be able to stand up, to say nothing of walk, without assistance.

To his right a line of monks, also in robes and heavy brocaded ponchos, chanted on cue, rang their bells whose handles were *dorjes*, the Tibetan thunderbolt symbol of wisdom. They also punctuated their chants by shaking small drums that had balls on strings attached to them. If you shake them with the proper wrist motion, they produce a dry, tart rattle. Periodically these monks took from the folds of their robes a square of fabric, about the size of a pillowcase—each square was different in design, some with a center of brocade, others appliquéd, yet others embroidered. These they spread on their laps as they continued to chant. At a pause declared by bell or drum they would fold them up again. The monk sitting closest to me at the end of the row had on a poncho of black and crimson that any Western woman would have instantly transformed into a ball gown.

The Tibetan year is based upon a lunar calendar of twelve months, with the new year usually beginning sometime in February. Each month consists of thirty days, with the full moon on the fifteenth day and the new moon on the thirtieth day. In the seventh month, during the first to seventh days, is the Zhotön, the Yogurt Festival. Held in Norbulingka, it is the scene of a week-long picnic of eating and drinking, with Ache Lhamo (Tibetan opera) performances in the garden and at other venues around town for the entire week. Don't miss the yak races in the Lhasa Stadium.

—Gary McCue, *Trekking in Tibet: A Traveler's Guide*

To the chief monk's left was a long table on which were lined up bowls, basins, and plates with various foods on them—rice, the barley dish *tsampa*, noodles, yak butter, and things I couldn't identify. This was the banquet table of the ghosts. We, the audience, composed of men, women, and children, sat in rows about ten feet before the fire. The chief monk wore a hat consisting of a mound of what looked like black hair in the shape of a *stupa*, a dome. It may have originally been hair since there were two braid-like tails that stuck out behind, but now it is part of the hat and probably made from yak hair. This tonsorial temple was surrounded by a crown composed of painted plaques. It made an anachronistic contrast with his horn-rimmed spectacles. The monks had similar headgear, but not as large and imposing.

While the chanting was going on, the two monks who were attending to the table brought basins and bowls one at a time to the chief monk, who threw fistfuls of their contents into the flames making the fire crackle while he chanted in a bass voice. In between the burning of food, to feed the lost ghosts, melted yak butter was poured from a great brass dipper, the size of a large soup bowl, in a gleaming yellow stream over two instruments, rather like branding irons, which were held over the fire by the head monk. At one point they ran out of yak butter and one of the spectators rushed out the gate and returned with several large yellow hunks which were then melted in the ladle before being poured into the fire that sprang up to consume the grease. The smoke, smelling sweetly of butter and the consumed grains, floated about the court.

Patrolling the roof of the temple was a German shepherd whose ribs were countable from my seat in the court. She would have been happy to eat what was being burned but a rope kept her from jumping off the roof. The part of the audience I was sitting in was primarily composed of poorly dressed older women. In front of us were a number of young couples with children who would occasionally, when the pressure of childish spirits was too much for them, tear out the door to cavort with each other and then return to sit quietly beside their parents. Even the youngest still in split pants, the ecologically correct Eastern solution to Pampers, seemed to understand that this was a solemn occasion.

To one side, near the chorus of monks, there was a row of older people who looked well dressed, well groomed, and well fed. I wondered if they were the founders of this feast since young monks brought them cups of butter tea and treated them with deference. When the ceremony was finished with a final flourish of drums and bells, the chief monk was helped down from his perch. Indeed, he did have difficulty standing and walking in his gorgeous heap of ceremonial draperies. His assistants removed them, folding them neatly. Then he went into the chapel and we all lined up to be blessed.

Karen Swenson has five volumes of poetry in print, An Attic of Ideals, East-West, A Sense of Direction, A Daughter's Latitude, *and* The Landlady in Bangkok, *which won the National Poetry Series. Nominated for the Pushcart Prize three times, she has taught at many colleges and conferences, including the Aspen Writer's Conference, which she also directed. Her frequent travels in Southeast Asia have been the subject of articles for* The New Yorker, The New York Times, The Wall Street Journal, *and* The New Leader. *She lives in Manhattan.*

PART THREE

GOING YOUR OWN WAY

TOM JOYCE

The Space Between

*Just when he thought he'd had enough Buddhist
lore, a monk brings him some more.*

IN LATE JUNE OF 1921, TWO MEMBERS OF A BRITISH RECONNAIS-
sance team set out from the Tibetan village of Tingri to survey the
northern approach to a mountain determined to be the highest
point on Earth. One of the mountaineers, George Mallory, made
mention in letters to his wife of a Buddhist monastery he and
Guy Bullock had encountered at the mouth of a vast glacial flood-
plain fanning out below the peak. Indigenous people had called
the massif Jomolangma—a shortened form of the Goddess
Miyolangsangma—but it was now christened with a proper English
name after India's Surveyor General, Sir George Everest. Mallory
referred to the monastic complex they visited as "Rongbuk,"
assuming it to be the Tibetan name for the glacier. Eighty years
later, I found out just how wrong Mallory had been.

Designated by that same corruption in every Tibetan travel
guide, except the one written by my friend and companion, Gary
McCue, this ochre mud-brick *gompa*—literally "a place in solitude"—had been virtually destroyed by the Chinese Peoples'
Liberation Army during the Cultural Revolution in the late 1960s.
It was rebuilt, predominately as a Western tourist attraction, twenty
years later. Gary had reasoned that since the Tibetan name of the

151

glacier was Rongphu, the monastery likely bore the title of Dza Rongphu. But now, as we sit in the cramped, candle-lit chamber of Tsongpa, one of the young monks in residence, we learn that even Gary's deduction had been in error.

"What is this monastery called?" Gary inquires in Tibetan, his strong hands cupped around a carved wooden *poba* of salty yak-butter tea.

"Do-ngak Chöling," replies the elfin monk, a tattered yellow ski jacket covering the upper half of his russet robes, green Chinese sneakers peeking out below their hem.

"It's something like 'Place of the Dharma, and Tantric Sutras,'" my friend muses.

The site, we learn, is dedicated to Padmasambhava, a sixth-century Indian monk who first brought the dharma to the forbidden land of Bhöt—the vast plateau beyond the "Abode of Snow." Known in Tibet as Guru Rimpoche, this legendary tantric yogi established the school of Nyingma, which once permeated Central Asia and is now known as the "old sect" of Vajrayana.

Tsongpa motions upward and south toward the glacier. *"Dza Rongphu drubphuk,"* he explains, practicing his halting English on us. "Guru Rimpoche there alone...many years."

"Of course," Gary nods excitedly. *"Dza* would be where the valley begins to ascend toward the Rongphu glacier, but it isn't the name of the *gompa* after all, it's the *drubphuk*—the cave where Guru Rimpoche meditated in seclusion. Mallory must have heard the words all slurred together and it came out '*Rong-bhuk*.'" We both have a good laugh at how easily our knowledge of geography has been corrupted by bad hearing. Gary turns to the diminutive monk, "How far from here is the cave?"

"Maybe one hour," Tsongpa confirms. "Tomorrow, you see."

We pitch our tents in a walled yak pasture below the monastery's gates, but thick clouds and intermittent rain obliterate any glimpse of the world's highest peak, which stands as sentinel over the valley. Excited by the prospect of another adventure, but weary from our month-long journey, I curl up in my down sack and dream of waking to a clear sunrise.

We had been trekking further west in the Rongshar and Menlung valleys, exploring the rugged country where the legendary Milarepa was reputed to have flown like an emaciated lammergeier through the canyons of Drin in the eleventh century.

There, we climbed steep walls to the village of Drintang, where Jetsun Mila had been poisoned by a jealous rival, and found below, near the viciously desecrated *gompa* of Chuwar, a place called Dreche Phuk—"the Demon's Tongue Cave"—where the ascetic had given up his mortal remains. Strangest of all, we were shown a granite boulder into which, according to legend, the celibate saint had plunged his erect penis as a display of disdain toward the seductive advances of two *dakini*— capricious female mountain spirits. It was a hole of impressive depth and diameter.

But nothing impresses me more than the sensuous, ice-glazed granite flanks of Jomolangma herself. At daybreak, I throw back the flap of my tent to greet her crystal-blue north face towering like a natural *chörten*, or *stupa*, above the living river of gritty ice that forms Rongphu Glacier. She is back-lit, crowned with a halo of morn-

---

Everest: there it was, before us, unspeakable in all ways. The Tibetan name, Chomolungma (Goddess Mother Earth), suddenly seemed so appropriate. The North Face rose unimaginably high from base camp, the jet stream plume off the summit just like the pictures we'd all seen. We had a hard time simply walking to the cluster of tents housing a Japanese climbing team, and couldn't imagine what was in their minds as they waited to risk their lives on a summit attempt. Gary Sheppard nudged me and handed me a long lens with a twinkle in his eye, "There's Larry." Indeed, off in the distance was our friend, taking a shit at the edge of the glacier. The excitement, or the blowtorch meal, or the yak we ate the week before, must have gotten to him and brought things down to human scale.

—James O'Reilly, "Notes from the Roof"

ing sun, and plumed with a soft feather of snow dancing in the
lapis jet stream above her head. Only the arrogant British Raj could
have been so insensitive as to re-name a goddess after a male colonial bureaucrat.

My breath condenses in the cold air while dressing in the confines of my tent. Encased in synthetic fleece, I make my way to the
chapel before breakfast, where the old chant master is leading a rag-
tag assembly of young monks and *ani*—Buddhist nuns—in morning prayer. On a cushion covered with dusty rugs, I remove my
boots and try to join the spirit of the *sangha*—the host of initiates.
But this proves difficult; several of the *ani* are coughing with tuber-
cular violence, some of the young monks are snickering at me as if
I were a Saturday morning cartoon, and everyone seems more intent
on eyeballing the alien in capillene while loudly slurping their bot-
tomless *pobas* of butter tea than the ritual du jour. Yet the chant
master croaks on as if it were just the same dharma, different day. In
the midst of this distraction, reminiscent of a high school assembly,
I cannot manage to silence my cerebral "monkey chatter," and leave
enshrouded in a state of spiritual dissonance, which even sweet
Sherpa tea cannot permeate.

"I've found the key master," Gary informs me at breakfast.

I stare at him blankly over warm *tsampa* pancakes. "Did I miss
something?"

"Tsongpa introduced me to the *go-nyer*, the caretaker who keeps
the key to Guru Rimpoche's cave."

"Of course," I nod, heaping Nescafé crystals into an aluminum
cup, "the key master. That would make sense. After all, some Chinese
soldiers with machine guns and mortars might get in and do mischief if the place were left unlocked."

Gary ignores my sarcasm. "Well, he's agreed to take us up to the
cave after breakfast."

"Excellent. Do you think he has any tricks for improving the
taste of *tsampa*?"

At 9 A.M., we await the Key Master within the butter-tea-and-
yak-dung-scented labyrinth of the *gompa*. Finally, he appears from

an alley, a lean fellow, cut with the lines of a lifetime in high altitude sun. His head is shaven, making it is impossible to guess his age— thirty-five or seventy-five for all I can tell. The Nyingma-pa monk wears a gray woolen sweater, threadbare at the elbows, over his deep claret robes. His leather street shoes are blown out at the sides; the sole is separating from the last. Evidently, they take their vow of poverty seriously at Do-ngak Chöling.

Gary makes the introductions: "This is Ngawang Sangye," he tells me. The lanky monk's face glows with simplicity and generosity, a child-like happiness so prevalent among his brethren. Although his teeth are rotting, Ngawang's smile is warm and endearing. He idly fingers an array of steel keys, some intricately shaped and intriguingly engraved, tethered to his belt by a cord of braided yak hair. Key Master beckons for us to follow him up a sloping moraine beyond the monastery walls, toward the glacier's tongue.

Along the high route that leads to Jomolangma's Base Camp, we encounter the scattered ruins of what once had been the enormous hermitage of Changchub Tarling, as well as those of Rongchung *ani-gompa*, an erstwhile nunnery. Here lies more evidence of the Chinese government's contempt for the "poison" of religion, and a testament to their efficiency in eradicating all aspects of it which didn't readily contribute to tourist revenues.

After about an hour of following the glacial tributary, we approach a rocky spur affixed with ropes stretched from a central mast across a defile that rises abruptly on the far side. The ropes are strung with a sequence of red, blue, green, yellow, and white squares of wind-tattered cotton, each imprinted with a black drawing of the "Wind Horse" and prayers lettered in Tibetan script. Beneath the mast, a little chapel is built into the slabs of glacial talus. We follow Key Master up steps carved into the spur, finally reaching a weathered wooden door.

Ngawang selects a plain steel church key from his tether, opens a padlock, then steps back to allow Gary and me entrance to the little chapel. Perhaps I've become jaded after exploring the treasures of the Potala, the Tsuglag Khang and Tashilhunpo monasteries, where enormous gilded images of Maitraya, Chenrezig,

Padmasambhava, and Tsong Khapa meditate infinitely within incense-scented chapels, where the rumbling drone of hundreds of chanting monks, and the sophisticated, multi-chromatic architectural ornamentation overwhelm every molecule of one's being. It is easy to appreciate spirituality in such an aesthetically pleasing environment, but in this wretched little place, where centuries of butter-lamp smoke has blackened the rough-hewn rock ceiling, and all but a few pitiful statues have been stolen by looters or sold to European collectors by monks in dire need of food and new shoes, I find myself sinking into ennui.

Key Master points to a hole in the floor and drops down a ladder into the blackness below. We follow with our mini-Maglites into a six-by-ten-foot cavern with a ceiling so low we have to stoop. The lean monk smiles a near-toothless smile, and lights a yak-butter lamp beside a tiny grotto in which a small effigy of Guru Rimpoche had been placed.

"Can you imagine," Gary asks, "being in seclusion, meditating for years down in this cave?" I stand in perfunctory admiration as Ngawang reverently reveals his dingy treasures with a fading flashlight. Gary fishes a few yuan from his belt pouch and tucks them alongside the greasy butter drippings and assorted coins scattered on the tiny altar. The monk nods and removes two filthy gray *katas*—scarves of greeting—from the shrine, placing them around our necks. They smell rancid and permeated with smoke from the butter lamps.

I am growing rapidly disdainful of the rote ritual piety and self-replicating dogma of Tibetan Buddhism, and am simultaneously ashamed by my lack of appreciation for our host's generosity. I want only to escape from this cold, damp, greasy little hole in the ground, to get back out into the crisp rarefied air and the pristine clarity of Jomolangma, more glorious, more compellingly divine, than any temple fashioned by human craft. Milarepa understood this, and repeatedly admonished the Khadampa priests for their corrupt materialism cloaked in false piety. I have reached utter saturation with man-made religion. It is time to leave these ascetics to their archaic cerebral fantasies and return to the spiritual reality of rock and ice.

As I climb back up the ladder, Gary and Ngawang are conferring in Tibetan.

"He says that there is a *kora* we can follow," Gary explains, referring to a clockwise circumambulation route around the premises, undoubtedly replete with various stations of sacred significance.

I sigh impatiently, "I'm anxious to reach Base Camp before sunset."

"Where's your sense of adventure?" Gary goads, a challenging grin creasing his sun browned angular face beneath a salt-and-pepper beard. "Let's see how it goes and bolt if necessary," he offers judiciously.

Tentatively, I agree, and the three of us set off through the defile, beneath the strands of rustling prayer flags flapping like the shreds of Christo's ill-fated curtain that briefly spanned Colorado's Rifle Gap.

After half an hour of walking the circuit, we have been shown several little shrines cut into the boulders where *shapjay* were found. These are generally agreed to be impressions left in solid stone by bodhisattva—a sort of Mann's Theatre of Buddhist sainthood—but most of the impressions look suspiciously like natural erosion to me, and bear little or no resemblance to human hands or feet. My impatience simmers to contempt.

"I've seen enough, Gary. Let's get out of here."

Gary makes our apologies to Key Master, and he nods graciously. But as we turn to go, Ngawang touches Gary's arm and points up the defile behind us. They exchange words and glances up at the tumble of enormous boulders re-arranged by the ever-shifting Himalaya.

Gary takes me aside. "Ngawang says there is one more stop on the *kora*—, the Long Hell Hole, he calls it."

"What's that?"

"Another cave of some sort," Gary replies. "He uses a word that means 'test.' Apparently, only those who have good intentions can get through it."

"Otherwise?"

Gary draws a finger across his throat and grins menacingly. "Well? Are you game?"

"I don't like caves, Gary," I admit as my gut begins to tighten.

"Questioning your intentions?"

"Just my karma. All right. Let's see this hell hole."

Ngawang instructs Gary and me to find a black stone and a white stone among the loose scree at our feet. Once we have located these items, we follow the monk several hundred yards up the slope, where he points to an opening in the rock and indicates we will need to remove our rucksacks in order to enter the narrow crevice. We dig out Maglites once again and stow our packs behind a boulder. Suddenly sweating, I strip to my t-shirt in the afternoon sun.

"Are you ready?" Gary asks, removing his wide-brimmed hat.

"No, but what the hell!"

Crouching, we follow the smiling Key Master into a natural tunnel created by the spaces between the stones. Soon we are crawling in a cool darkness, climbing over obstacles, dropping down into channels formed by a landslide some millennia before the Buddha was a thought in the great Universal Mind. After what seems like an eternity, the passage abruptly narrows to a point where I must contort my body to negotiate the opening in the rock. My shoulder blade scrapes on a rough surface and my boot sole wedges into a crack. With the Maglite clenched between my teeth, I wrench free. Discovering that the two stones I'm carrying have become an awkward handicap, I tuck them into the cargo pocket of my trousers, noticing that my hands are shaking with cold—and fear. Suddenly, the monkeys of the mind begin to shriek:

Are you insane? Why did you ever agree to do this? To prove you're not a coward? To prove you're as tough as Gary? What if this smiling monk is really a lunatic? What if he can't find the way out? You'll never be able to retrace your steps. Are you out of your fucking mind?

It must be obvious by now that even the thought of spelunking breaks me out in a cold sweat. In my panic, I remember a recurring childhood dream: I am deep in a cave just like this one—crawling gradually into a narrower and narrower space, deeper and deeper into a cold dark tunnel. I somehow know that there is an exit just ahead, but soon there is not enough space to squeeze through. My head gets stuck in the gap. I can't breathe…. The Freudian implications are obvious, but perhaps there are Jungian archetypes at work here as well, Gnostic implications of spirit imprisoned in matter, psyche frozen in stone…or maybe it was just a feverish hallucination.

But I am not able to reason through the etiology just now, as I shiver and sweat simultaneously. We down climb a twelve-foot chimney and emerge into a grotto. I shine my wide beam up onto the wet rock twenty feet above my head, then down its concavity to my right; there is an opening in the floor. Cautiously approaching the pit, I discover a low rim of stones built up around it like the lip of a well. Clearly this is a place of ritual, perhaps one that predates even Guru Rimpoche. The ancient Bönpo of Tibet were animists led by shamans like the infamous Naro Bönchung, defeated at Gang Ti-sé—Mount Kailash—in a black magical duel with Milarepa. Looking into the dark hole before me, I can only guess what may have taken place in this grotto deep beneath the glacial moraine…but I try not to.

Ngawang hurls his black stone into the pit with a flourish, and I listen to it clatter off the well shaft for several seconds. When Gary and I have replicated his actions, the monk turns to the opposite side of the grotto. My flashlight reveals a six-foot conical pile of white stones. Key Master tosses his shard to mingle with the others, and again, we follow his lead.

I shine my beam on Ngawang's face; he is smiling as if in possession of some numinous secret. Key Master begins a subdued discourse, which Gary attempts to translate faithfully: "He says 'the black stone represents all the karma you carry through life…It is just a burden, so you must throw it away…The white stone represents you—your spirit…By placing it with all the others who have come here, you are re-dedicating yourself to the liberation of all beings.'"

The monk turns to Gary and taps his Maglite. "He wants us to turn them off."

With great trepidation, I oblige.

"This is how your journey will be after you die," Gary translates. "There will be no butter lamps to light your way…It will be dark, and you will be cold and afraid…"

No shit!

"You will be surrounded by all your demons—the projections of your human mind...Fear of loss will cause your desire to cling to things you no longer need."

Like life? Is it wrong to cling to life?

"This is what you will find in the *bardo*...the space between one life and another...You will discover that you are not separate from all other beings...Together, you must help each other face fear...and prepare yourself to blow out the flame of desire."

Should I panic yet? Jesus! This guy has decided it's time to die and he's taking us with him. No one will know where we are. No one will be looking for us. How the hell are we ever going to find our way out of here?

Although certain I've been in more dire circumstances than this, I'm hard pressed at the moment to remember a single instance. We are in Key Master's hands now, totally at the mercy of his intention and whim. There is no alternative but to hope — to trust — that this little monk is not as insane as he appears in my state of high anxiety. There is nothing else I can do, no way out, no course of action but surrender.

I wait in the dead silent darkness — the space between my last thought and the next...

After an eternity in suspended animation, a lamp flashes on. Ngawang is smiling as before, obviously pleased with his little near-death demonstration. He motions us to the base of a boulder in the grotto, where Gary shines his beam down into a crevice.

"There's a tiny stream under here."

"*Chinlap,*" Ngawang replies, motioning me closer. *"Drub chu."*

Gary smiles, "A blessing. We're supposed to drink the water of attainment."

"Why not?" I agree, reaching into the crevice to feel the icy trickle. Wetting my fingers, I bring them to my parched lips. The water is sweet and mineral laden. When Gary has taken his blessing, Key Master heads off into the underground labyrinth without a word.

We follow closely on his tattered leather heels. Perhaps I'm just disoriented, but it seems that the way out bears little or no resemblance to the way in. Then, after fifteen minutes of squeezing through the gaps between one cold stone and another, I see light. It is the most glorious sight I've beheld in my entire life.

We scramble up a slick, narrow ramp and emerge on a flat boulder sloping sharply to the ochre earth outside the cave. Sliding down out of the talus tomb, the sun kisses my face like a long-absent lover; the cool, rarefied air bites my nose, and I am ecstatically happy to be alive. Endorphins subside; I feel giddy, physically lighter, mentally sharper. It seems that all the problems of life, once weighing so heavily on me, have been effortlessly reduced to trivial annoyances, or vaporized in the blinding midday sunlight.

I am new.

Key Master stands before us with his paradoxical grin, simultaneously wise and childlike. He speaks to me through Gary, "Now, you are reborn…now, you can start over…from this moment."

Tears well in my eyes. I grope for something to say as I grasp the monk's hands in mine, but his sage nod tells me that no words are necessary. He understands exactly what I am experiencing—the ineffable. After all, he too was once initiated.

"Tujay chay." I thank him from the bottom of my heart with a voice that seems to echo another lifetime.

Gary digs deep into his oversized pack, producing a pair of white, Indonesian-knock-off running shoes, and presents them to Ngawang. "I've been carrying these around for months, waiting for the right opportunity to give them to a deserving soul," Gary explains with a wry grin. Key Master accepts the shoes as if they are inestimable treasures. One man's knock-off is another's salvation. He takes Gary's head in his hands and confers a blessing that ends in gleeful laughter.

With all the time in the world, keys jangling from the braided lanyard at his side, Ngawang Sangye begins back down the trail toward Do-ngak Chöling, clutching his new shoes like a contented child returning home from his birthday party.

Bereft of analysis, I stroke the coarse beard on my face in silent emptiness. Electricity seems to flow from my fingertips, dancing across my cheeks like fireflies, crackling through my hair like winter static, pulsing up the back of my neck on a trajectory to the crown of my head, exiting toward some destination beyond my ability to envision.

"Do you suppose we're alive or dead?" I ask only half-facetiously.

Gary squints for a long time back toward the mouth of the cave, then shakes his head as if waking from a lucid dream. "Probably somewhere in between," my friend concludes, pulling the canvas brim of his hat down over his eyes.

I shoulder my rucksack in euphoric silence, cinch up, and point what remains of my ego in the direction of the Goddess Miyolang-sangma, napping peacefully behind her afternoon veil of silver clouds.

Tom Joyce is a writer, photographer, and graphic designer who lives in the San Francisco area. He is currently working on a documentary film project called The Heretic's Pilgrimage.

MARK JENKINS

Instant Karma

Questions of free will and causality enliven
a rough trip in the hinterlands.

I KILLED THE RAT. EVEN THOUGH THE WOMAN WHO SWEPT THE courtyard told me I would bring bad karma upon myself. The rat was menacing the bunk room. It was a big, oily sewer rat. Every night it crept into the room after we were asleep and clawed into our backpacks, gorging itself. One night it leaped onto the face of a Danish girl and got its claws tangled in her long blond hair. She woke up screaming. Enough is enough.

The woman who swept the stone courtyard wore a traditional Tibetan gown, trim and dark, and had plaited her raven hair into a thick braid. She came from a remote village and was a devout Buddhist. She looked into my face and told me no one sold rat traps in Lhasa. In the market I found almost everyone sold heavy, serrated, spring-loaded metal rat traps. I bought one and baited it with a cube of yak meat and placed it under my bunk. I heard the loud snap around midnight, the desperate thumping, a final jerk. I pulled my sleeping bag over my head and slept soundly.

In the morning the woman was solemn and anxious, but the travelers staying in the bunk room were relieved. Killing the rat is how I became friends with Maury and Brigitte.

"Thanks," Brigitte said. "No one else would have done it."

"I know I wouldn't have," Maury said.

Brigitte was a Canadian physics student, a climber with blue, round doll's eyes. She was traveling alone. She carried her Tibetan phrase book everywhere she went, and despite all the laughter she provoked she was actually learning Tibetan. She would eventually be invited to Geneva to earn her Ph.D.

Maury was a tall, beach-blond Aussie, a former lifeguard who became an itinerant carpenter in Vancouver, building decks half the year and traveling the other half. He loved to dive and knew every brilliant blue-water lagoon from Honduras to Hong Kong.

That evening, with a ratless night to look forward to, Maury and Brigitte and I went out together to celebrate. On the way to the restaurant Maury bought a case of bottled beer and carried it lightly on his shoulder. We laughed so hard and stayed out so late that we were locked out and had to pound on the great wooden gate to get in.

The next day, hanging out in the courtyard in the cold sunshine, I asked each of them if they were up for something illegal.

"What do you think, mate?" said Maury, breaking into his habitual smile.

"Always," said Brigitte. I didn't know if this was true or not.

I wanted to go to Lhamo Latso, one of the holiest lakes in Tibet. I'd been hearing about the lake since my first journey to Tibet, in 1984. One day in the slums of Delhi, where the beggar children with limbs broken backward by their parents peer up from the ground, I had found a book titled *The Power-Places of Central Tibet* for sale between an Indian tome on sexual positions and a photo-biography of the Beatles. In it there was a description of Lhamo Latso: "It is Tibetan belief older than Buddhism that every individual, every family, and an entire country, possesses a 'life-spirit' called *la*. This *la* is embodied in natural phenomena, such as mountains, lakes, trees, and so on. When the place of residence of the *la* is damaged, the individual, family, or nation suffers directly. Thus when a lake that is the home of the *la* dries up, this omen of death and disaster can inflict the terrible result that is presaged. The 'life-spirit' of Tibet is identified with Lhamo Latso."

Lhamo Latso is also the geographical life-spirit for all Dalai Lamas. It is a surprisingly small lake, a tiny oval barely recognizable on a map, located a hundred miles southeast of Lhasa near the head of the Metoktang Valley. Over the centuries, most Dalai Lamas made a pilgrimage to this oracle. By staring into its cold, lapping waters, each Dalai Lama could divine essential clues to who his reincarnation would be. When the 13th Dalai Lama died suddenly in 1933, the Regent of Tibet made a pilgrimage to Lhamo Latso, where, transfixed by the turquoise water, he had a vision that gave exact details for finding his spiritual leader's reincarnation, Tenzin Gyatso, the 14th (and current) Dalai Lama—until then an unknown two-year-old boy living in a village in Amdo.

I had food, tents, and camping gear left over from an aborted expedition, but neither Maury nor Brigitte had come to Tibet prepared to live out in the cold, so we went shopping. In lieu of a cheap Chinese army slicker that Maury thought too expensive, he bought himself an enormous white plastic gunnysack. We cut out holes for his head and arms, and he pulled it on and tied a rope around his waist.

"You look like a priest from the Middle Ages," Brigitte said.

"You know it gets cold above 15,000 feet," I told him.

"No drama," said Maury—Aussie for "don't worry"—and donned a green felt fedora he'd purchased instead of a Tibetan sheepskin cap.

Brigitte borrowed my fleece pants and bought herself a Tibetan scarf and a floppy wool cap. She would stay bundled in them for the next two weeks.

The Chinese were requiring foreigners to hire a guide, a driver, and a jeep and to obtain (i.e., buy) three or four permits for any travel outside Lhasa. We couldn't have received permission to go to Lhamo Latso in any case; it was deep inside an off-limits chunk of Tibet the size of Texas, and four days of hard mountain hiking from the nearest road.

We sneaked out of town before dawn, catching a lift on a local bus overloaded with Tibetans bundled up like Inuits, the bus driver eyeing us in a shard of mirror. We hid under the seats at security checkpoints. Where the bus U-turned we jumped out and started walking away fast, not looking back, not turning around, expecting to be stopped and questioned and perhaps jailed, but it didn't happen. We negotiated a ride with a well-connected local, sardined into the back of his jeep, and he drove us straight past every dusty roadblock with a grin and a wave.

At dusk the jeep dropped us near the head of the Metoktang Valley. We slipped across the Tsangpo River on a tank-wide suspension bridge that was inexplicably unguarded, hiked up into the mouth of the canyon, and pitched camp in a muddy field encircled by apricot trees. I couldn't believe how lucky we'd been. Lying in my bag, I must have said so out loud.

"No such thing, mate," whispered Maury from the other tent. Brigitte was already curled up asleep beside me.

"What's that?"

"No such thing as luck."

In the morning, mist wreathed the valley. To either side, treeless slopes reared up a mile in the sky. We walked the track in shade, the ground hard-frozen, and watched the sunlight coming. When the light finally sailed into the bottom of the valley the temperature leaped 50 degrees. In minutes winter metamorphosed into summer. The river began to cough and jerk and then run free, the pastures turned from frost-white to green, and shouting shepherd kids sprouted on the hillsides. That's how the world works above a certain altitude. Of course, it could just as easily have been snowing.

"So, Maury," I said. "You don't believe in luck?"

He had his pants hiked up, revealing the funny, laceless, ankle-length Blundstone boots that Aussies like. He'd taken off his fedora and was strolling hat in hand. "Luck isn't something you can believe in," he said. "Luck is the word used by people who don't believe."

"Good things happen and it's not just a matter of luck?"

"Nope. They were supposed to happen."

"And bad things?"

"Same." Maury was practicing twirling his fedora on the tip of his finger and catching it. "Everything happens for a reason, Mark."

Brigitte was just ahead, practically skipping even with a heavy pack. She was implacably cheerful, just like Maury. You couldn't get either of them to say a bad word about anything or anybody if you tortured them.

"So you must believe in karma."

"I do."

"And reincarnation."

"They go together." Maury flashed a smile and flipped the fedora up onto his head.

To me, it seemed like the oddest coincidence that I should wind up walking to Lhamo Latso with a man who actually believed in reincarnation. But then Maury would have said that that's because it wasn't a coincidence at all.

That night we camped in the bleak medieval village of Tseqgu. Brigitte danced among the snot-faced urchins practicing her Tibetan until they clutched our fingers with their callused, dirt-blackened hands and pulled us into a tiny stone hut. We had to stoop and could see almost nothing in the dim light. We were led through an indoor pen separating the goats and sheep

---

For years now I have been trying to remember, every moment of the day, that great teaching of the Lord Buddha which says "Holy company brings desirelessness, desirelessness brings peace of mind, peace of mind brings freedom from illusion, freedom from illusion brings immediate liberation." This is difficult to practice, yet one can find real happiness only by avoiding desire and hatred. Whenever I feel unhappy or worried I look into myself and find the root of my unhappiness hidden in a dark corner of selfishness. Milarepa has said that by pretending and deceiving we cheat and mislead ourselves, so I carefully watch my mind all the time.

—Rinchen Dolma Taring,
Daughter of Tibet

---

from the humans but allowing the animals' body heat to half-warm the cramped black space. An old man plunging a yak-butter churn with gnarled hands greeted us and invited us to sit on a dirt bench beside a red-glowing hearth. Steaming red potatoes were poured into a basket on the floor and the children squatted on their haunches and wiped green mucus across their red cheeks and we all ate together.

The next morning there were three inches of snow on the ground. While we were packing up our tents a shivering, barefoot boy, ragged and filthy and carrying a water jug heavier than himself, passed our tents. I looked at Maury.

"OK, mate," he said. "If it's bothering you so much, this is what I believe: Every thought, every word, every action produces karma. Our karma carries on from life to life. It's a spiritual progression. Bit by bit, act by act, life after life, we create our own karma. Acts of kindness in this life beget gifts of kindness in the next. Acts of cruelty in this life beget suffering in the next. It's self-fulfilling retribution and reward. It's a spiritual quest for learning, and we all have a choice as to what path we will take."

Brigitte asked Maury how the actions of others affected an individual's karma.

"Depends on how you respond," he said. "It's up to you."

In the honey light of late afternoon we reached the forlorn but still magnificent Chökorgye Monastery. Chökorgye was built in one of the ancient geomantic hot spots of Tibet—a vast triangular plain at the confluence of three rivers and surrounded by three mountains symbolizing a perfect harmony of three elements: earth, water, and air. The monastery's castle-like walls form an equilateral triangle, a quarter-mile to a side. Gendun Gyatso, the second Dalai Lama, founded the monastery in 1509 as a place of rest and worship for those making the pilgrimage to Lhamo Latso.

We popped up our tents outside the walls of the monastery, across the vast triangular commons from the black wool tents of the Tibetan nomads. Lion-dogs—immense mastiffs with the solid bodies of rottweilers but the matted coats and lion ruffs of chows— were staked outside these tents, barking themselves hoarse.

The Chökorgye Monastery was razed by the Junggar Mongols in 1718, rebuilt, and destroyed again by the Chinese in 1959. Inside the walls were the beheaded skeletons of hundreds of stone buildings, including several temples. Before the tanks and dynamite, there were 500 monks at Chökorgye; now, we discovered, there were only two:

an old man and a young man living amid the ruins, quiet and transparent as spirits. They thought we were pilgrims—and we were, although I didn't know it then. To reach Lhamo Latso, they told us, you follow the wide stone path leading northeast from the monastery. We would find our way.

The lion-dogs barked all night, lunging and snapping taut their heavy chains, mistaking gusts of wind for intruders. We collapsed our tents in the predawn dark and left the gear on the broken stones of the former temple as the monks had suggested. Slipping back out below a whistling sky, we moved along the wall past piles of stone tablets all engraved with the same hypnotic chant—*om mani padme hum, om mani padme hum, om mani padme hum,* "hail to the jewel in the lotus"—as if the wind itself were using the tablets as a hymnal.

> Sometimes in Tibet, when we see there is not freedom to do anything under the Chinese, we get very sad and very angry at times. Sometimes I wish I could burn down something, but after that I think this is not the right way. We offered our body, speech, and mind to the three jewels so that is what we must do. We gave our vow not to take any life. We must avoid these poisons: attachment, anger, hatred, and ignorance.
>
> —A Tibetan Nun

To stay warm, we simply hiked swiftly. By the time we crossed the Metoktang River it was light enough to switch off our headlamps. We walked through a yak herder's camp where great black beasts snorted columns of white steam. A woman in angular swaths of black was milking one of the yaks. Brigitte went over to speak with her, but the woman fled to her black tent.

It was steep going into a hanging valley, and then level again. Cold squalls kept coming and going. I was making my case for the irrationality of reincarnation and waiting for Brigitte, the scientist, the physicist, to chime in.

"Matter cannot be created or destroyed, only reformed," she said at last. "If you want to infer something spiritual from that—"

"Brigitte!"

"Well, Mark, it's up to you."

Maury was walking ahead of us with his arms crossed and his fedora pulled down over his ears. "We not only come back in a new form," he declared. "I believe we choose the form we come back in."

"What!" This was too much. "Who would ever choose to come back as that dying barefoot child we saw carrying water yesterday morning?"

"I don't know," said Maury, his tone implying not that it couldn't happen, but that he himself didn't have an example.

"C'mon, Maury, this is preposterous. Forget about coming back as a beetle or a rat; just take a child who dies of starvation or AIDS or malaria. Who would choose that life? For that matter, take any kid who is abused by his parents and tell me he chose to be reincarnated into that kind of suffering."

Maury glanced back over his shoulder. "I suppose it depends on the kind of lives, the hundreds or thousands of lives he's lived before."

It was too cold to talk anymore. We finally reached the 17,300-foot pass overlooking Lhamo Latso—"a sharp cragged ridge," according to *The Power-Places of Central Tibet*, "upon which is built the Dalai Lama's throne, and from this eminence the divine rulers of Tibet once sat to gaze into the lake...to divine the future." The throne itself was buried beneath untold thousands of prayer flags frozen into an icy mound, and the wind was cutting us in two. The sacred lake didn't look any different from a thousand other inhospitable high-altitude tarns found everywhere in Tibet.

Maury and Brigitte and I tried to stay up high and stare down into the oracle-lake because we all want a vision, we all want something mysterious and inexplicable and portentous to happen to us—especially those of us who doubt that such things can happen. We braced ourselves amid the creaking flags and peered down into the hard blue lake until our eyes blurred and our faces froze and our feet began to slip. To me it was just like standing on the summit of a mountain: no divination, no enlightenment, just the howl and bite of cold doing all it could to freeze solid the blood in three beating hearts.

That night bullets of snow strafed our tents and the lion-dogs yelped and the monastery stood silent as stone. The next day we crossed Gyelong Pass in a whiteout. The day after that we woke to eight inches of snow, and more falling.

By now we'd each settled into our roles, which of course were not roles at all but who we really were, so there was harmony. I was the navigator, plotting our course over the earth and through the mountains on 1:500,000 declassified military maps, reading between the brown lines. Brigitte was the bubbly, fluid linguist who got us invited into every Tibetan home or tent we came near for boiled potatoes and yak-butter tea. And Maury was the incorrigible optimist, the blast of fresh air, the man who could not not smile no matter how deep the snow or how hungry we were, even when it got so cold we all had to cram into one tent and sleep in a pile to keep from freezing to death.

One evening we followed a mule cart stacked high with hay into the village of Woka Taktse. There was a dirt road trickling out of this village and a jeep for hire, and so our journey would end. The Tibetan women in their bright blue tunics and heavy wool aprons were on the flat roofs of their mud homes, beating stalks of barley and singing softly in the twilight.

Maury and I were talking, and I was telling him how lucky I was to have been raised in a big family where everyone was loved.

"No such thing."

"Love?"

Maury hooted. "Luck, mate. Luck!"

"What about you, Maury? What was your family like?"

"Ah, well…"

"Well what?"

"It was a learning experience."

"What's that mean?"

Ahead, Brigitte was being led by the hand by a bowlegged old woman. It was almost dark, but the air was still warm. Maury doffed his fedora and ran a hand through his scarecrow hair and told me that he had lived in terror as a boy because his father was a drunk. A

mean-spirited drunk who all through Maury's childhood viciously
beat him and his mother.

Mark Jenkins is on the staff of Outside *magazine and writes a regular
column entitled "The Hard Way."*

Red River Valley

Time travel in Gyantse takes on new meaning
when you're making a movie.

THERE ARE TIMES, TRAVELING, WHEN YOU FALL INTO EXTRAORDI-
nary circumstances—doing things you couldn't even imagine you
might be doing. Like right now, standing in a monastery courtyard,
adjusting my sword and pith helmet, with a make-up artist streak-
ing dirt and bloodstains on my face.

When three buses disgorge their loads of People's Liberation
Army soldiers at the monastery, we know we're onto something big.
Why so many soldiers? For security? For an execution? The fresh-
faced recruits stand at attention while a commander barks at them.
Then one platoon proceeds to remove their camouflage fatigues
and put on khaki uniforms, and wigs, mustaches, sideburns, and pith
helmets. One of them picks up a pole with a ragged Union Jack
mounted on it and waves it around. They are the British Army!

"Stiff upper lip, lads—hold the flag high!" shouts Nick, a
Hollywood actor. We're in the courtyard of Nenying Gompa, a
monastery south of Gyantse in central Tibet. The massive fort at
Gyantse was the last major barrier on the road to Lhasa when the
British invaded Tibet in 1903–1904, forcibly seeking to open it to
trade, and to flush out any Russian agents lurking in Lhasa. We're
dressed as British officers—in real life, five travelers recruited in

Lhasa as extras in the Chinese movie, *Red River Valley*, a fictionalized
account of the British invasion.

Having heard about the film, I jumped at the chance to be on
the inside of the movie-making process, to see how the director
would handle political cor-
rectness with such a hot pota-
to as Tibet. Getting into the
movie is a matter of luck and
timing: I happened to be sitting in the right café in Lhasa
when the movie recruiters
went about their talent quest.
A rum bunch they rounded
up—two Americans, a
German, a Spaniard, and
myself. Actually, our main
qualifications for the role are
our big noses and round eyes.
A wardrobe assistant shows me
how to wrap leggings, and
thrusts a 303 rifle in my hands.

There are two Hollywood
actors on the set—Paul
Kersey, a soap opera star, and
Nick Love, from Los Angeles.
Nick enlightens us on the
story line: "All you have to
know about the script is that
everybody dies at the end.
The heroines are blown up,
the Tibetans are all blown
away, a lot of Brits die—even
I die a few pages before the
end. After that, I can go home, thank God."

Nick plays Colonel Rockman, who bears an uncanny resemblance—with scruffy goatee—to the real British commander,

> Gyantse, Tibet, is the Wild
> East, a one-yak town. Yet
> this dingy little burgh, this wind-
> blown village, played a major
> role in modern Tibetan history.
> The turn of the century was
> the era of the so-called "Great
> Game," the covert struggle
> between Britain and Russia
> for control of Central Asia. By
> 1902, the Tsarist Empire was
> rapidly expanding eastward, and
> Lord Curzon, Viceroy of India,
> feared Russian expansion into
> Tibet—and perhaps further. In
> a letter to London in 1902, he
> vowed to "frustrate this little
> game while there is yet time."
> So, in 1904, the colonial govern-
> ment in India launched an expe-
> dition that has been called "one
> of the most contentious episodes
> in British imperial history."
> —Garry Marchant, "The
> Road to Gyantse"

Colonel Younghusband. However, he has seen fit to affect a Scottish brogue in keeping with the script, oblivious to the fact that Younghusband was definitely not a Scot. Off-camera, he reverts to his regular English accent. Kersey, who is supposed to play a British reporter, sometimes comes up with a London accent, and other times lapses into a Los Angeles lilt.

To see history spring to life is magical for me, having researched this era. In the real invasion, Younghusband didn't die—he thrived. Fewer than 40 British soldiers died in battle, compared with some 2,700 Tibetan soldiers killed. Everything in Tibet is medieval, and that includes weapons. Tibetan muskets and swords were no match for British weaponry: in one engagement, 600 Tibetans, believing their amulets would protect them from bullets, were mowed down by Maxim machine guns. The amulet-makers later claimed that the amulets were only good against *copper* bullets, and obviously the British had used another metal. The British stayed two months in Lhasa, failed to find any Russian agents in the woodwork, negotiated a useless treaty with some head lamas, then withdrew—leaving behind a telegraph line and a couple of trade agents. The Chinese director's problem is how to rewrite history to suit the theme of heroic Tibetan resistance to the British barbarians, who also happen to be the military victors.

Camera, horses, action: pretty soon we're in the thick of things, among droves of neighing, farting horses with jingling bells mounted by nervous PLA-Brit riders. The energetic director, Feng Xiaoning, seems to be in a dozen places at once in his roles as scriptwriter, director, cinematographer, and chief PLA-consultant. He signals the start of a scene where the British Army files slowly past some Tibetans on pilgrimage. Paul Kersey is grovelling on the ground, trying to get into character. He plays Lieutenant Jones, a sensitive British war reporter who sympathizes with the Tibetans and falls in love with a beautiful Tibetan woman (well, actually, a Chinese actress dressed in Tibetan robes). The interpreter wants to know if Paul has read up on this scene. "Of course I've read the fucking script," he tells her sharply. Our job is to march past the camera in close-ups; behind us, slightly out of focus, are scores of PLA-Brit soldiers.

The eerie thing is that if you ignore the film crew, the illusion of being with the British expeditionary force of 1904 is complete. Long lines of horses and riders saunter through desert terrain under cobalt-blue skies; in the background the imposing ruins of a Tibetan fort command a hillside. Adding battle atmosphere, an assistant runs amok with a sizzling censer that billows black smoke everywhere. This device makes the horses skittish—a horse bolts through the ranks with a novice PLA rider dangling off the saddle. In my rush to get out of the way, I trip over my sword. The PLA commander bawls the PLA rider out; the Tibetan horse-handler changes mounts. We do the scene again. And again. About ten times altogether, I think.

The PLA men are total klutzes—and very dangerous when handling rifles with blanks and fixed bayonets. During an infantry charge a PLA-Brit soldier stumbles and nicks Markus, the German extra, in the back with a bayonet. Only his leather bandolier saves him. Even more hazardous are blank bullets—life-threatening if fired too close. Comically, the PLA men have great trouble with timing. In one scene, the director shrieks *"Cut!"* when a soldier prematurely fires a blank. When a second recruit misfires, his PLA commander goes absolutely ballistic—he wades in there, grabs him by the ear, and drags him howling off the set.

In the background is Nick, riding a black stallion, which has been specially imported—it towers over the Tibetan horses. Nick gets his kicks from shouting orders at the PLA-Brits like: "You silly blighter—get out of the way!" or "Steady lads, hold your fire!"— none of which the recruits understand. Nick is the best-dressed Brit—he carries a revolver, sports a set of field glasses, and wipes his brow with a white handkerchief. He also flips the handkerchief forward when signalling the start of an all-out attack: it is his favorite theatrical prop.

Our least favorite prop is swords. The sword is a very awkward attachment—it can get stuck between your legs when running, which means you trip over the damn thing. If you run, you have to hold the sword, but then you can't operate a rifle, which requires both hands. Discreetly, we're all trying to offload our swords.

Ridiculous, too, are the vintage backpacks supplied—made of some moth-eaten animal skins. They're useless for carrying anything and heat your back up, but they make good cushions for sitting on between takes.

The last scene of the day calls for charging into Nenying Gompa courtyard and firing away with blanks at unarmed monks. "I can't shoot a lama," protests Keith, the American extra. A pause here while fellow American Tom convinces Keith that he is actually only shooting shaven-headed PLA soldiers dressed up as monks. "Oh, that's okay—I can do that!" says Keith. In the background, crowds of curious Tibetan villagers—and real Tibetan monks from Nenying Gompa—watch the filming in progress. A day in the life of a motion-picture extra: we rush into the courtyard, fire away at monks, scale the steps of the monastery. Smoke billows over the courtyard (smoke appears to be the special signature of this director—we are never without smoke); dead bodies litter the place.

In early 1904, British troops partially destroyed Nenying Gompa, killing the armed monks who defended it. British reporters glossed over this, unaware of the temple's sacred significance, but Chinese chroniclers single out the desecration as evidence of British barbarism: one source claims the temple courtyard was "a lake of blood." Ironically, Nenying Gompa was rebuilt after the Brits departed, only to be destroyed again by the Chinese during the Cultural Revolution (it was then rebuilt again). It has probably never occurred to the Chinese that they might be guilty of the same thing as the British, albeit on a much grander scale. The Chinese have occupied Tibet by force for nearly fifty years. The death toll of Tibetans under Chinese occupation is estimated to exceed a million; scores of monasteries have been reduced to rubble.

Cut to: Nenying Gompa, upper floor. After the shooting scene, we set about emptying the monastery of paintings, statuary, and other treasures. We file past the camera in the background, loaded with booty. In the foreground, Jones argues with Rockman, debating the finer points of imperialism (Rockman sounding off in a thick Scottish accent):

✳

JONES: But we're destroying their priceless cultural heritage.

ROCKMAN: It is exactly because they are priceless that we must act as proper stewards. We have an imperial and scientific responsibility.

Lieutenant Jones, the pacifist, sees a kind of innocence, unchained freedom, and harmony between man and nature in Tibet. Colonel Rockman, the boorish imperial warmonger, sees a medieval world—and the British Empire bringing science and civilization (and toilets!) to the heathens, for which they should be bloody grateful. Looting is a hotly disputed facet of the British invasion—it went on largely because British soldiers wanted souvenir trinkets from the campaign.

It is during the shooting of this scene that I solve The Mystery of the Dogs. When I visited this monastery ten years earlier on a bicycle trip through Tibet, the most vivid image that stayed with me was the scores of dogs lying around the courtyard. You had to tread warily in case they decided to wake up, gang up, and shred your ankles. But I haven't seen a single dog this time, so I'm wondering if my memory is playing tricks on me and this is a different monastery. Until the looting

---

As we descend into the next valley, we encounter one of the strangest artifacts of that early twentieth-century expedition. Telephone poles made of mud, in places with wires still strung from the short crossbars, stretch off into the distance, a strange remnant of the Empire from Britain's brief period in Tibet. The resourceful British signals unit accompanying the Younghusband expedition built this line as the army advanced, connecting the expedition to Darjeeling. One pole has 1910 daubed on it in red paint, obviously a memento of a later scrawler. More modern wooden poles now in use run parallel, going on and on across the windswept, dusty valley.

—Garry Marchant, "The Road to Gyantse"

scene. As we venture deeper into the monastery, we pass an alcove where there are…scores of dogs huddled together, all curled up. They most likely bolted at the first sounds of movie gunfire. They will obviously be sitting this one out.

Back to the movie: I'm trying to find out more about it, but I must be discreet. I can't openly interview the director, but I manage to ask the odd question. According to the director, *Red River Valley* is the first full-length movie ever shot in Tibet, and the highest-budget movie (at $1.8 million) made by prestigious Shanghai Film Studios. Filming takes place at half a dozen locations in Tibet—one on a glacier at over 18,000 feet—and several more locations in western China.

One small oversight: there are very few Tibetans in the movie. The plum roles are played by Mandarin-speaking actors and actresses from Shanghai or Beijing (the movie will later be dubbed in Tibetan). The "Tibetan" hero is a Chinese actor who struts around the set shirtless, with a red headband, looking like Rambo. Everyone speaks Mandarin: the only Tibetan actor we've seen mumbles mantras. The two heroines are name-brand Chinese actresses decked out in Tibetan jewelery. One of them is the beautiful Ning Jing, a woman with a Sharon Stone gaze, and figure, who has starred in a number of top movies. The director has custom-built this role for her—"imported" her into the story. At the start of the script, in western China, beautiful young Xue Er is about to be sacrificed to the River Gods by a band of peasants. Her brother saves her, and while fleeing villagers, she is rescued by a Tibetan nomad family, and thus takes on Tibetan dress. She, in turn, helps rescue the two British characters from an avalanche.

Tibetans have higher cheekbones and bigger noses than Han Chinese, and yet all the monks are played by PLA troops, as are the Tibetan soldiers and British troops. Maybe real Tibetans with real weapons pose a real problem—they might get carried away when fighting PLA soldiers dressed as Brits. *Red River Valley* could well be called "the Red Army movie"—the PLA provides all the extras, the explosives, and special effects. Despite this, the movie is a fascinating departure from the usual dreary Chinese propaganda spiels. It's a shoot-em-up action movie, more in the style of Hollywood epics like *The Man Who Would Be King.* But make no mistake: moviemaking in China that is funded by the state is a species of propaganda, whether blatant or refined.

On the set of *Red River Valley*, the PLA provides all the military extras and—double-bonus—arranges all the blowing up that needs to be done. And I am on the inside of this Chinese movie-propaganda machine. I am undercover. I have never felt more like a spy in my life. This is great! Never, ever, invite a writer along as an extra on a movie shoot—they come up with their own script on the proceedings. If Nick or Paul found out I was a writer, I'd be out on my ear. Or up against the wall for execution by PLA extras.

Day Two on the set: several PLA men show up with wigs and mustaches that make them look like Wild Bill Hickok. They point at Jorge, who finds this all hysterically funny. Jorge is a Spanish backpacker with beard and shoulder-length hair. On arrival, he asked if he should cut his hair: the answer was negative. Instead, the director has decided to copy the hairstyle with a few of the PLA extras—though this is extremely dubious, historically. The only long-haired possibilities on the Younghusband expedition would have been members of the press. Jorge is putting in some sterling performances. He tries to hog the zone facing the camera, convinced that the movie will be shown at Cannes.

Back to the day's shooting: we spend a lot of time charging through breaches in walls, shooting at anything that moves. Ever tried sprinting up a hill at 13,000 feet? You're out of breath in a flash. And it doesn't help to yell at the top of your lungs *"Chaaarge!"* or *"At them!"* or *"Aaaiieeyyy!"* After each take, all you can do is collapse and catch your breath.

The interpreter primes us for the next scene: "Wait for the third explosion, then run through the hole in the wall and start shooting." On the other side are wild-looking PLA-Tibetan troops armed with swords, blunderbusses, and rattan shields. We wait, we count, we charge. *"Bastarrrrdos!"* yells Jorge. Just as I race through the breach, a fourth explosion goes off. Then a fifth. Then a sixth. Dust is flying everywhere. This isn't acting anymore, it's sheer terror. All of a sudden, a wall of flame shoots up, engulfing Jorge. Scene over, we rush to see what happened. Jorge's fine, if a tad shell-shocked. The flame was faked: by staging surprises, the crafty director has elicited looks of real horror from his novice actors. But you couldn't have gotten Jorge to repeat that scene, not for all the tea in the PRC.

Later that day, a Chinese heroine is hurled sideways by a miscued bomb-blast and showered with dirt. The wardrobe seamstress rushes in to dust her off and give her bruised back a massage. The seamstress! She probably sews you up if you get skewered by a bayonet, too.

In the afternoon, more killing of unarmed monks (well, actually, they're armed with wooden planks this time). Mercifully, we do not have to participate: for hand-to-hand combat, the PLA-Brit clones do the job, and rather efficiently, I might add.

It's been a long day, we're exhausted. Back at the hotel in Gyantse, a look of horror from the woman at the reception desk—I've forgotten to remove my bloody make-up. A kind of battle is still on, anyway: after an unsuccessful attempt the previous night, we rally our forces to crash the hotel's evening buffet, which is a big step up from the movie-crew rice-slop that masquerades as food. We gleefully make off with our trophies: plates piled high with vegetables and meat. The British troops are hungry.

Day Three: I feel like I've been in the British Army for a year now—too many bombs and bayonets. We've come to the stark conclusion that there are no stuntmen on the set. After almost getting our bollocks blown off the day before, we wise up and ask for a script preview. This morning starts with page 75: a British officer is shot from behind a large Buddha statue (awfully bad karma). *A battle of Tibetan swords and spears against British bayonets. Outside the castle, a wall is blown open with a cannon and bodies shoot into the air. Followed by the rattling of machine guns.* Sounds like a whole lot of stones, arrows, spears, and bullets—it will be a miracle if we survive today's shooting.

Actually, we don't. The director decides to kill us off by sundown. Keith is decapitated with a broadsword by the Chinese

Rambo actor. An extra special fate—only possible in Tibet—is in store for Tom. Confronted by a mad white yak, he fails to reload his rifle in time and is pinned to a wall by the beast's gigantic horns. His last words are: *No no Noooo! Arrgggh! Oh my Gaawwd!!* as he is gored and re-gored. The air hisses out of his stomach and his head clicks sideways—and blood runs out of his mouth. The film crew pack away the stuffed yak, and that wraps up our bizarre couple of days on the set. Director Feng Xiaoning wishes us well, and leaves us with this startling thought about *Red River Valley:* "It's an anti-war movie," he deadpans. "Shows the futility of war."

Back in Lhasa, in a Xinhua Bookstore, I come across a Chinese war-comic that shows the Tibetan struggle against the British marauders to defend the "Chinese motherland." Obviously a popular theme in Chinese-produced books—patriotism versus pith helmets. It's all there—dead monks, evil Brits, handy Chinese advisers, and a caricature of Younghusband. Just like us, but add the PLA platoons. Historically, however, there were no Chinese advisers or military officers helping the Tibetans as *Red River Valley* claims.

FAST FORWARD

Mid-1997: Red River Valley *is released across China, causing "a patriotic sensation" according to Xinhua news service in Beijing. More than this, it is the patriotic duty of government employees to see the movie—in numerous cities, including Lhasa, workers are handed free tickets (compulsory viewing). Blame it on the Brits: the movie is released in time for the British handover of Hong Kong to the Chinese, along with another epic movie—*The Opium Wars—*making for a double round of Brit-bashing.*

Although Red River Valley *flops in Hong Kong itself, the Chinese think highly enough of the movie to nominate it for the Gold Wine Cup Award at the Shanghai Film Festival. Paul Kersey and Nick Love return to China for a ten-day publicity tour as the movie premieres. Paul apparently has conducted an off-screen romance with his on-screen lover: he marries the female lead of the movie, Ning Jing. Their son is born in Los Angeles a few months after the movie premieres.*

I finally get my hands on a video copy of Red River Valley. *Here the full script is revealed: a number of other Western extras appear as British soldiers except in a different location. The dialogue is all in Mandarin, but when the Brits speak, they do so directly in English, with Mandarin subtitles. This results in classic one-liners like: "Perhaps it is a blood-red sun that never sets on the British Empire." Also revealed is why Rockman adopts a thick Scottish accent. Feng Xiaoning is a crafty director indeed. In one scene, an English-speaking Chinese military commander confronts Rockman with the fact that Scotland is part of England, yet Scotland wants to separate— and argues that, in similar fashion, Tibet is an inseparable part of China.*

Michael Buckley is the author of Heartlands *(from which this story was excerpted), and also contributed "The Lost Kingdom of Guge" in Part Two.*

Approaching Lhasa

*In the early twentieth century, an amazing
Frenchwoman, determined to reach Lhasa, crossed
mighty passes with a young Sikkimese monk.*

WE OUGHT TO HAVE LEFT THE *DOKPAS'* CAMP IN THE MIDDLE OF THE
night to cross the pass at noon. But we were tired, and the warmth
that we felt, lying next to a big fire, kept us sleeping longer than we
had planned. I shrank also from the idea of starting without eating
and drinking hot tea, for on the higher level we would find no fuel.
What would happen? What would the road be like? We could not
guess. Was the pass even practicable? People had only told us that it
might be. Yongden, of course, felt reluctant to go so far to fetch
water, inasmuch as the few places where the stream flowed freely in
daytime might be covered with ice after dark. Anyhow, he went, and
we drank our tea. But the day broke before we had left the place.

Later in the morning we reached a *latza*, which, from a distance,
we had taken as marking the top of the pass. Behind it extended a
completely barren valley enclosed between a high ridge of crum-
bling reddish stones on one side, and perpendicular cliffs of various
pretty grayish and mauve shades on the other. In the middle of this
valley we again saw the river, the water of which we had drunk at
our breakfast. It fell nearly straight down in a narrow gorge from the
upper valley to the lower one. I looked for traces of *dokpas'* summer
encampments—those low stone walls forming enclosures in which

cattle are penned, but there were none. I could understand from the barrenness of the landscape that cattle were probably never brought so high.

A nearly straight reddish line—the sharp summit of a ridge it seemed—blocked the horizon at the end of that desolate valley. The distance, without being considerable, appeared great enough to people ascending with loads on their backs, in the rarefied air of these high altitudes. Still, the hope of seeing the end of the climb gave us courage, and we endeavored to accelerate our pace. One thing, however, made me uneasy—I did not discover any *latza* on that ridge, and Tibetans never fail to erect at least one, at the top of a pass. The explanation came when we had reached the point from which we had supposed that we would descend the opposite side of the mountain.

How could I express what we felt at that moment? It was a mixture of admiration and grief. We were at the same time wonder-stricken and terrified.

Quite suddenly an awe-inspiring landscape, which had previously been shut from our sight by the walls of the valley, burst upon us.

Think of an immensity of snow, an undulating tableland limited far away at our left by a straight wall of blue-green glaciers and peaks wrapped in everlasting, immaculate whiteness. At our right extended a wide valley which ascended in a gentle slope until we reached the neighboring summits on the skyline. In front, a similar but wider stretch of gradually sloping ground vanished in the distance, without our being able to discern whether it led to the pass or to another tableland.

Words cannot give an idea of such winter scenery as we saw on these heights. It was one of those overpowering spectacles that make believers bend their knees, as before the veil that hides the Supreme Face.

But Yongden and I, after our first admiration had subsided, only looked at each other in silence. No talk was needed; we clearly understood the situation.

Which was the way, we did not know! It could just as well be to our right, as ahead of us. The snow did not allow one to see any trace of a trail. It was already late in the afternoon, and to miss the road meant to remain wandering all night on these frozen summits. We had a sufficient experience in mountaineering in Tibet to know what it would mean—the exploration would be ended at its first step, and the explorers would never live to tell their tale.

I looked at my watch; it was three in the afternoon. We had still several hours of daylight before us, and, happily, the moon would shine brightly at night. We had not yet cause to be really alarmed— the important thing was to avoid missing the road and to make haste.

I looked once more at the valley on our right, then decided: "Let us proceed straight forward." And so we went.

I grew excited and, although the snow became deeper and deeper, I walked rather quickly. We had not been able to follow the advice of the Tashi Tse villagers and carry much food with us. Our host could only sell us a small quantity of *tsampa*. His neighbors had hardly enough for themselves. They informed us that we could buy some from the servants of the *pönpo*. To avoid giving them cause to talk we had said that we would go to the *zong* early the next morn-ing, which, of course, we didn't! My bag was, therefore, rather light, whereas Yongden, carrying the tent, its iron pegs, and sundries, was much more heavily loaded.

I forged quickly ahead. Dominated by the idea of reaching the top of the pass, or of discovering if we were going in a wrong direc-tion. I tramped with the utmost energy through the snow that reached my knees.

Was the lama far behind? I turned to look at him. Never shall I forget the sight! Far, far below, amidst the white silent immensity, a small black spot, like a tiny Lilliputian insect, seemed to be crawling slowly up. The disproportion between the giant glacier range, that wild and endless slope, and the two puny travelers who had ven-tured alone in that extraordinarily phantasmagoric land of the heights, impressed me as it had never done before. An inexpressible feeling of compassion moved me to the bottom of my heart. It could not be possible that my young friend, the companion of so many of my adventurous travels, should meet his end in a few hours on that hill. I would find the pass; it was my duty. I knew that I would!

There was no time for useless emotion. Evening was already beginning to dim the shining whiteness of the landscape. We ought by then to have been far beyond and below the pass. I strode on, now through the snowfield, jumping sometimes with the help of my long staff, proceeding I could not say how, but progressing quickly. At last I discerned a white mound and emerging from it, branches on which hung flags covered with snow and fringed with ice. It was the *latza*, the top of the pass! I signaled to Yongden, who appeared still more distant and tiny. He did not see me at once, but after a while he too waved his staff. He had understood that I had arrived.

There the scenery was grand beyond all description. Behind extended the waste I had crossed. In front of me was a precipitous fall of the mountain. Stretching far below, black undulating crests vanished into the darkness. The moon rose as I looked around in a trance of admiration. Its rays touched the glaciers and the high snow-robed peaks, the whole white plain, and some silvery unknown valleys toward which I was to proceed. The impassive landscape of the day seemed to awaken under the blue light which metamorphosed it, sparks glittered to and fro, and faint sounds were wafted by the wind.... Maybe elves of the frozen waterfalls, fairies

There is a saying in Tibetan that likens the Buddhist concept of "mind" to a horse: a powerful tool rendered useless without training and discipline. Likewise, *lungta*, often translated as "wind horse," is not only the name given to the prayer flags embossed with the image of a horse delicately balancing the jewels of Buddha's teachings. *Lungta* is also a Tibetan Buddhist practice, a series of initiations and teachings that is both the "universal foundation" (*klung*) implied by vast space and the "excellent horse" (*rta mchog*), a symbol of traveling with wisdom, transmuting obstacles, illusion, and misfortune with the greatest speed.

—Sienna Craig, "Riding in the Rain Shadow," *Tricycle*

of the snow, and djin-keepers of mysterious caves were to assemble
and play and feast on the illuminated white tableland; or perhaps
some grave council was to take place between the giants whose
heads wore helmets of cold radiance. What mysteries could not have
been discovered by the inquisitive pilgrim who, hidden, dared
remain there motionless till dawn. Not that he could ever have
related the wonder of the bewitching night, for his tongue would
soon have been stiffened by the frost!

Tibetans do not shout *"Iha gyalo"* after dark. I complied with the
custom and threw only in six directions the old Sanskrit mantra,
"Subham astu sarvajagatam [May all beings be happy]."

Yongden, who, after having understood that he neared the *latza,*
had taken courage and quickened his pace, caught up with me. We
began to descend. Traces of a track were visible now and then, for
on that side of the mountain the snow was not deep and the
ground, a yellowish gravel, was often visible.

What might have been the exact level of the pass we had crossed
I would not venture to tell, as I could not make any observation.
Still, from the comparison of the plants and various other particu-
lars, one who has tramped for years through many mountain ranges,
in the same country, may make a rough guess. I had carefully looked
at the lichens, and observed a few other things; and I felt nearly certain that the pass was about 19,000 feet high, even higher perhaps
than the Dokar La I had crossed about two months before, higher
than the Nago La and others that reached from 18,299 to 18,500.

Although we knew that we should have to walk a part of the
night before we should reach a spot where fuel would be available,
we rejoiced at having found the pass open and at having crossed it
safely. In this agreeable mood we reached a valley whose bottom
was almost entirely covered by a frozen stream. There, on the ice,
no trace of a track was of course visible, and we began again to roam
to and fro in search of some sign to show us our direction. To follow
the course of the frozen river was the safest way, if we did not find
any better one. It would take us to a lower level, no doubt, but it
could also happen that the stream would disappear into a narrow
gorge or fall over a cliff. Still, I had decided to continue on the

ice—at least as long as the valley was open. But then I found the track again, near the foot of the hill, and we had only to follow it down, proceeding slowly.

The walk was rather agreeable beneath a beautiful moon. Here and there we began to see a few bushes scattered in pasture grounds. Otherwise the country was quite barren. We could not think of stopping without lighting a fire, for motion alone kept us warm. No shelter whatsoever was in sight, and the cold wind from the snow rushed through the valley, which had now become rather wide.

We tramped until two o'clock in the morning. For nineteen hours we had been walking, without having stopped or refreshed ourselves in any way. Strangely enough, I did not feel tired, but only sleepy!

Yongden had gone in the direction of the hills in search of fuel, and I found some near the river, in a flat place, which must have been a camping place in the summer, where travelers from the Po country go to the Dainshin province, either to trade or on robbery expeditions.

I called the young man back, gathered as much fuel as I could, and, certain that nobody was wandering in that wilderness, we decided to pitch our tent in a low place among a few bushes. The flint and steel which, according to Tibetan custom, Yongden carried attached to his belt in a pouch, had become wet during our passage across the snowfields, and now it did not work at all. This was a serious matter. Of course we were no longer on the top of the range and we had only a few hours to wait before the sun would rise; but even if we escaped being frozen, we were not at all certain that we should not catch pneumonia or some other serious disease.

"Jetsunma," said Yongden, "you are, I know, initiated in the *thumo reskiang* practice. Warm yourself and do not bother about me. I shall jump and move to keep my blood moving."

True, I had studied under two Tibetan *gompchens* the strange art of increasing the internal heat. For long I had been puzzled by the stories I had heard and read on the subject and as I am of a somewhat scientific turn of mind I wanted to make the experiment myself. With great difficulties, showing an extreme perseverance in my desire to be initiated into the secret, and after a number of ordeals, I succeeded in reaching my aim. I saw some hermits seated night after night, motionless on the snow, entirely naked, sunk in meditation, while the terrible winter blizzard whirled and hissed around them! I saw under the bright full moon the test given by their disciples who, on the shore of a lake or a river in the heart of winter, dried on their bodies, as on a stove, a number of sheets dipped in the icy water! And I learned the means of performing these feats. I had inured myself, during five months of the cold season, to wearing the single thin cotton garment of the students at a 13,000-foot level. But the experience once over, I felt that a further training would have been a waste of time for me, who, as a rule, could choose my dwelling in less severe climates or provide myself with heating apparatus. I had, therefore, returned to fires and warm clothes, and thus could not be taken for an adept in the *thumo reskiang*, as my companion believed! Nevertheless, I liked at times to remember the lesson I had learned and to sit on some snowy summit in my thin dress of *reskiang*. But the present was not the time to look selfishly after my own comfort. I wanted to try to kindle a fire that had nothing miraculous about it, but which could warm my adopted son as well as myself.

"Go!" said I to Yongden, "collect as much dry cow dung and dry twigs as you can; the exertion will prevent you from getting cold. I will see after the fire business."

He went convinced that the fuel was useless; but I had got an idea. After all, the flint and steel were wet and cold. What if I warmed them on me, as I had dried dripping sheets when a student of *thumo reskiang*? *Thumo reskiang* is but a way devised by the Tibetan hermits of enabling themselves to live without endangering their health on the high hills. It has nothing to do with religion, and so it can be used for ordinary purposes without lack of reverence.

I put the flint and steel and a pinch of the moss under my clothes, sat down, and began the ritualistic practice. I mentioned that I felt sleepy on the road; the exertion while collecting fuel and pitching the tent, the effort to kindle the fire, had shaken my torpor, but now, being seated, I began to doze. Yet my mind continued to be concentrated on the object of the *thumo* rite. Soon I saw flames arising around me; they grew higher and higher; they enveloped me, curling their tongues above my head. I felt deliciously comfortable.

A loud report awakened me. The ice on the river was rending. The flames suddenly died down as if entering the ground. I opened my eyes. The wind was blowing hard and my body burned. I made haste. The flint and steel and moss would work this time; I was convinced of it. I was still half dreaming, although I had got up and walked toward the tent. I felt fire bursting out of my head, out of my fingers.

I placed on the ground a little dry grass, a small piece of very dry cow dung, and I knocked the stone. A spark sprang out of it. I knocked again; another sprang out…another…another…a miniature fireworks…. The fire was lighted; it was a little baby flame which wanted to grow, to eat, to live. I fed it and it leaped higher and higher. When Yongden arrived with a quantity of cow dung in the lap of his dress and some branches between his arms, he was joyfully astonished.

"How have you done it?" he asked.

"Well, it is the fire of *thumo*," I answered, smiling.

The lama looked at me.

"True," he said." Your face is quite red and your eyes are so bright…"

"Yes," I replied, "that is all right. Let me alone now, and make a good buttered tea quickly. I need a very hot drink."

I feared a little for the morrow, but I awakened in perfect health when the sun touched the thin cloth of our tent.

In 1923 Alexandra David-Neel was the first Western woman to pass through the gates of Lhasa. Twelve years earlier, she had met the Dalai Lama in India and had become enchanted with the Tibetan religion. Then she met Yongden, a young monk whom she would later adopt and with whom she shared all her travels. Together they went to Burma, Bhutan, Japan, and Korea, before returning to a monastery on the Sino-Tibetan frontier. It was there that for three years she perfected the ancient practice of thumo reskiang, *the ability to raise body temperature through meditation. David-Neel's purpose in traveling and studying was to prepare herself for a pilgrimage through treacherous mountain passes to Lhasa, the place she called her spiritual home but a place at the time closed to women. The Frenchwoman wrote scholarly books on Tibetan mysticism and in 1937 went to live in China for eight years. She died in Provence in 1969 at the age of 100.*

PICO IYER

Mondays Are Best

One of the greatest sights in the holy city of Lhasa
is one you are not truly welcome to attend.

ONE MORNING IN LHASA, I AWOKE TO FIND SNOW BLANKETING THE
mountains, and a fine rain misting the town. As if in a dream, I
made the long ascent up to the Potala Palace, whose thirteen white
and brown and golden stories preside over the town with silent
majesty. Inside, the secret rooms were heavy with the chanting of
holy texts. The smell of butter lamps was everywhere, and flashes of
a sky, now brilliant blue, outside. Banners fluttered in the wind,
prayer bells sounded. Sunlight and silence and high air.

In some rooms, ruddy-cheeked girls and women in many-colored
aprons bowed before monks who poured blessings of water in their
hands; in others, ancient men placed coins and bank notes on the
altar. And into the empty spaces, the slanted sunlight came softly,
filtered through red or golden curtains. Uplifted by the chants, the
smiles, the holy hush, I felt myself to be a clean and empty room,
thrown open to the breeze.

And then came the golden afternoon. Then lightning over distant purple mountains. Then nightfall, and silence, and the stars.

Yet the greatest of all the sights in the holy city, according to the
wisdom of the Banak Shol, was the sacred rite known as the
Celestial Burial. Each morning, at dawn, on a hillside five miles out

of town, the bodies of the newly dead were placed on a huge, flat rock. There a sturdy local man, dressed in a white apron and armed with a large cleaver, would set about hacking them into small pieces. Assistants would grind the bones. When at last the corpses had been reduced to strips of bloody flesh, they were left on the Promethean stone for the vultures.

For Tibetan Buddhists, the ritual was a sacrament, a way of sending corpses back into the cycle of Nature, of removing all traces of the departed. For the visitors who had begun to congregate in larger and still larger numbers to watch the man they called "the Butcher," the rite was the last word in picturesque exoticism.

I was no different, and so one morning, I got up at four o'clock and walked for more than an hour through the night, crossing a field full of bones and wading through an icy stream that left my thighs stinging with the cold. By the time I arrived on the sacrificial rock, three Westerners were already seated, cross-legged, around a fire, murmuring Buddhist chants and fingering their rosaries. Twenty others stood around them on the darkened hillside, faces lit up by the flames. As the sky began to change color, three Tibetans picked up a body, wrapped it from head to toe in bandages, and gave it to the flames. Then, as the body burned, they handed some of us sticks of incense to hold, while the chanting continued. Afterward, with customary good humor, they brought us glasses of butter tea and chunks of bread the color of red meat.

Then they marched back to the rock, where the corpses of two more affluent citizens had been placed. One of the Tibetans tied an apron around his waist, picked up his ax and set about his work. As he did so, a gaggle of onlookers—most of them Chinese tourists from Hong Kong—started to inch closer to the sacred ground, chattering as they went. The man muttered something to himself, but continued about his task. Still, however, the visitors edged closer, giggling, and whispering at the sight. The Tibetan stopped what he was doing, the gossip continued. And then, all of a sudden, with a bloodcurdling shriek, the man whirled around and shouted again and, waving a piece of reddened flesh, he came after the visitors like a demon, slicing the air with his knife and screaming curses at their blasphemy. The tourists turned on their heels, still the Tibetan gave chase, reviling them for their irreverence. Terrified, the Chinese retreated to a safe position. The man stood before them, glowering.

After a long silence, the Tibetan turned around slowly and trudged back to his task. Chastened, we gathered on a hillside above the rock, a safe distance away. Before long, however, we were edging forward again, jostling to get a better glimpse of the dissection, urgently asking one another for binoculars and zoom lenses to get a closeup of the blood.

"Sometimes I think that we are the vultures," said a Yugoslav girl who had come to Tibet in search of an image glimpsed in a dream a decade before.

"Oh no," said a Danish girl. "It's always wild on Mondays. The butcher takes Sundays off, so Monday's always the best day to come here." She turned around with a smile. "On Mondays, it's great: there are always plenty of corpses."

Pico Iyer is one of the most popular travel writers of our time. He's journeyed the world covering distant places for publications like Time, Harper's, The New York Times, *and* The New Yorker. *His books include* Tropical Classical, Cuba and the Night, Falling Off the Map, The Lady and the Monk, *and* Video Night in Kathmandu, *from which this story was excerpted.*

Journeys with a
Buddhist Pilgrim

The very landscape of Tibet changes you,
day by day, breath by breath.

WE HAD CROSSED THE FEARED 18,000-FOOT PASS IN PERFECT EASE
and under a cloudless sky. The sun was so hot during the ascent that
I had discarded my warm things, but hardly had we entered the
shadows on the other side of the pass when we were plunged into
icy cold that made me regret not having kept my warm clothing
at hand. Tibet is a country where one is ever up against the unexpected and where all accepted rules of nature seem to be changed.
The contrast between sunshine and shade is such that if for any
length of time one part of one's body would be exposed to the sun,
while the other remained in the shade, one could develop simultaneously blisters, due to severe sunburn, and chilblains due to the icy
air in the shade. The air is too rarefied to absorb the sun's heat and
thus to create a medium shadow temperature, nor is it able to protect one from the fierceness of the sun and its ultra-violet rays.

The difference in temperature between sun and shade can be as
much as 100 degrees Fahrenheit, according to some observers, and
I can well believe it, for when riding I often found my feet getting
numb with cold, while the backs of my hands, which were exposed
to the sun while holding the reins, got blistered as if I had poured
boiling water over them, and the skin of my face came off in flakes,

before I got sufficiently acclimatized. In spite of applying various ointments, my lips cracked open, so that eating and drinking became difficult and painful, but fortunately after three or four weeks my skin grew sufficiently sun-resistant to make me immune against these troubles for the rest of my journey. Even Tibetans, except those who live permanently in the open air, like herdsmen, farmers, or muleteers, often wear face-masks when traveling to protect themselves from the fierce sun and the still fiercer winds, which at certain seasons sweep over the highlands, carrying with them clouds of fine stinging sand that penetrate even the heaviest clothing. To meet a caravan or a group of masked and armed men somewhere in the wilderness, far away from the haunts of men, was a rather frightening experience, as one never could be sure whether the masks were worn merely for protection against the inclemencies of the climate or for hiding the faces of robbers who, especially in times of unrest, infested the more remote regions of Tibet.

However, I was not unduly worried about these things at that time (though I knew that fighting was going on in neighboring Chinese Turkestan), because after leaving the last check post on the Ladakh side at Tankse, I branched off from the caravan route into the no-man's-land which stretched from the region of the great lakes, Pangong and Nyak-Tso, towards the Aksai-Chin plateau. In those days there were no frontiers between Ladakh and Tibet in this region. It was one of the few spots in the world where man and nature had been left to themselves without interference of man-made "authorities" and governments. Here the inner law of man and the physical law of nature were the only authorities, and I felt thrilled at the thought of being for once entirely on my own, alone in the immensity of nature, facing the earth and the universe as they were before the creation of man, accompanied only by my two faithful Ladakhis and their horses. The horses more or less determined the choice of our camping-places, as we could stop only where there was sufficient grazing ground for them as well as water.

In spite of the feeling of smallness in the vastness and grandeur of the mountain landscape, in spite of the knowledge of human limitations and dependence on the whims of wind and weather, water and grazing-grounds, food and fuel and other material circumstances, I had never felt a sense of greater freedom and independence. I realized more than ever how narrow and circumscribed our so-called civilized life is, how much we pay for the security of a sheltered life by way of freedom and real independence of thought and action.

When every detail of our life is planned and regulated, and every fraction of time determined beforehand, then the last trace of our boundless and timeless being, in which the freedom of our soul exists, will be suffocated. This freedom does not consist in being able "to do what we want," it is neither arbitrariness nor waywardness, nor the thirst for adventures, but the capacity to accept the unexpected, the unthought-of situations of life, good as well as bad, with an open mind; it is the capacity to adapt oneself to the infinite variety of conditions without losing confidence in the deeper connections between the inner and the outer world. It is the spontaneous certainty of being neither bound without clinging to any of their aspects, without trying to take possession of them by way of arbitrary fragmentation.

> M ay all beings have happiness,
> and the causes of happiness;
> May all be free from sorrow
> and the causes of sorrow;
> May all never be separated from
> the sacred happiness which is
> sorrowless;
> And may all live in equanimity,
> without too much attachment
> and too much aversion,
> And live believing in the
> equality of all that lives.
> —The Buddha

The machine-made time of modern man has not made him the master but the slave of time; the more he tries to "save" time, the less he possesses it. It is like trying to catch a river in a bucket. It is the flow, the continuity of its movement, that makes the river; and it is the same with time. Only he who accepts it in its fullness, in its eternal and life-giving rhythm, in which its continuity consists, can master it and make it his own. By accepting time in this way, by not resisting its flow, it loses its power over us and we are carried by it like on the crest of a wave, without being submerged and without losing sight of our essential timelessness.

Nowhere have I experienced this deeper than under the open skies of Tibet, in the vastness of its solitudes, the clarity of its atmosphere, the luminosity of its colors and the plastic, almost abstract, purity of its mountain forms. Organic life is reduced to a minimum and does not play any role in the formation and appearance of the landscape or interfere with its plastic purity, but the landscape itself appears like the organic expression of primeval forces. Bare mountains expose in far-swinging lines the fundamental laws of gravitation, modified only by the continuous action of wind and weather, revealing their geological structure and the nature of their material, which shines forth in pure and vivid colors.

The roles of heaven and earth are reversed. While normally the sky appears lighter than the landscape, the sky here is dark and deep, while the landscape stands out against it in radiating colors, as if it were the source of light. Red and yellow rocks rise like flames against the dark blue velvet curtain of the sky.

But at night the curtain is drawn back and allows a view into the depth of the universe. The stars are seen as bright and near as if they were part of the landscape. One can see them come right down to the horizon and suddenly vanish with a flicker, as if a man with a lantern had disappeared round the next corner. The universe here is no more a mere concept or a pale abstraction but a matter of direct experience; and nobody thinks of time other than in terms of sun, moon, and stars. The celestial bodies govern the rhythm of life, and thus even time loses its negative aspect and becomes the almost tangible experience of the ever-present, ever-recurring, self-renewing *movement* that is the essence of all existence. As the sky is hardly ever hidden by clouds, man never loses contact with the celestial bodies. The nights are never completely dark. Even when there is no moon a strange diffused light pervades the landscape, a truly "astral" light, that reveals the bare outlines of forms without shadows or substance and without color, yet clearly discernible.

Even the waters of rivers and brooks rise and fall in accordance with this celestial rhythm, because during the twelve hours of day-time the snow on the mountains melts due to the intensity of the sun's rays (in spite of the low temperature of the air), while at night it freezes again, so that the supply of water is stopped. But as it takes the water twelve hours on the average to come down from the mountains, the high tide of the rivers begins in the evening and ebbs off in the morning. Often the smaller water-courses dry out completely during the daytime and appear only at night, so that one who unknowingly pitches his tent in the dry bed of such rivulet may suddenly be washed away at night by the rushing waters. (It happened to me, but fortu-nately I managed to save myself and my equipment.)

The great rhythm of nature pervades everything, and man is woven into it with mind and body. Even his imagina-tion does not belong so much to the realm of the individual as to the soul of the landscape, in which the rhythm of the universe is condensed into a melody of irresistible charm. Imagination here becomes an adequate expression of reality on the plane of human con-sciousness, and this consciousness seems to communicate itself from individual to individual till it forms a spiritual atmosphere that envelops the whole of Tibet.

Thus a strange transformation takes place under the influence of this country, in which the valleys are as high as the highest peaks of

---

The driver pulls up to a house and Mr. Toe says there is a place on the roof that we can sleep. A kindly looking woman with really long braided hair shows us the way up the stairs with a candle in hand. We step out onto the pitch-black roof and are suddenly swallowed by the magnitude of the sky. We are not on top of a building looking at the stars, no...we are in the stars, thrust up into the galaxy. They are all around us. Our host gives us a few extra seconds of wonderment before continuing on to the small room in the far corner.

—William Eigen, "At Large in the Common World"

Europe and where mountains soar into space beyond the reach of humans. It is as if a weight were lifted from one's mind, or as if certain hindrances were removed. Thoughts flow easily and spontaneously without losing their direction and coherence, a high degree of concentration and clarity is attained almost without effort and a feeling of elevated joy keeps one's mind in a creative mood. Consciousness seems to be raised to a higher level, where the obstacles and disturbances of our ordinary life do not exist, except as a faint memory of things which have lost all their importance and attraction. At the same time one becomes more sensitive and open to new forms of reality; the intuitive qualities of our mind are awakened and stimulated—in short, there are all the conditions for attaining the higher stages of meditation or *dhyana*.

The transformation of consciousness which I observed here (and each time I returned to Tibet) was in a certain way similar to that which I experienced during my first stay at Yi-Gah Chö-Ling, though on a bigger scale, because here the connections with the world I had been familiar with were completely severed, and the physical effects of high altitude, climate, and living conditions greatly contributed to this psychological change. The spiritual importance of this change is not lessened by explaining it on the basis of physical reactions. Yoga itself is based on the interaction of physical, spiritual, and psychic phenomena, in so far as the effects of breath control (*pranayama*) and bodily postures (*asana*) are combined with mental concentration, creative imagination, spiritual awareness, and emotional equanimity.

The rarefied air of high altitudes has similar effects as certain exercises of *pr,n,y,ma*, because it compels us to regulate our breathing in a particular way, especially when climbing or walking long distances. One has to inhale twice or thrice the quantity of air which one would need at sea-level, and consequently the heart has to perform a much heavier task. On the other hand the weight of one's body is substantially reduced, so that one's muscles seem to lift one almost without effort. But precisely this is a source of danger, because one is not immediately conscious that lungs and heart are

at a great disadvantage, and only the fact that one is very soon out
of breath, and that the heart begins to race in a frightening manner,
reminds one that it is necessary to control one's movements carefully. Tibetans themselves walk very slowly, but at a steady pace,
bringing their breath in perfect harmony with their movement.
Walking, therefore, becomes almost a kind of conscious hatha yoga
or breathing exercise, especially when accompanied by rhythmic
recitations of sacred formulas (*mantras*), as is the habit with many
Tibetans. This has a very tranquilizing and energizing effect, as I
found from my own experience.

At the same time I realized the tremendous influence of color
upon the human mind. Quite apart from the aesthetic pleasure and
beauty it conveyed—which I tried to capture in paintings and
sketches—there was something deeper and subtler that contributed
to the transformation of consciousness more perhaps than any other
single factor. It is for this reason that Tibetan, and in fact all tantric,
meditation gives such great importance to colors.

Colors are the living language of light, the hallmark of conscious
reality. The metaphysical significance of colors as exponents and
symbols of reality is emphasized in the *Bardo Thödol* (*The Tibetan
Book of the Dead*, as it is commonly known), where transcendental
reality is indicated by the experience of various forms of light, represented by brilliant, pure colors, and it is interesting that a serious
modern thinker like Aldous Huxley has come to the conclusion
that color is the very "touchstone of reality."

According to him, our conceptual abstractions, our intellectually
fabricated symbols and images, are colorless, while the given data of
reality, either in the form of sense-impressions from the outer world
or in the form of archetypal symbols of direct inner experience, are
colored. In fact, the latter "are far more intensely colored than the
external data. This may be explained, at least in part, by the fact that
our perceptions of the external world are habitually clouded by the
verbal notions in terms of which we do our thinking. We are forever attempting to convert things into signs for the most intelligi-
ble abstractions of our own invention. But in doing so we rob these
things of a great deal of their native thinghood. At the antipodes of

the mind we are more or less completely free of language, outside the system of conceptual thought. Consequently our perception of visionary objects possesses all the freshness, all the naked intensity, of experiences which have never been verbalized, never assimilated to lifeless abstraction. Their color (the hallmark of giveness) shines forth with a brilliance which seems to us preternatural, because it is in fact entirely natural in the sense of being entirely unsophisticated by language or the scientific, philosophical, and utilitarian notions by means of which we ordinarily re-create the given world in our own dreary human image."

The Tibetan landscape has "all the naked intensity" of color and form which one associates with a preternatural vision or prophetic dream, which distinguishes itself from ordinary dreams by its super-real clarity and vividness of colors. It was precisely in a dream of this kind that for the first time I saw colors of such luminosity and transparence in the form of mountainous islands that rose from a deep blue sea. I was filled with incredible happiness and thought to myself: these must be the paradisiacal islands of the southern sea, of which I have heard so much. But when later I actually saw some of these lovely palm-fringed islands of the south I found none of those colors I had seen in my dream.

But when I came to Tibet I recognized those colors, and the same happiness came over me as in that unforgettable dream. But why should I have seen those mountains rising out of the deep blue sea? This puzzled me for a long time, until one day we were traveling through a hot, narrow gorge, hemmed in by light yellow rocks which not only intensified the glare of the midday sun but captured its heat to such an extent that one could have imagined traveling somewhere in the tropics or through a gorge in the Sahara, instead of at an altitude of more than 14,000 feet. It was so warm that during a halt by the side of a placidly flowing stream I could not resist the temptation to take off my clothes and enjoy the luxury of a bath and a swim—much to the astonishment of my Ladakhi companions! I felt greatly refreshed, but the effect did not last long, as the gorge became hotter and hotter the farther we proceeded and even the water of the stream became steadily less until it disappeared in a shallow lemon-yellow lake. After that the gorge became narrower and completely dry—and with it our spirits. We just trudged wearily along, and I was wondering how long we would have to continue in this fashion when suddenly a strange phenomenon stopped me in my tracks. At the far end of the gorge the rock-walls receded, and a radiantly blue object flashed into sight. It was as luminous and as sharply set off from the background as the surface of a cut jewel from its gold setting, and it emanated an intensely blue light, as if it were illuminated from within. It was so utterly unexpected and different from anything I had seen that I simply gasped, unable to find any reasonable explanation or connection with what I saw. I felt so baffled and excited that I called out to my companions, fearing to be the victim of a hallucination: "Look there! What is that? Look!"

"Tso! Tso! Pangong-Tso!" they shouted, and threw their caps into the air triumphantly, as if they had conquered a mighty pass; and indeed there was a *lha-tse*, a pyramid of stones, left by previous travelers to mark this auspicious spot, from which the first glimpse of the great Pangong Lake could be had. We too added our stones, grateful to be released from the oppressiveness of the gorge. But I still could not believe my eyes. "Impossible," I thought. "This cannot be water. It looks like some unearthly, self-luminous substance!"

But soon we were out of the gorge and its deadening heat, and before us stretched a lake like a sheet of molten lapis lazuli, merging into intense ultramarine in the distance and into radiant cobalt blue and opalescent veronese green towards the nearer shore, fringed with gleaming white beaches, while the mountains that framed this incredible color display were of golden ochre, Indian red and burnt sienna, with purple shadows. Yes, this was the luminous landscape of my dream, rising out of the blue waters in brilliant sunshine under a deep, cloudless sky!

The mountains to the left had sharp-cut, almost stereometrical forms; those of the opposite side formed a range of softly modeled giants, crowned by eternal snows and mighty glaciers, known as the Pangong Range, running parallel to the fjord-like Pangong and Nyak-Tso Lakes, which form an almost consecutive sheet of water of more than 100 miles length. The two lakes are actually a sub-merged valley, divided merely by what probably was an ancient rock-fall.

When reaching our next camping-ground at the foot of the snow-range, a little above the lake, I felt so inspired by the colors of the lake and the mountains and the immense rhythm that pervaded this landscape that I forgot hunger and tiredness and immediately returned to the place from where I had the first overwhelming impression of the lake and the glaciers above it. So I walked back a few miles with my drawing-board, papers, and a box of pastels, munching some dry *kulchas* on the way, until I found the spot that I had marked in my mind while passing it, but where I had not dared to delay, as I did not know how far the next camping-place might be. I worked fast and with such enthusiasm that I finished two or three sketches in a short time, keeping in mind that I should be back in camp before sunset. But my excursion almost ended in disaster. Retracing my steps toward the camp, I suddenly found myself confronted by a raging stream that had not been there before! In my eagerness to get to my sketching place I had not noticed that I had crossed several shallow beds of dried-out water-courses. Now the melted waters from the glaciers came rushing down and threatened to cut off my retreat. Knowing that every minute was precious, I splashed through the icy waters, and after this crossing two or three water-courses in succession I finally reached the camp somewhat out of breath, but happy to have succeeded in capturing something of the unforgettable beauty and freshness of my first impressions of this memorable lake.

The following days we traveled along the shore of the lake at the foot of the snow mountains, whose far-flung slopes gradually flattened out and formed an almost even stretch of land above the lake, interrupted only by dry beds of mountain streams. Very few streams had a continuous flow of water, so that grazing-grounds were few and far between and paradoxically we suffered from lack of water during the greater part of the day, in spite of having miles and miles of water at our feet. But first of all the shore was not always in our reach, as the ground over which we traveled was slightly raised and suddenly broke off into the lake, except for such places where the water-courses from the glaciers had carved out shallow beds, along which one could approach the pebbled or sandy beaches—and secondly, even if one reached the shore, there came a greater surprise: the water was undrinkable because of its high content of magnesium!

This too was the reason for the incredible clarity and color of the water. The magnesium, though colorless in itself, kept the water absolutely free from organic matter or any form of life, whether plant or fish or crustaceans, and consequently the water was so transparent that on windless days, when the surface of the lake was as smooth as a mirror, it was impossible to see where the water ended and the beach began. I still remember the shock when for the first time I approached the edge of the water, and I suddenly felt its icy touch, because I had not noticed that the pebbles, which looked no different from those on the dry beach, were already under the water. The water was as invisible as the air! Only when it got deeper, the ground assumed a greenish-blue tinge and finally disappeared in the luminous blue that made this lake such a wonder.

The colors of the lake and its surroundings never ceased to fascinate me. In the evenings, when the waters of the glaciers flowed into the lake, they would form lighter streaks on the dark blue surface, while the mountains would glow in orange, red, and purple tints, under a sky of the most sublime gradations of rainbow colors.

The weather suddenly became mild, almost sirocco-like, and one day we crossed a blindingly white and intolerably hot sand desert (mixed with pebbles), stretching for miles between the slopes of the snow mountains and the lake. Though it was in the middle of July, I never expected such heat at an altitude of 14,000 feet. But, as I said before, Tibet is a country of surprises and contrasts: one day one may be in a blizzard and the next in a hot desert or in a sandstorm.

Not long after we had left the "burning desert" we came upon a lovely oasis of blossoming shrubs and grassland watered by a placidly winding stream that meandered through a wide, slightly undulating plain between the lake and the receding mountains. The blossoms of the shrubs reminded me of heather, both in form and color, but the stems of the shrubs were sturdy enough to supply us with ample firewood, a luxury which we had not enjoyed for many days, having had to content ourselves with the scanty yak-dung that we picked up on the way, or with the roots and twigs of thorny shrubs found near water-courses or in the dry beds. Dry yak-dung was rare, because we were off the beaten track, but even on the caravan route nobody would pass by a precious piece of yak- or horse-dung without picking it up for the evening campfire.

The value of yak-dung cannot be easily imagined by those who have never lived in Tibet or in the woodless regions of Central Asia. It is the main fuel of the country and burns almost smokeless with a hot, steady flame. Since I had only as much kerosene as the basin of my primus stove could hold, I could use the latter only in emergency cases or on rare occasions, like in the rock monastery. Since then I had not had a roof over my head, though shortly after crossing the Chang-La we had camped near villages. But after Tankse we had not found any human habitations except for a few huts near a cultivated patch of barley at the foot of the Pangong Range.

Thus fuel was always a major problem and as important as the water and the grazing-grounds for the horses. To find all these necessities of life combined in this uninhabited oasis was a pleasant surprise. So we settled down to a blazing campfire in a little depression near the winding stream, protected from wind and cold. It was a most idyllic spot, with a superb view of the snow mountains on the one side and the big fjord-like lake on the other.

I felt so happy and carefree that I decided to camp here for few days, to explore the surroundings, and to devote myself to painting and sketching, as well as to some quiet spells of meditation. Here in the utter stillness and solitude of nature, far from the haunts of man, under the open sky and surrounded by a dream landscape of "jewel mountains," I felt at peace with myself and the world.

Strangely, there was no feeling of loneliness in this solitude and no need for talk or outward communication. It was as if consciousness itself was stretched and widened out to such an extent that it included the outer world landscape and space and human beings— those present as well as those with whom one was connected in the past; indeed, the past seemed to rise into the present on its own accord. This latter tendency I observed especially when there was even the slightest increase in humidity, when the air became heavy or sultry, when there was a tendency to cloud formation, and even more so when the sky was overcast.

But even before any visible signs appeared I found that my dreams had a direct connection with the changes of atmosphere, so that I could almost with certainty predict sudden changes of weather. I remembered the popular saying that if you dream of dead people it will rain. I took this to be a mere superstition, as I could not see any reasonable connection between the dead and the rain. But now I observed that whenever I dreamt of a person who was very dear to me and who had been intimately connected with my childhood, but who had died some years ago, rain was to follow exactly within three days. Generally there was not a cloud in the sky and not the slightest indication of any change in temperature or humidity when such a dream occurred, but with unfailing regularity a heavy rainfall, a thunderstorm, or a blizzard would follow. Due to the comparative rarity of rain in this part of the world I observed these facts for the first time during this journey, and from then on I made good use of them. Whenever traveling in Tibet in later years I took notice of my dreams and regulated my itinerary accordingly.

> When we get back our own country, Tibet can never be the same as before. The next generation will not be fooled by superstitions and delusions; they will be more knowledgeable, and by preserving our religion and culture at the present time we can make sure that in future the Truth will be practiced by all Tibetans. Lord Buddha himself has said that whether we have great teachers or not the Truth is there—and no one can alter it, neither can anyone improve it.
>
> —Rinchen Dolma Taring,
> *Daughter of Tibet*

My own explanation for this phenomenon is that our consciousness is sensitive to atmospheric pressure and that with increasing "heaviness" (whatever it may be due to) our consciousness descends into the deeper layers of our mind, into our subconsciousness, in which the memories of our individual past are stored up. The greater the pressure, the farther we go back into the past, and this is revealed in our dreams by meeting again those persons who were closest to us in our childhood and who, in the majority of cases, passed away by the time our childhood had become a remote remembrance. In the high altitudes of Tibet one not only becomes more sensitive to these things but one is also more conscious of one's dreams. Tibetans themselves rely a great deal on their dream consciousness and they are seldom proved wrong in their judgment.

Besides dreams they have many other methods of contacting the deeper layers of their mind: meditation, trance, certain forms of oracles, and various natural and "supernatural" (psychic) portents. All these methods have been tried out for millenniums, and their results have been found sufficiently satisfactory to guide people in their daily life. Tibetans would be greatly surprised if one would doubt these facts, which are matters of practical experience and have nothing to do with beliefs or theories. To them the attempts of modern psychologists, who try to "prove" extrasensory perception by scientific methods, would appear crude and laughable: one might just as well try to prove the existence of light which is visible to all but the blind. The circumstances under which these modern experiments are carried out are in themselves the greatest hindrance to their success. In their attempt at "objectivity" they exclude the emotional and the spiritually directive elements of the human mind, without which no state of real absorption or concentration can be created. Their very attitude bars the doors of psychic perception.

In Tibet the capacity of concentration and self-observation, as well as our psychic sensitivity, is increased a hundredfold in the vastness, solitude, and silence of nature, which acts like a concave mirror that not only enlarges and reflects our innermost feelings and emotions but concentrates them in *one* focal point: our own consciousness. Thus there is nothing to divert the mind from itself, not even the grandeur of nature, because nature never interferes, but on the contrary stimulates and heightens the activity of the mind. Mind and nature enter into co-operation rather than into competition. The immensity of nature and its timeless rhythm reflect the similar properties of our deepest mind.

It is mostly the effects of other minds that interfere with our consciousness, the quiet stream of inner awareness, of thought and imagination, reflection and contemplation. In the uninhibited or sparsely inhabited regions of the world the mind expands unobstructed and undeflected. Its sensitivity is not blunted by the continuous interference of other mind activities or by the meaningless noise and chatter of modern life, and therefore it can enter into communication with those minds that are spiritually attuned to it, either by affection or by sharing certain experiences of the inner life.

This explains the frequency of telepathic phenomena among the inhabitants of Tibet—not only among the highly trained, but even among the simplest people. I am reminded here of an incident which Sven Hedin reports in one of his travel books. On his way into the interior of Tibet he had to cross a vast stretch of uninhabited territory with his caravan. Before setting out he met some nomad herdsmen who knew the territory, and with great difficulty he persuaded one of two brothers to act as a guide for his caravan. He was a shy young man and declared that he was not accustomed to travel in a "crowd" and that he would guide the caravan only under the condition that he would be allowed to go ahead alone, as otherwise he would not be able to concentrate on the landmarks and the direction of the route. Sven Hedin respected his wish, and the caravan followed him without any difficulties or untoward incidents, until one day the young man fell ill and died under inexplicable circumstances. There was no other choice for the caravan but to return the same way they had come. But while they were still several stages away from the place from where they had set out with their young guide his brother came to meet them, and before anybody could tell what had happened he said that he knew that his brother was dead and described the spot and the exact circumstances under which he had died. He had seen it with the mind's eye!

In this case a close relationship favored the telepathic contact between two individuals. But I remember a case that concerned me personally and in which a third person acted as a transmitter or medium without my cooperation or knowledge. After a year's traveling in Western Tibet without postal communications I was worried about my aged foster-mother, fearing that she might be seriously ill or that she might have died in the meantime. Li Gotami thereupon—without telling me about it—consulted a Tibetan friend of ours, who was well trained in tantric methods of meditation, to perform a *mo* or oracle, according to an ancient book of omens in his possession. The answer was that my foster-mother was alive and that there was no cause for worry, but that her legs were swollen and caused her much trouble. I was somewhat skeptical about this answer, because it did not seem to have any connection with any of her former ailments. But a few weeks later I received a letter which proved that the *mo* had been correct.

Lama Anagarika Govinda was born in Germany in 1898. He was the founder of the Buddhist order Arya Maitreya Mandala. In his early years he went to India and a got a chair at Tagore University. His keen interest in Pali-Buddhism and monastic life led him to Ceylon (now Sri Lanka) and Burma. He visited Tibet several times and lived for two consecutive years in Central and Western Tibet with his wife Li Gotami. During these years he received teachings and inspiration from the Theravada, Mahayana, and Vajrayana traditions. He finally settled in India, where he held posts in various Indian universities and held exhibitions of his paintings, several of which he had made together with his wife when still in Tibet. He died in 1986.

FOSCO MARAINI,
TRANSLATED BY ERIC MOSBACHER
AND GUIDO WALDMAN

The Visions of the Dead

*Many decades ago, an Italian explorer
became friends with an old lama.*

KIRIMTSE IS A TINY VILLAGE LYING ON THE SAME PLATEAU AS
Pemogang ("Knee Hill"). But, while Pemogang has a Bon temple,
at Kirimtse there is a fine Buddhist temple, belonging to the *Nima-pa* sect ("the Ancient Ones"). One might have expected a certain
rivalry between the two villages, but I could find no trace of such a
thing, at any rate on the surface. The people of Kirimtse say that
the people of Pemogang are Bon-po just as casually as the people
of an Italian village might say of those of the next village that they
were water-diviners or were good at grafting, or some such thing.
In other words, they talk of them as a group of neighbors who
happen to have special characteristics but are fundamentally the
same as themselves.

Only one person made a slight grimace when I told him I was
going to Pemogang; he was Lama Ngawang, of Kirimtse. But Lama
Ngawang is a rather special individual, and a law unto himself. He
is an old grumbler, with an incredible number of years on his head
and incredibly few hairs in what might be described as his beard.
His opinions are always ready, clear and precise, and he always states
them in very outright fashion.

I shall not easily forget our first encounter. I came down from the mountains that enclose Kirimtse on the west. The weather that afternoon from bad had become appalling. I remember the clouds growing grayer and grayer, the mountain that rose interminable until it vanished into the clouds, and finally the rain which came down and laid a gray mist over the whole landscape. Eventually I felt I had lost my way. Fortunately I came upon a *chorten*. I stopped, heard voices, and found I was just outside the village. I went straight to the monastery-temple. It was a big, solid, white-washed building, with high walls enclosing a courtyard, which one entered by passing through a wooden doorway; the door squealed open. The courtyard was deserted. I was wet, cold, hungry and tired. I called out. An old woman appeared on a wooden balcony.

"Come in!" she said. "There's a fire alight!"

I went up the creaking stairs and found myself in a smoky room, half kitchen and half sacristy. An old lama was sitting in the corner near the window. His spectacles were perched on the top of his nose and he was reading prayers aloud. Every now and then he broke off to sip a little tea, but his attention was not distracted, and he did not so much as look at me.

"Lama Ngawang is reading the scriptures," the old woman whispered, with great and obvious reverence. "Don't disturb him! Sit here near the fire and dry yourself. But where do you come from? What have you been doing in the mountains at this time of day? Don't you know there are *rii-gompo* (mountain demons) who suck one's life out and leave one empty? Drink a little tea! The lama won't be long."

Her lama-husband (it is normal for lamas of the *Nima-pa* sect to marry) continued reading impassively. My clothes steamed and started getting dry, and I felt better every minute. It was getting dark and the kitchen-sacristy filled with shadows. It was an irregular-shaped room, blackened with soot. Against one wall were pots and pans, flour sacks, a pile of logs, bowls, saddles, Tibetan slippers, cups, and packets of tea; on the other were books, a few pictures on cloth, statuettes, a little drum, lamps, peacock quill-pens, offerings of butter, a bronze thunderbolt—in short everything needed by a pious lama in the exercise of his duties.

Soon afterwards, while I was holding a cup of tea between my fingers to warm them, I felt a hand on my shoulder and heard a low, almost cavernous, voice.

"*Oé! Oé!* And where do you come from?"

It was Lama Ngawang, who had got up and walked barefooted over to the fireplace. Later I found out that he started practically every sentence with "*Oé! Oé!*" in the tone of voice of one saying: "My boy, just you listen to me!" The first time I heard it it struck me as rude, and it made me take a momentary dislike to him. But I soon discovered I was mistaken; the lama was an enchanting old gentleman. He was one of those persons of great faith and great directness of speech, who know exactly what they want, and want it because if reflects their unshakeable idea of what is good and right.

The next time I went to see him the weather was fine. The temple courtyard was flooded with warm, bright sunshine. All round I saw flowers growing in rusty old petrol tins. Who knows how they had got there? The courtyard naturally served also as a threshing-floor, and herbs and beans had been laid out to dry in the sun.

I went upstairs to Lama Ngawang. He greeted me with a broad smile, the kind that comes from the heart. He had not believed me when I had said I would come back. But here I was. He was delighted.

"Will you have some tea? *Oé! Oé!* Drolmá! Bring some tea for the *chiling-pa* (foreigner). But you were really crazy to come up here so late the other day, and in the rain too! Who knows what you might have met on the mountains at night! Did you say *Om mani?*"

The lama looked hard at me.

"Yes, yes, of course I did."

It would have been impossible to have answered no. Who would have had the heart to disappoint an old man with such a firm and impregnable faith? To Lama Ngawang everything was obvious, clear, beyond dispute. Soon afterwards he asked me about my country.

"Are there monasteries where you come from?" he asked "*Oé! Oé!* You don't come from a barbarous country, do you?"

"No, I do not come from a barbarous country, Lama Ngawang," I answered. "In my country there are many monasteries."

"And many lamas?"

"Many lamas."

"And you read the scriptures."

"We read the scriptures."

"Bravo, bravo, then you're like us, you're a civilized people too! *Oé!* Drolmá! Did you hear? They're like us! They're civilized people too!"

I suppose I should have explained the difference between the two countries in religion and in so many other things too, but I lacked the courage. The lama's happiness at what I said filled his face with light and warmth. I thought of how Christians of former ages must have looked when merchants from Central Asia told them of scattered communities of faithful Nestorians in the empire of the Mongols. Lama Ngawang is a straightforward, simple man, who has lived in an isolated village in the mountains for seventy years and more, and to have undeceived him would have been useless and cruel.

> If we don't show love and compassion to those people who do not know about this, then what is the difference between who has the knowledge of compassion and love and those who do not have this knowledge?
>
> —A Tibetan Nun

Then we went down to see the temple. On the steps we were stopped by an old village woman, who was accompanied by a little girl. The old woman spoke rapidly to the lama. When she had finished he turned to me.

"*Oé!* The little girl is ill, you must cure her," he said.

I tried to explain that it was impossible, because I was not a doctor.

"What? You're not a doctor? But you *chiling-pa* are all doctors! When needs be, we are all doctors too…And you have so many extraordinary medicines! *Oé! Oé!* Have a look at the girl, and prescribe her a good medicine."

I had to give in, and try to find out in my own way what was wrong with the girl. Alas! No very great medical knowledge was required. She was thin, pale, flushed, and said she had pains in her chest. I made her spit on a piece of paper, and she spat blood, bright, purple blood. Poor little girl! What could anyone do for her? Air better than that of Kirimtse would be hard to find, I said she must rest and eat well.

"I know what is the matter with her," Lama Ngawang announced. "There is some devil who wishes her ill. I shall exorcize him. Drolmá! *Oé!* Drolmá! Bring me the *damaru* (the little drum)!"

The exorcism lasted for some time. When the old woman and the girl had gone Lama Ngawang stood at the temple door with his feet apart, looking like an ancient tree that had survived appalling tempests. With a threatening gesture he said something about the "accursed demons who never leave us in peace." The effect of his words was that it must be clear to all, in heaven and on earth, that he, Lama Ngawang, and they, the demons, were irreconcilable enemies.

In the little temple of Kirimtse, as in all other Tibetan temples, there are many frescoes. Two are of special interest. One shows the Great Paradise of Padma Sambhava; the other shows the Visions of the Dead (*shi-trö*). Let us for a moment contemplate the painting of the Visions of the Dead, and consider what are the effects on a civilization of adopting a belief in a single mortal life, and compare it with the effects of a belief in successive incarnations.

Belief in only one life—the Western belief—leads to a strained, tense, hectic outlook. Time presses, and our single, never-to-be-repeated youth runs through our fingers like pearls dropped irremediably into an abyss. Loves and hates swell to the size of irremovable mountains. Virtue adorns the soul like a flashing sword and sin weighs it down like a lump of granite. Everything is unique, final, immense: an interjection in the biography of the ego, set for chorus and orchestra. Finally death presents itself, not as a stage in a journey, but as the end: an event of outstanding, terrifying importance.

The career of the individual is thus simple, but full of care and responsibility. Creation is followed by life in time. There is freedom of action, and one's deeds can be salutary or harmful, or actually fatal to the eternal principle within. Finally death cuts short the process of becoming, and henceforward the past is congealed and irremediable. Sin inexorably demands its punishment. Earthly life is followed by the judgment, and beyond that there is eternity. We have made our single appearance on the stage of life, to which there is no return. "You only live once," as popular wisdom puts it. You only die once too.

But a belief in reincarnation, in a succession of lives, leads to an outlook both more grandiose and less dramatic, to a broader but cooler picture of the universe; a calming, analgesic picture, full of time and patience. In such a universe there are certain cruel questions which lose their sting, including the cruelest of all questions— why should innocent children suffer? In such a universe the suffering of children enters into the order of things; it is the consequence, the punishment, of evil done in previous lives. The whole picture is more serene and more logical. Life is not so much an episode as a state; true, it is theoretically a provisional state, but a provisional state that lasts for an untold number of centuries. The cosmic life of man could, at a theoretical minimum, consist of one terrestrial life only, but in ordinary cases it consists of innumerable successive lives. Death is therefore not a tragic, supreme culmination, a single, fearful event, a crucial moment from which there is no return, but is, like life, an experience that is repeated at certain intervals, a normal transition to which one must become accustomed, a process as natural as sunset at the end of the day. Hence Buddhists have always been great thanatologists, great students of death. Preoccupied as they are with the problem of escaping from the flux of becoming in order to attain the ineffable serenity of being, they have been able to study death with the simplicity and detachment of an industrialist studying a phase of production. To them death is not a mystery, but a problem.

The results of their long and profound labors in this field of intellect and intuition were collected as early as the fourteenth century in a book that is of cardinal importance in the spiritual life of Tibet. This is the *Bardo Tö-döl* ("The Book that Leads to the Salvation of the Intermediary Life of the Sole Fact of Hearing It

Read"). Like a *Baedeker* of the world beyond, it gives astonishingly detailed descriptions of the visions that appear in the mind of the dead, from the first until the forty-ninth day after it has left the body; that is to say, until the moment that it is on the point of entering a new bodily envelope. These visions constitute a synthesis of the lamaist conceptions of reality and of the universe. From the purity of the undifferentiated Absolute, of which gleams are obtained in the first stages of this temporary life after death, there is, as time passes, a gradual transition to ideal thought, then to individuated thought, and finally to matter. Just as the West, considering life from the biological aspect, sees the development of the species repeated in the development of the individual, so does Lamaism, looking at life from the cosmic aspect, see in this intermediary state of life after death (*bardo*) a repetition of the evolution of reality from the Absolute (Buddha) to illusion (*samsara*).

Let us try to be more specific. After death, as we have mentioned, the conscious principle enters upon an intermediary state of being, which lasts for forty-nine days. From this it can either emerge into liberation (*nirvana*) or return to *samsara*, the vortex of life. The *Bardo Tödöl* tries to set it on the path of esoteric knowledge of the fundamental Buddhist truths, enabling it to experience "an immediate revulsion from the phenomenal plane of exis-

Those interested in the Tibetan technology of dying might want to read two versions of the classic work: *The Tibetan Book of the Dead: The Great Liberation through Hearing in the Bardo* (translated with commentary by Francesca Fremantle & Chögyam Trungpa), and also *The Tibetan Book of Living and Dying*, a version in which Tibetan teacher Sogyal Rinpoche interprets Tibetan Buddhist views of the process of dying for a Western audience. No matter what your religious beliefs, there's a good chance the ancient text will shake your metaphysical timbers and lead you to a better life.

—JO'R and LH

tence and an impulse towards the sphere of the absolute." (Tucci.) The fundamental truth of Buddhism is that *samsara*, "the vortex of life," is nothing but empty appearance and illusion, that only the Absolute really exists, and that it is only by identifying oneself with it (becoming Buddha) that one can be liberated from *samsara*.

The crucial phase in the cosmic history of the individual occurs in the first days after death. The conscious principle becomes aware of a pure, colorless luminosity. He who recognizes the Absolute in this and is able to fuse himself with it is saved, and has ended his cycle of lives. The alternative is descending a step towards the multiple, towards becoming, illusion and suffering. In the days that follow, the whole cosmic evolutionary process is represented in vast, symbolical visions which the conscious principle gradually experiences as it detaches itself from the body. The possibilities open to it present themselves in successive dichotomies, alternatives of liberation and enslavement. Understanding the first means re-entering the cycle of rebirths at a higher level; being bound to the second means being dragged lower because of the operation of *karma*.

On the walls of the temple of Kirimtse are large-scale paintings of the terrifying gods, terrifying to the conscious principle of him who is still bound to the illusions of life and believes he really sees them, but mere shadows to him who has reached a sufficient stage of maturity to understand their essential vacuity. These paintings show a stupendous population of fantastic forms, not creatures of the artist's imagination, but painted according to meticulous instructions set forth in the scriptures. Above all there are the Heruka, the terrifying manifestations of the *Dhyani* Buddhas, dancing in union with their own *shaktis*. Around them is unleashed a maelstrom of witches, with the heads of crows, tigers, scorpions, dogs, and other fantastic, raging animals.

The Lama Ngawang raised his lamp (the temple was very dark) and threw light on the picture. In the uncertain, tremulous light the monstrous figures seemed to come to life.

"*Oé! Oé!* Examine them well!" the lama said to me, turning and looking at me over his spectacles. "Examine them well, because one day you too will see them. When that happens, you mustn't be afraid.

Oé! They are nothing but imagination, shadows, fantasies. If you remain perfectly calm and don't get frightened, it means salvation."

"But at bottom I'm afraid of death, Lama Ngawang."

"*Oé!* You are foolish, *kuk-pa du*." He looked at me severely again over his spectacles. "Everything dies, it's nothing to be afraid of! Who knows how many times you have died already! You must always be ready. If you die here, I'll read the *Bardo tö-döl* in your ear, and you'll see that it'll help you. *Oé!* Look well at the figures, they are void, nothing, illusion!"

The Lama Ngawang went to the end of the temple, took a piece of incense, lit the end of it from the lamp he held in his hand, put it in front of a statue to Padma Sambhava, bowed, and we went out.

Not far from the temple of Kirimtse there is a little *gön-kang* where the masks for the sacred dances are kept. When I mentioned the place (which I had heard about from a peasant to whom I talked on the way) Lama Ngawang turned out to be entirely opposed to the idea that I should visit it.

"What? You want to go to the *gön-kang*? No, no, it would be an act of madness! *Oé! Oé!* The gods there dislike being disturbed. Good heavens! The *gön-kang*? What are you thinking of? Besides, you would be running a grave risk; you don't know what might happen to you. You might become ill, you might even die. *Oé!* The gods of the *gön-kang* are very touchy; even a trifle can upset them!"

I knew that it was useless to tempt him with money. Lama Ngawang is incorruptibility personified. The first time I saw him I noticed a fine painting on cloth in the apartment of honor behind the kitchen, a portrait of a lama to whom some monks were bringing offerings. I asked the Lama Ngawang if by any chance he would be willing to sell it, but I found myself up against a brick wall.

"*Oé!* Where are we? What? Sell a saint?"

Today, after a great deal of insistence, I succeeded in getting him to agree to let me enter the *gön-kang* to see the masks and pictures. I hoped to be able to photograph them. Should I succeed? Lama Ngawang gave the keys to a peasant who accompanied me.

"No, no, I shan't come with you," he said firmly at the monastery gate. "I shall have nothing whatever to do with it! *Oé!* The gods there are very easily angered. Don't they have tutelary deities in your country? Well, then..."

The peasant opened the big locks of the *gön-kang* door. Behind it was another door, on which there was an extremely effective painting of the face of one of the terrifying deities. We went inside. The place was small, dark, ancient, low-ceilinged, and full of old armor and the carcasses of animals. On the walls were frescoes of local demons, painted with a fine vigor, and in a corner was a gilded pavilion with some statues. The masks, about thirty of them, hung from the ceiling, carefully wrapped in cotton handkerchiefs. I asked the peasant, as if it were the most natural thing in the world, to take some of them down, because I wanted to photograph them. The young man grumbled, but obeyed.

As the dirty, grayish cotton handkerchiefs were removed those fantastic personages with the soul of the wind and the look of wood came alive in the darkness of the temple. There were the terrifying gods, there was Namka-bazin (the murdered and deified monk), there were masks representing the *shi-trö* (the visions of the dead), huge bird faces, faces of mythological dogs, faces of animals of the forest. The peasant forgot the ritual prohibitions, put on one of the masks, and did a few steps of the ritual dance. It was not he who danced, but the face.

With some difficulty I persuaded the peasant to take the masks outside and to put them on, so that I might photograph them. Suddenly I heard somebody shouting from the corner of the square outside the *gön-kang*. It was Lama Ngawang who had come to see what was going on and had "caught" us.

"Put back the masks immediately!" he shouted. "Don't you know they must never see the light? *Oé!* Are you mad? Now evils will descend upon the whole village! If anyone is ill, the fault will be yours! If the harvest fails, the fault will be yours! If animals die, the fault will be yours!..."

I tried to calm him.

"Lama Ngawang, I assure you nothing will happen," I said. "If anything happens, it will be my fault. I'll take all the evils upon myself!"

Lama Ngawang approached me, looked at me very seriously, and said nothing. He had understood. He had understood from the light-heartedness with which I spoke that I did not believe. I felt at once that I had hurt him. I was very sorry for it, but I had no chance to remedy it. The peasants who had gathered interrupted our silent colloquy.

"Did you hear, Lama Ngawang? Did you hear? The foreigner takes all the evil upon himself! Don't worry!"

They laughed. They looked at me as if I had the plague, and they were glad. Lama Ngawang accepted the situation. He forgot the anger that he had perhaps felt for a moment. He let me go to the devil as the expiatory sacrifice. I even managed to photograph him against the inner door of the *gön-kang*, next to the face of the terrifying god.

"*Oé!* Don't forget to send me a copy!" he said when I said good-bye. But he spoke coldly. I had disappointed him.

The other evening, when I got back to Yatung, I found waiting for me a letter from Pemà Chöki, from Gangtok. She described at length the celebrations that had taken place, at court and in the temple, in connection with the dedication of a new *chorten*. I answered describing my visit to the Lama Ngawang, and I told her how I had finally managed to photograph the masks.

At ten o'clock this morning the post came again. There was another letter from Pemà Chöki, sent by express post from the palace at Gangtok. She told me she was greatly worried at my having dared to take photographs of the *gön-kang*, and at my having carried the masks out into the daylight. "At times the gods can be a bad medicine," she wrote. "I implore you to go back to Kirimtse and have a *kar-sö*, a purification ceremony, conducted by the lama. If you don't believe in these things, please do it all the same for my sake. I'm worried." I was touched by the princess's letter. Apart from her evident concern for me, it was like being asked by a child: "How is it that Father Christmas doesn't get dirty when he comes down the chimney?" or: "Is it true that little Jesus had the loveliest toys in the whole world?"

This morning I woke up shivering, and with a bad pain in my back. It must have been a touch of lumbago. Piero produced a most plausible explanation, reminding me that yesterday it was very cold and damp. But I immediately remembered my light-hearted promise, a few days ago, to take upon myself all the evils that might ensue from the removal of the masks from the *gön-kang*. Then I laughed. Then I felt frightened. It was very stupid. But we are all surrounded by the unknown. Could my promise really have had some occult significance? My reason said "Nonsense." But what is reason worth, after all?

So I climbed up to Kirimtse under the midday sun (which chased the pain away and made me feel better immediately). I found Lama Ngawang sitting in his usual place beside the window, reading. Drolmá, his wife, was boiling *chu-kar* plants in a big saucepan, to dye some woolen cloth red. I drank a cup of tea and waited.

"So you've come back?" was the lama's eventual, cool greeting. "How are you? *Oé!* Have you heard that a mule has died at Pemogang? Luckily they are Bon-po at Pemogang. Otherwise they'd say it was because of the masks. And you? Why aren't you ill?"

"As a matter of fact, Lama Ngawang, I've got pains in my back."

"Just as I said! Just as I said! That's all right! If you're ill after your act of stupidity, we can rest assured that we shan't have to suffer the consequences!"

The lama's manner towards me had changed greatly for the worse. During my first visits I had felt in him the gladness of a man speaking to a distant brother, to whom he is linked by the same faith, and I had not had the courage to undeceive him, because I had felt how much this meant to him, and I did not want to spoil his pleasure. But now we had become strangers. The only link between us was a link in a game of magic. I had performed certain acts, said certain words, set in motion a concatenation of inevitable cause and effect. He was an onlooker. His only surviving interest in me was as a participant in the unhappy incident with the masks; I was a pawn in his game of chess with the invisible.

"Lama Ngawang," I said to him after some time, as I ate one of the fried biscuits which Drolmá offered me, "I've come up here because of that business the other day, when we took the masks outside. Now I want you to say a *kar-sö*, to pacify the gods of the *gönkang*, in case they're offended. I've brought you five silver rupees."

Lama Ngawang spun round towards me, bent his head forward so that his glasses dropped to the tip of his nose, looked at me, smiled and opened his arms.

"We'll do it straight away," he said. "*Oé!* Drolmá! Bring me my cloak, we're going downstairs!"

Then he looked at me again, as if to say: So I made a mistake after all.

"*Oé!*" he said. "You've done well to come soon. Bravo! Bravo!"

Our former friendship was re-established as firmly as ever. I knew it was based on a misunderstanding, but I was glad....

The time came for us to leave Yatung, and today we left. The porters arrived and selected their loads. Many acquaintances came to say goodbye. The *ku-tsab* sent us a big loaf and some bottles of arak from Chumbi, and Mingyur was there with a white silk sash.

A man came hurrying from Kirimtse. "Lama Ngawang sends you this gift," he said to me, handing me a parcel. I opened it. It was the portrait of the lama that I had so often admired in the hall of the Kirimtse monastery, and had tried in vain to buy. Tears were in my eyes when I packed it among my things. I shall keep it always in memory of old Lama Ngawang, a straight, upright, generous and just man. What does the faith in which one was born matter? Civilizations present us with pictures of the universe just as they teach us how to eat certain foods. To dress in a certain way, to have certain ideals in connection with women when we make love to them. But in the last resort all that matters supremely is heart and character.

Fosco Maraini was born in Florence in 1912. His father was Italian, his mother English, and from childhood travel was in his blood. An anthropologist by training, after his first visit to Tibet he was trapped in Japan by the outbreak of war, and taught in the University of Kyoto from 1941 until he was interned in 1943. In addition to his writing, he has been a broadcaster, documentary filmmaker, and professor at the University of Florence. During 1959–64 he was Fellow at St. Antony's College, Oxford. A keen mountaineer, he is the author of Karakoram *and* Where Four Worlds Meet.

PART FOUR

In the Shadows

SANGITA LAMA WITH
RAJENDRA S. KHADKA

✦ ✦ ✦

Zone X in Zhangmu

*A group of Nepali friends cross
the border to see what's up.*

THE BUZZ IN THE BUSINESS CIRCLE OF KATHMANDU IS THAT THE
Tibetan border town of Zhangmu, or Khasa to Nepalis, has now
become a "mini-Bangkok." Like the famed "Alice's Restaurant" of
New England, in Zhangmu too, you can get anything you want—
from faux leopard-skin pillbox hat to fabulously faux fashion models. Or so we were told, but we wanted to verify it for ourselves.

One cool October morning, eight of us (five men, three
women) left Kathmandu early in the morning in our rented Toyota
SUV for Zhangmu, a road trip of about seventy-five miles on the
winding, mountainous Arniko Highway. Arniko was a thirteenth-
century Newari artisan of Kathmandu Valley who, Nepalis assert,
introduced the distinctive pagoda style of building to China via
Tibet. Arniko went on to become a master builder and architect in
the court of Kubla Khan.

Around twelve-thirty in the afternoon, we arrived at the Nepali
border town of Tatopani where we went through the formalities
of obtaining a formal document from the Nepali customs and
immigration department. Although a passport with Chinese visa is
normally required to enter Tibet, an agreement between Nepal and
China allows those living within eighteen miles of the border to

227

travel back and forth into each other's territory after being granted an official chit from an appropriate government official. The ostensible purpose of such easy access is to allow traders to continue the traditional barter economy.

At Tatopani, as we crossed the Friendship Bridge into Liping in Tibet, we could already see along the ridgeline of Zhangmu, the tall, cement buildings glittering in the sun. But when we looked back toward Tatopani, we only saw a few huts and shops and naked hills. Thus, right away, we felt that we Nepalis continue to remain impoverished and undeveloped. We hired another taxi in Liping for the remaining nine-mile journey to Zhangmu. The narrow, winding, rather dilapidated road is often jammed with trucks laden with goods headed for Kathmandu.

We prayed silently as we stood in line at the Chinese immigration post in Zhangmu. Our friends had warned us that if any one of us was not allowed to enter, we should not argue. We were to simply and quietly disappear—and come back and stand in line an hour later. Some had tried three times before they were waved in. In fact, one of our friends, Sampurna, was stopped by a rather angry Chinese official. Sampurna stepped aside, but then the same official told him to go in. We did not try to fathom this infamous mercurial nature of the Chinese, but scurried in, lest he change his mind again. We had also been told to return to Nepal by five in the evening. Our Nepali time was around two in the

Arrested by the P.L.A. on the Tibet-Nepal border, my companions and I were led off to separate rooms for interrogation. The soldiers in charge of me confiscated everything remotely related to the Dalai Lama. It took a good deal of pantomime and a photograph of a little girl for me to convince them that the colorful drawings in my possession were not in fact Buddhist mandalas, but the work of my four-year-old daughter.

—James O'Reilly, "Notes from the Roof"

afternoon, but the Tibet time, which is on the Beijing clock, was just before noon. Officially, we had five hours to explore Zhangmu, but our Nepali merchant friends had also told us that usually the Chinese didn't mind if we spent the night and returned the next day, which was our intention.

We found two rooms in Friendship Lodge, again recommended by a friend, because it was run by a Tibetan woman who spoke Nepali. The five men stayed in the larger room, and we three women in the smaller room. Each of us had to pay eighty Nepali rupees (just under one U.S. dollar). There was a common bathroom for all to use. Happily, we discovered that Nepali currency is accepted everywhere in Zhangmu because the Tibetan and Chinese traders use it to buy noodles, butter, flour, and other goods from Nepal.

Shops, banks, and impressive office buildings line the half-mile paved road that snakes about downtown Zhangmu. While one sees corn or paddy on the terraced hills of Nepal, in Zhangmu, the "crops" on the hills are tall concrete structures. The architecture of these buildings makes you think that you're in a miniature Chinese city instead of Tibet. And seeing many Chinese taxi drivers, I wondered who hired them to drive along that short strip of paved road.

For the past twelve years Zhangmu has been the central exit point of Chinese goods entering Nepal, and the town was full of Nepalis buying and selling, eating in restaurants, unloading trucks and strolling about while chatting and laughing with their Chinese counterparts. Many Chinese spoke a smattering of Nepali, and Nepalis spoke broken Chinese. But what impressed—and puzzled—us was the predominance of young, beautiful Chinese girls fashionably dressed in short skirts, tight t-shirts, modern hairstyles, a clean and attractive presence overall. To us, especially our men, these slim and sexy beauties appeared to be fashion models on a catwalk, but we wondered how and why such visions of loveliness had landed in this remote outpost of civilization, if you can call it that. Why had such "angels" rushed in where even fools feared to tread?

After resting in our rooms, we stepped out in the evening again, and discovered that the citizens of Zhangmu were bustling about with increased energy and purpose. Once again, the "angels" of Zhangmu attracted us like moths to bright lights. Inside beauty parlors, they were applying make-up and getting their hair done. There were many more women on the streets; some had stylish hats on and many were clutching cigarettes between their fingers. Again we wondered where they were going at this hour of the evening. From the windows of the buildings lining the street, we occasionally saw lovely ladies gazing down at us pedestrians, but when we looked at them carefully, we were convinced that they were not the wives, daughters, or daughters-in-law of those homes. Also, through some of the windows from which the women were gazing out, we could see posters of naked women on the walls, but we still didn't get it.

At the street-level shops, we saw groups of women chatting and knitting sweaters at the entrance, and we wondered why they would knit sweaters standing up at the entrance instead of inside in their rooms. Once we reached the end of the paved street at the end of the town, we

---

It was getting dark, most of the stalls had been shuttered, and the crowds were thinning. But following bargain-hunting locals to a hawker with a pile of t-shirts, I still hoped that I'd find the perfect "Made in Tibet" t-shirt. Sure enough, there was one with a Potala Palace design and another with dancing yaks. Although I remembered the warning that they fall apart after one washing, I bought two and showed them to Amar, who confirmed that they were locally made and not from Nepal. "How can you tell?" I asked. "That's easy," smiled Amar. "The Tibetan ones carry labels that say 'Made in Panama.'" And so it was. When I got back to Kathmandu and presented Tashi with the Potala Palace t-shirt, he was very happy—and was still beaming several washings later after it hadn't fallen apart. "A very good sign for Tibet," he remarked.

—Daniel B. Haber, "Not Quite 'Made in Tibet'"

turned around, and it had become dark—and it was then we noticed that where the women stood at the entrance knitting, the rooms inside were illuminated with a soft, red light. Above the entrance also was a garland of red lights. We stood in front of the knitting ladies and peered beyond them into the softly lit interior. One large room had been partitioned into several small "cabins" just large enough to accommodate a bed. And as men walked by, the knitting women would invite them in with a wave or a smile, or other such appropriate gestures, but they never came out on the streets to grab or drag the men in. Friends had told me that not just Lhasa or Shigatse but even Zhangmu, just beyond our scruffy, impoverished border, had become a hotbed of discos, bars, night-clubs, restaurants, shops, and brothels. While sprawling Kathmandu has perhaps a half dozen discos, tiny Zhangmu has at least eight or nine. I later learned that these Chinese ladies of the night came from mainland China itself and that most of their clients were our own Nepali merchants and traders.

We returned to our lodge for dinner and came out to explore the irresistible and colorful Zone X of Zhangmu. It was now after nine P.M. We didn't have to go far. Attached to our lodge, at the street-level shop, we saw the glow of a red bulb. The women who were inside beckoned our men friends. But we moved on when women called them again from another red-lit room, and here two of our friends ventured inside. We waited for them in the street. They came out a few minutes later, smiling, "The women asked us to drink beer and hang out with them."

We kept on strolling, and entered a place that advertised itself as a nightclub. On the second floor of this rather large but ancient-looking building, there was a disco. Those welcoming the guests, tending bar and taking orders, were all women. While it appeared as if the place was run totally by women, we had our suspicion that it was actually men who were the real operators, but they were lurking behind the scenes.

Two women asked us to sit down on a sofa. A man with a micro-phone was lip-synching a slow, romantic, Chinese song that was on TV. A few couples were slow-dancing, their hands on each other shoulders and hips. A Chinese woman asked us in Nepali what we would like to order. We asked for beer. The TV music switched from Chinese to a fast-paced English song. We all got up and danced. Perhaps because of our presence, the music now was English, so we continued to dance.

Then we sat down to rest and drink our beer. The Chinese man with the microphone began to croon yet another dreamy Chinese song. A young, lovely, slim Chinese girl in a short skirt asked one of our friends, sixty-year-old Ganesh Man, to dance with her. The music was slow, and the Chinese "angel" put her hands on Ganesh Man's hips and began to step and sway with him, leading him and teaching him to keep time with the rhythm. Ganesh Man, despite his years, was a quick learner and was soon dancing effortlessly with his angel. Very soon, only he and his girl were on the dance floor while the rest of us watched them indulgently. Ganesh Man is a simple farmer in Kathmandu, and we agreed among ourselves that perhaps he had never had so much fun in his life. When we left after about an hour, Ganesh Man tipped his angel 100 Nepali rupees.

As we were leaving this disco, we discovered that the floor below was in fact a brothel. A passage, perhaps three feet wide, led away from the stairs. There were Chinese women milling about. Our men friends wondered what was going on, so they went in. I followed them. On the right side of the passageway, a large room had been once again curtained off into several smaller rooms with a bed each. Father down the passage, there were more women knitting sweaters and gossiping at the entrance of each cabin area. In what appeared to be a parlor, fashionably dressed women were playing mah-jongg. I entered and tried to talk to them. While some appeared taken aback, others became quite angry. I got the impression that they did not like women approaching them. But when the men appeared, they were all smiles.

We left this disco-brothel and visited yet another nightclub when we saw that there were many other Nepali men inside. It was dark inside, and crowded. The dance floor was in fact jammed with Nepali men. Others were seated at tables, drinking and chatting with Chinese girls. A Chinese woman in a traditional Chinese dress appeared on the stage and said something on the microphone. The dance floor emptied and everyone went back to their tables. Soon, young Chinese couples wearing a variety of traditional Chinese dress appeared. A fashion show began! Keeping in mind the predominance of Nepali patrons, a few models "catwalked" in traditional Nepali dress of *daura-surwaal* (string-tied shirt and jodhpur-style trousers), Nepali cap; the women wore sari and blouse. Meanwhile, I noticed that at the open entrance of this street-level nightclub, a crowd of local Tibetan women, tired from a hard day's work of loading and unloading trucks, were watching people like us eating, drinking, and enjoying ourselves. I wondered what they thought of us.

It doesn't take long to realize that the entire trade and commerce in Zhangmu is in the hands of the Chinese. And when you observe the local Tibetan inhabitants, it appears that they are struggling in life, that they remain backward

> Standing above the Tashilhunpo, one of Tibet's most vibrant and active monasteries, we saw two pilgrim women coming our way, stretching out to place a goat hoof on the ground to mark their progress as they prostrated around the sacred temple. Below us the view stretched to a stark valley ringed with mountains. The sun was pleasantly warm, the air quiet, the scene timeless and serene. But then we noticed how small the traditional Tibetan quarter was compared to the ugly expanse of the Chinese city and military garrison below us, clear evidence of the squeeze being put on Tibet and Tibetans by their Chinese rulers.
>
> —Larry Habegger, "Glimpses of Tibet"

when compared to their Chinese occupiers. The Tibetans still wear their ragged *bakkhus* (traditional Tibetan robe) and they both braid their hair, thus, from a distance, it is difficult to distinguish men from women; it also appears as if they have not taken a bath in a long time. However, they appear healthy and sturdy.

I also noticed that certain Tibetan women use a single conch shell as a bracelet. The hand is inserted through the openings in the shell. I was told that they were from the Amdo region of Tibet. The Amdo work in groups in cities as far away as Shanghai, Beijing, and Guangzhou. And in Zhangmu, they work loading and unloading hundreds of trucks that arrive every day from various parts of China. It occurred to me that the women were stronger than the men when it came to lifting and carrying the loads. I was told that not too long ago, the Amdo folk were all over Zhangmu, running businesses and doing every sort of work, but their numbers slowly thinned out. It used to be that just over a decade or so ago, Nepali traders flocked to Bangkok and Hong Kong to purchase goods for the Kathmandu market, but no longer. These cities have been replaced by Zhangmu.

As we staggered back to our lodge after three A.M. (our own Nepali time, not the artificial Beijing/Zhangmu time), I realized that if a Kathmandu consumer wanted to buy a fake "Head & Shoulders" shampoo or fake orgasms, he no longer had to travel to exotic and expensive places, but that a capitalist paradise of consumption and possession was to be found quickly and cheaply nearby in "Communist" Zhangmu. Indeed, the epitaph of Communist China could easily be a rephrasing of the opening line of Marx's Communist Manifesto—that a specter is haunting China, but not that of communism but "free" market capitalism.

Sangita Lama is a Nepali journalist based in Kathmandu. She is currently at work on a book about the Nepali Women Millennium Everest Expedition. Recipient of various journalism fellowships, she has traveled for work and pleasure in France, Germany, Pakistan, Sweden, and Thailand. Rajendra S. Khadka is a dutiful son, faithful husband, eagle-eyed editor, slothful scrivener, and turgid traveler. A former Berkeley resident, he is now a "Facilitator" par excellence in Kathmandu where his mission statement is: "Ask, and Thou Shalt Receive." He is also the editor of Travelers' Tales Nepal.

JEFF GREENWALD

A Day in the Life of Ghang Sik Dondrup

The author makes a surprise acquaintance — and
is drawn into an international intrigue.

I WAS STANDING BEHIND THE COUNTER OF THE POTALA PHARMACY
in Lhasa, squeezing shots of Buddha brand nasal spray up my snout,
when the nomads walked in.

There were two of them, both in their late twenties. They wore
olive-green fatigue jackets, and their long, unwashed faces descended beneath ragged, fur-lined hats. The older of the two carried a
cardboard box, riddled with air holes and tied with a leather belt.

The nomads walked up to the counter and set the box down,
undoing the strap and waving the pharmacist over for a look. He
peered into the box and shook his head rapidly, backing away.

When the pharmacist retreated I took his place. I couldn't quite
make out the creature inside. I thought it might be a fox, or a bad-
ger, but its head was buried in a corner. The younger brother reached
in, placed his hand under its middle, and pulled it out of the box.

As he set it on the floor my brain did a back flip. I was looking
at one of the world's most beautiful and elusive animals: a baby
snow leopard.

The cub was a healthy creature, muscular and plump, creeping
across the cement on lunar-lander paws. Its coat was thick silk, a
dappled storm-gray that would ultimately turn blizzard-white. The

leopard couldn't have been more than a month old; when I held it to my chest it nuzzled into my arm, nursing on the fabric of my shirt.

I looked at it, it looked at me, and a chill ran up my spine; for I recognized, beyond question or doubt, the beginning of an obligation I could not refuse.

A small crowd gathered, forming a semi-circle around the cub. One of the onlookers—a student, guessing from the plastic pencil-box he carried—spoke a bit of English. Through him I was able to learn a little bit about the animal, and the circumstances of its abduction to Lhasa.

The nomads had come from a village in the mountains above Yangbajain, six hours by truck from Lhasa. A snow leopard had been decimating their livestock, they claimed, and they had been forced to destroy it. After shooting the cat—an adult female—the nomads discovered the extra mouth that had compelled her to stalk human settlements in the first place. They bundled up the cub, and brought it to the city in hopes of selling it. The reason for their visit to the pharmacy was suddenly clear. Snow leopard bones are a prized Chinese tonic, and the animal could fetch a high price from an interested buyer.

"How much do they want for it?" I asked.

My young interpreter furnished the reply: "Two thousand yuan." This came to exactly $232.56.

This was a major quandary. To begin with, I simply didn't have 2,000 yuan on me. But even if I did—even if I were to buy this snow leopard outright—what would I do with it? Baby snow leopards are adorable, but they grow up fast. And while a carnivorous Himalayan beast would undoubtedly be a useful sidekick in Oakland, the logistics of bringing home a Class One endangered species were beyond me.

I watched in restless frustration as the nomads placed the docile cub back into its box, fixed the leather strap, and left.

I followed them. They seemed bewildered by my presence, but as they spoke no English there was literally nothing they could say. We crossed Xingfu Donglu, the busy main avenue, and made our way toward the Peoples' Cultural Park.

The woman collecting admission fees exchanged a few words with the nomads and spoke into an intercom. We were soon joined by a dour-faced man in a blue blazer. Whether he was Chinese or Tibetan I could not tell. He pushed his black bicycle toward a compound of official-looking buildings, and we followed close behind. My presence did not please the man. He turned around, regarded me with disdain and waved me back; I could come no further. I ignored him. A minute or two later, as we were about to enter the compound itself, he demanded that I go back. I looked him dead in the eye, and spoke calmly.

"You listen to me, pal. I *come* with this animal. If you want to call the police, be my guest. Nothing less than physical force is going to keep me away from that cub."

My words were lost on this non-English speaker, but not my intent; he nodded gamely. He offered no objection as I tailed him into a narrow, whitewashed alleyway, where I was immediately attacked by guard dogs.

There was a rusted cleaver lying on a nearby oil drum. I seized it, brandishing the blade at the charging hounds. They zipped nimbly by, renewing their challenge at a safe distance. I kept hold of the weapon as we were led through the alley and into the man's home.

We entered an open courtyard, a lush terrarium filled with exotic cacti and blooming bushes. A parrot perched on a swing, shitting profusely onto the ground. In a nearby room I could see a widescreen television with a large clock sitting on top. Gaudy chandeliers and knick-knacks were much in evidence, staples of the Han Chinese taste in consumer goods. The man's wife held the dogs at bay, and offered us chairs. I set the cleaver down.

The cat was freed from its box. As it began lapping at puddles on the leaf-strewn cement, a loud debate ensued. Though I speak scant Tibetan, I comprehended the exchange. The animal, the man insisted, was not a snow leopard; its color was wrong. The nomads disagreed, however, as did his wife. She left the courtyard and stepped into an adjoining room, returning a moment later with a rolled carpet beneath her arm. It was the pelt of a full-grown snow leopard, creamy white with prominent black spots, framed in a brocade of red Chinese silk. The nomads nodded, gesturing with their hands. Now the animal was small, they said; when it matured its coat would lighten, taking on the pearlescent hue of the carpet. The wife concurred: "*Chik paray*," she insisted over and over again, nodding first at the animal, then at the rug. "It's the same."

The snow leopard, it seemed, faced two possible fates: it could be ground up into an aphrodisiac, or crafted into a floor covering.

But the blazered official, for reasons I didn't understand, chose to pass. Perhaps he was biding his time; perhaps he was inhibited by my presence. The three of us quit the compound, taking the cardboard box with us.

We returned to the main avenue, where the nomads entered a small restaurant. I assumed they were stopping for lunch but, to my surprise, they ordered only warm milk for the cub. A few scraps of raw meat were also placed in the box, but the leopard seemed blasé. He was too young, I guessed, for a solid-food diet.

A small group of tourists came in. Their guide was Tibetan, a slight young man in a t-shirt and jeans. I explained the situation, and he agreed to interpret while I asked a few more questions.

The Tibetan nomads, I learned, did not want to see the cub harmed—though they apparently had nothing against selling the animal off to a Chinese merchant who had no such qualms.

By now a crowd had gathered, composed mostly of Tibetans. Through the interpreter, I advanced a plan. It was wrong to kill the snow leopard, I agreed. Though I had little cash, I knew another tourist who did. If he would buy the leopard, we could donate the animal to the local zoo.

The nomads smiled, slapped me on the back and gave me the old thumbs-up as the young interpreter walked me to the nearest phone.

"This is very, very good," the guide said, his arm around my shoulder. "Sometimes, I think, Western people more Buddhist than Tibetans. The Dalai Lama teaches like this: Compassion. You have compassion for this leopard. Oh! That is very, very good."

I felt a slight twinge of panic, wondering what the hell I was getting myself into.

I phoned the Holiday Inn, angling for the wealthiest Westerner I knew. But Bill Thompson, a National Geographic photographer I'd met a few days ago, wasn't in his room.

All was not lost. I had one back-up plan. If the nomads would agree to wait at the restaurant, I'd return to the Yak Hotel and speak with someone there. My interpreter put this suggestion forward, and the nomads nodded silently. The older one stepped forward, and spoke to the guide.

"He wants to come with you."

We caught a minibus to the intersection near Sonam's restaurant and walked to the Yak from there. The nomad was jittery, cowed by the presence of so many affluent foreigners. I took his hand and led him up the stairs, the cardboard box clutched beneath his arm.

During my week in Lhasa I'd had numerous intense conversations with Brock Owen, a soft-spoken Tibetan scholar from Georgia. Brock lived at the Yak almost full-time, poring over obscure

---

I dreamed that to the east
beyond this high majestic mountain
A colossal pillar was standing.
At the top crouched a great lion.
His mane of turquoise flowing everywhere,
He spread his claws upon the snow,
His eyes gazed upward,
And he roamed proudly on the vast whiteness.
I tell this to the Lama Buddha of the Three Ages.

I took it as a happy omen
And rejoiced at this great fortune.
I wish you to tell me its meaning.
— Milarepa, Eleventh-century Tibetan saint

---

manuscripts and cohabiting with Francesca, his beautiful Chilean girlfriend. I found his room, pushed aside the hanging brocade and knocked with my fingertip. Brock opened the door and squinted at me through the slit in the curtain.

"I'm with a Tibetan nomad who speaks no English," I said. "May we come in?"

Brock and Francesca were stunned by the sight of the snow leopard—stunned, and fatally charmed. I told them all I knew, and explained my plan for donating the cub to the zoo.

"But you cannot give it to the zoo!" Francesca cried, hugging the cub to her breast. "It is a torture place. It is no better than death."

"She's right," Brock said. "The zoo is a joke. We'll have to find some other way to deal with it. But first things first: how much does this guy want?"

"Two thousand yuan."

Brock snorted. "*Jesus.* This is bullshit. Another classic scam. Know what he's doing? He's *ransoming* the animal. I mean, if he's so concerned about the cub, why doesn't he just give it to the zoo himself?"

I shrugged. "Maybe he's trying to recover the value of his lost livestock. I don't know. And what do you mean, a 'scam?' Is this a common occurrence? Have you seen other snow leopard cubs for sale?"

"No...." Brock softened, and took the animal from Francesca. He scratched it between the ears. "You think he'll take a thousand?"

"Might as well offer; all he can say is no."

Brock set the cub back into its box, unlocked a green metal trunk and removed two bundles of 10-yuan notes. He counted out the money, and placed the stacks on the carpet in front of the nomad.

"One thousand yuan," he said in Tibetan. "Take it or leave it."

The nomad smiled, but shook his head. Brock calmly leaned over, collected the money, placed it back in his trunk and snapped the lock shut. "Goodbye," he said, and turned back to the manuscript he'd been leafing through when we walked in.

There was a beat, and the nomad coughed sharply. "He's changed his mind," Francesca guessed. Indeed he had. Brock silently re-opened the trunk, removed the bills and handed them over. The nomad folded them into a thick wad with a huge, innocent grin on his face. He dropped into a crouch, and removed the leather strap from around the cardboard box. When he had recovered his belt he stood up to go.

"Wait a minute." Brock opened a drawer in his dresser and extracted, from a small stack, a picture of the Dalai Lama. This he presented to the nomad, who pressed it to his forehead with a prayer. Brock nodded, piercing our visitor with a stare.

"Just so he knows," he said quietly, "where our motivation comes from."

When the nomad had left, Francesca examined the cub. "He's a boy," she declared.

"A boy, hunh?" Brock sat down beside her. "Well, he obviously needs a name."

My own suggestion—Bob—was quickly vetoed, as was Francesca's more poetic Spanish inspiration, Nubita.

"He's got to have a local name," Brock insisted. He pulled a Tibetan lexicon from a shelf and leafed through it knowledgeably. "Okay. Here we go. This is perfect: *Ghang Sik Dondrup*."

"Meaning what?" Francesca was dubious.

"The Snow Lion Whose Every Wish is Fulfilled."

Brock ran down to the corner to buy some human infant formula and a bottle; Francesca went off to find a larger box. When Brock returned he had a plan of sorts, though how it would be carried out was anybody's guess.

"The zoo is out," he drawled. "Somehow, we've got to get this animal out of China. He has to be smuggled, overland, into Nepal. From there it's a matter of getting him into Darjeerling, India. There's an excellent zoo there, with a special habitat where they breed and take care of snow leopards. That's what has to happen, and it has to happen soon—because this thing is going to grow. In another six weeks he'll be like this—" he spread his arms about three feet apart—"and he'll know how to use those claws."

The problems with smuggling the snow leopard out of Tibet were two-fold. First of all, possession of a Class One endangered species was a criminal offense. The second problem was keeping the animal hidden in the interim. If confiscated by the authorities, it could command a very high price: thousands of dollars, Brock guessed.

Getting the snow leopard over the border would be the hard part. Once in Nepal, the situation eased. There were dozens of naturalists and wildlife specialists in Kathmandu, many of whom would know how to handle the animal. International phone calls could be made, faxes could be sent without fear of government snooping, and a vast web of official and non-official allies could be recruited for help.

"I'll do it," Francesca offered. "I have to go to Nepal in a week. And I'm already smuggling things that are harder to hide than a snow leopard."

I raised my eyebrows. "Like what?"

"Like two hundred bottles of Chanel No. 5 perfume."

That evening I found Bill Thompson and brought him to the Yak. He fell in love with the animal, and vowed to do whatever he could. He'd be flying back to the States tomorrow, and offered to use his network of National Geographic contacts to help the cause.

"The person I really need to call," he said, "is George Schaller. You've heard of him, right? He's the guy Peter Matthiessen trekked with in *The Snow Leopard*. I've worked with George; he's the director for science of the Wildlife Conservation Society in New York. He's done loads of stuff with Chinese pandas, and he's the leading expert on snow leopards as well. If anyone can help you, it's him."

This was excellent news. We thanked him profusely, and I took him out for a brandy and cheesecake before saying goodnight.

I was awakened at six A.M. by a steady pounding at my door. It was Bill Thompson, on his way to the Lhasa airport. He was in quite a state.

> Among George Schaller's many books are two on Tibet: *Tibet's Hidden Wilderness* and *Wildlife of the Tibetan Steppe*. While the latter is a technical study, it will still please many students of Tibet and Tibetan wildlife, with its many quotes from old expeditions and excellent descriptions of habitat and behavior. You'll amaze your traveling companions by being able to do more than pointing and shouting, "Wild ass!"
>
> —JO'R and LH

"You'll never fucking believe this," he said. "I got back to my hotel last night, and just as I was opening my door the people in the next room came out. Guess who?"

I gazed at him blankly.

"George Schaller!"

It was a miracle. Schaller, his wife, Kay, and a grasslands specialist named Dan Miller had checked into the Holiday Inn the night before, back from an assignment in Mongolia. Bill had told the naturalists about the snow leopard, and George had gone apeshit—not with enthusiasm, but with trepidation. Huge penalties awaited us if we were caught in possession of the animal—let alone smuggling him out of Tibet.

"Call Dan Miller this morning," Bill advised. I nodded groggily, freezing in my purple underpants. "Contact him first, and let him discuss the situation with Schaller." We shook hands, and he left.

After breakfast I returned to my room to find a note from Miller. His advice—and Schaller's as well—was that we turn the cub over to the Tibet Forest Bureau, which would figure out what to do with him. At ten o'clock I called the Holiday Inn and spoke to Schaller personally. He agreed to come by, but only if he could bring a liaison from the Bureau with him.

Brock and Francesca were livid.

"The minute any Chinese official knows about this it's finished," Brock said. "Why the hell can't Schaller come over here by himself? Is he too busy and important? Well, I'm sorry. The three of us are risking our necks over this animal, and I'm not willing to hand him over to the Chinese government at the first opportunity. I'd rather see him get to Kathmandu, regardless of the risks, than end up in a little cement box in some Chinese city, enriching a bunch of scumbag officials. These guys rent panda bears out for a million dollars a year to foreign zoos."

I telephoned Schaller again. "Listen," I said. "I've spoken with my friends, and we all agree. We'd like a candid meeting with you before getting any officials involved."

I'd expected an argument, but Schaller was surprisingly receptive. "Okay," he said. "I'll be at the Yak within an hour."

George Schaller was a tall man with a high forehead and the calm, no-nonsense mien of a Kansas City Sheriff. He was capable,

I guessed, of being entirely clinical; but as he stroked the cub we watched a lifetime of scientific objectivity melt away.

"In all my years studying snow leopards," he said, "I don't think I've ever seen a juvenile this young. He's…well, he's beautiful."

Brock and Francesca held hands, beaming like the surrogate parents they had become.

Both Dan Miller and Kay Schaller—a copper-haired woman who looked like she did her crossword puzzles in pen—concurred. The animal must be protected at any cost; the only question was, how.

Schaller and Miller had meetings through the afternoon, but the six of us got together that evening for a brainstorming dinner at Drölma's. It was a bittersweet event, as Schaller examined and rejected various strategies for dealing with the cub.

"Forget the idea of taking him to Nepal," he warned. "Even if you can get him there—and that's a huge risk—he probably wouldn't last a week. Snow leopards live at very high altitude, where few micro-organisms survive. Not only is Kathmandu 8,000 feet lower than Lhasa, it's the middle of the monsoon. There are dozens of diseases to which the animal has no natural immunity. Within a couple of days you'll have a sick snow leopard on your hands—and what will you do then?"

"In that case," Francesca said, "why not just take him back into the mountains? At least he can fend for himself."

"Absolutely wrong." Schaller said. "Returning cats to their natural habitats is extremely difficult. Snow leopards learn to hunt with their mothers; it would take months to wean the cub, and a year or more to train him to hunt in the wild. Even then, he'd probably only be able to take down domesticated animals like goats and sheep—which would eventually lead him to the same fate as his mother."

"I understand the argument against smuggling him to Nepal," I said, "but can't you use your contacts to at least get him out of China? There must be a zoo that'll take him. Someplace like the Bronx Zoo, where there's a good snow leopard exhibit…."

Schaller shook his head. "There's a problem with that, too. Since snow leopards are an endangered species, no reputable zoo will accept one without paperwork. It would be like a stolen Rembrandt showing up at the door of the Met; there's not a chance they would take it. The same would hold true for Darjeeling, or any other zoo."

Someday, he said—in a year or two, perhaps—it might be possible for Khang Sik Dondrup to be sold or traded to a high-budget Western habitat where he could live out his years in comfort (and, presumably, with company). Until then, there was only one solution. George and Kay would be leaving Lhasa in a week. They would discuss the matter with the Tibetan government, bring the cub to Beijing and use whatever clout they had to assure he was well taken care of. It was less than ideal, but it beat the alternatives.

"I guess the most important thing is that he lives." Francesca stared into her beer, her voice edged with bitterness. "But it's also his quality of life I'm thinking about. From everything I've heard the Beijing Zoo is horrible. They sell kids toy guns so they can pretend to shoot at the animals."

"Not this one." Kay handed Francesca a tissue, and gave her husband a long look.

"He'll be all right," George Schaller said. "I'll do my best."

I left for Golmud the next morning. Peach and banana sellers lined the sidewalk near the main bus terminal, and I stocked up on fruit and water. Chinese police in green uniforms were everywhere. The Dalai Lama's birthday, Brock explained, was only four days away.

The Tibet-Qinghai bus looked like a soft drink can that had been dropped from the top of the Empire State Building. I lashed my backpack to the roof, climbed down, and grasped Brock's hand.

"Did you ever stop to consider," he said, "that the entire reason for your around-the-world trip—everything that went into thinking about it, writing the book proposal, and actually doing it—might have all been a karmic scheme to save that snow leopard?"

"If that's true," I replied, "it's been worth every minute."

Jeff Greenwald is the author of five books, including Mr. Raja's Neighborhood: Letters from Nepal, Shopping for Buddhas, *and* The Size of the

World, *a chronicle of his around-the-world overland voyage, from which this story was excerpted. His most recent book,* Scratching the Surface: Impressions of Planet Earth, from Hollywood to Shiraz, *is an anthology of his best short travel pieces from the past twenty-three years. He was a pioneer of internet travel writing (www.jeffgreenwald.com), and his work has appeared on Salon.com, in many Travelers' Tales books, and in diverse national and international magazines. He divides his time between Oakland, California and Kathmandu, Nepal.*

PAMELA LOGAN

Rebuilding Palpung

Restoring a remote Tibetan monastery is a colossal task.

THE FIRST SIGHT OF PALPUNG BROUGHT A GASP FROM JOHN, Razat, and Harry—and me, too; no matter that I had been here twice before. Some 200 meters over our heads, planted on a lookout, Palpung's walls loomed gargantuan, steep, and impregnable. The main temple was like a boxcar that had slid down the mountain and come to rest just on the verge of flying off a ski jump. Peripheral buildings, ridiculously small by comparison, were scattered around the main temple. A rabble of Derge-style log houses ran behind the monastery, on the saddle that connected it to sacred Wuchi Mountain. Water for the community came from a thin trickle flowing down a crease in the mountain, whose pasture-covered slopes rolled upward and out of sight.

From Pewar, it had taken just over three hours to get here, but the hardest part was yet to come: a steep, dusty, backbreaking climb from the valley floor. We rode past the log houses containing the township headquarters, which were lined up facing the Bei Chu. Then we turned our backs to the river and faced a steep path that snaked upward—up and up and up—to Palpung as it loomed on its eagle's perch.

In a photograph, Palpung's main temple looks smaller than it re-

247

ally is, for the eye wants to believe that its lowest row of windows belong to the first floor. But no, these are second-floor windows, and that makes the building twice as large as it appears at first glance. All my reports and photographs had been for naught: John Sanday was little prepared for the immensity that confronted him. "This is a mammoth, mammoth task," he would say later. "At the moment, all we're doing is irritating the elephant—a little gnat scratching at its side."

Walking around Palpung was like exploring a medieval castle. The ceilings were high, the rooms great, but all were sunk into musty gloom. Black soot covered beamed ceilings and obscured antique frescoes. There were so few inhabitants that we seldom saw anyone except our direct hosts. The three men and I stayed in the long-abandoned quarters of Khyentse Rinpoche, who had fled into exile in 1959. I stored my gear in a dusty, butter-blackened cabinet that once housed sacred texts. Most rooms were either empty or littered with refuse. Windows, already small and admitting little light through their paper-covered wooden lattices, were boarded up. The monastery was a maze of dark, dungeon-like chambers—most of which were too dark and uncomfortable even for rats to infest.

Like Pewar, Palpung suffered from a leaking roof that had rotted interior load-bearing timbers. The wood looked fine on the outside, but when I touched the inside of a fallen split log, it crumbled like stale bread in my hand. Palpung's exterior rammed-earth walls, despite being more than a meter thick at the base, had huge cracks. Although its structural ills resembled Pewar's, what was different was the immense size of the place and how each movement propagated through the structure like a house of cards. The building was slowly bending to the force of gravity, settling like snow to match the rounded contours of the hill beneath.

To start off our inspection tour, Shongshong led us down into the basement, a maze of empty rooms and uneven dirt floors broken by protruding bedrock. Once upon a time, this was a storage area and stables. We looked at the immense outer walls and saw how cracks had penetrated all the way through. In the basement chambers was a forest of timber columns that Shongshong had inserted to stop the building from sagging. "Here it sank twenty centimeters, here it sank ten centimeters, here it sank forty," he explained, pointing to various places on the ceiling as he showed us around.

Back in Chengdu, John Sanday had scoffed at Shongshong's request that I purchase two twenty-five-ton jacks and haul them out here. But now, seeing the thunderously heavy weight that rested on rotting columns, John was a believer. As our inspection party worked its way upward, John and Razat brainstormed about what to do. Razat asked, "Is there any way on the ground floor we can tie things together?"

"Exactly what I was thinking," John replied. "My gut feeling is that you need to do an enormous amount of research and analyze the movement throughout the whole structure, to see if there is a pattern. This is going to take an enormous amount of time."

In the days that followed, the two architects set to work like master detectives to figure out why the building was sinking, and why the walls and floors didn't meet at right angles anymore. They measured angles, pulled up floorboards, and excavated clay. At another, less important building,

I had been to Nenang Valley nearly every year for the past decade to visit the Karmapa Lama, head of the Kagyu Sect of Tibetan Buddhism. He was only seven when I first met him, a shy but spirited boy whom I would catch peeking from behind the curtains of his towering room when I would leave. I sensed an aloofness, almost a listless boredom on my last visit. Two months later, I saw on the BBC news that he had escaped to India, following so many other Tibetan refugees. After destroying more than 6,500 monasteries in Tibet during the Cultural Revolution, the Chinese have made some attempt to rebuild several of them, mostly for the sake of tourism. But in reality, so many of the spiritual teachers have escaped into exile leaving these buildings devoid of their great masters, nothing more than empty shells.

—Alison Wright,
"Shell Game"

John conducted an experiment in crack-repair by putting an invisible steel "stitch" in the wall. Gradually, he pieced together a theory of why some parts of the building were going south, others west, and still others straight down.

The monastery's problems were more than structural, however; it had a serious morals problem, just as Situ Rinpoche had told us. The place just stank of giving up. Litter left in the courtyard was still there, unswept, days later. Despite Situ Rinpoche's letter of introduction, the monks gave us a halfhearted welcome. The villagers who were helping John with his experiments were uninterested. "They just don't care," he complained. "At Pewar, if we needed something all we had to do was ask the abbot Tenzeng Nyima. At Palpung, who do we ask? Poor old Shongshong! And he doesn't even belong to this monastery! I've had lazy workers at other places, but at least the people cared about conserving their building. Here, they don't."

But John wasn't a quitter. He called a meeting of all Palpung's monks. That afternoon, they assembled in the reception room, some seventeen maroon-robed lamas, most of them wrinkled old men. As they lowered themselves painfully onto cushions, I felt a jolt of embarrassment that we had the chutzpah to drag those sagacious ancients out of their nice warm quarters. But those guys needed waking up, and John was going to give it to them.

After some decorous preliminaries, John let them have it. Harry translated into Chinese; then Malu, who was proving an able and intelligent interpreter, translated into Tibetan. John berated the monks for Palpung's lack of cleanliness and for the lack of spirit. He told them what he was trying to do, what a great treasure they had in this spectacular building, how unique it was, and how proper conservation would bring Palpung to world prominence again. He said, "We can't repair and conserve Palpung alone; you can't do it alone; Shongshong can't do it alone; Situ Rinpoche can't do it alone. We all must work together."

"Any questions?"

Silence.

Then a voice. Shongshong's voice.

I don't know exactly what he said, because Malu and Harry

declined to translate; and anyway the speech took long enough as it was. Shongshong went on and on in a low, sincere voice—reverently, humbly, unstoppably. With my smattering of Tibetan, I knew that he was relating the whole history of the monastery, who had built it, why and when, who had repaired it, why and when and for how much money, what had happened during the Cultural Revolution, what had happened since, and how he, Shongshong, was ready to do his utmost in making it right again, making it a fit place for Situ Rinpoche to return to.

I was beginning to wonder how many more hours we might be trapped here when Shongshong reached a punctuation mark of some kind, and we five started struggling to our feet, awkwardly, as our legs had gone to sleep from sitting for so long. The monks stared at us with grave attention as we staggered toward the door. How to get them to realize the meeting was over? At last I looked at them and said, "*Ndro!*" (Let's go!) Suddenly, the ice melted and they began moving and talking and getting to their feet also. Meeting adjourned.

Later, after dinner, John explained to me his plan of attack: "The first step is to set up a major survey, do a month of analysis, work out what the building's future use will be," he said. "We'll chop the whole thing up into a series of manageable annual projects. For each section, we'll strip out the earth to see the structure, then we'll undertake consolidation, replacement, and reconstruction. Probably five annual projects. It's daunting. But we can get it done."

Shongshong was way ahead of John on this score. Taking a piece of paper from John's notebook, he sketched a picture of how he felt the building should be divided up and attacked piece by piece, starting at the most dangerous area around the central courtyard. John looked over Shongshong's plan and pronounced it excellent.

However, before any actual work could begin, John and Razat would need to come again, this time for a longer stay, to draw up detailed plans. I sighed to think of how much money Wong How Man and I would have to raise.

It had now been eighteen days since we left Chengdu. Harry was laboring hard to carve a habitable niche out of Palpung's dust. ("I will teach these monks what is the meaning of clean!" he vowed.) Assisted by the ever-helpful Malu, he created edible meals out of flour, butter, yak meat, and our dwindling store of imported comestibles. Never-theless, John and especially Razat were feeling the homeward call.

There was, however, a problem about leaving. The telephone at the township headquarters was out of order, so if we rode out of the usual trailhead at Göncheshi, we'd have an uncertain hitchhike to town. But there was another way, a direct trail back, circumventing the highway. According to Shongshong, it was a seven-hour trip— just two hours longer than the usual route. It did, he cautioned, involve several passes.

My executive decision: Okay. Let's give it a try.

By now it was November and frosty as our caravan climbed away from Palpung. Our guides, half a dozen local men and women, walked beside the horses, which carried team members and belongings. As we crested the first pass, the sun left us and snow began drifting down. Half an hour later we were walking in a blizzard. Stupidly, I had left my arctic outerwear packed inside my bag, now on another horse somewhere at the other end of the line. To ward off frostbite I dismounted and began to walk. But we were all still in high spirits, snapping photos of each other surrounded by swirling white. Harry was quite the horseman by now, twirling his rope and spurring his mount faster.

An hour or so later, as we left a straightaway and turned to descend into a valley, the sun came out, and with it a wave of euphoria. *"Taiyang chu laile!"* (the sun is out!) shouted Shongshong in a burst of uncharacteristic exuberance as the mist parted and we saw a stockade of peaks encircling a valley of stunning white. I was still walking, and what with my picture taking, was falling behind. The guides urged me onto the back of my white mare. We went on, trotting briskly beside a burbling river that was already leading us upward, to another pass.

At around one in the afternoon, we reached a cluster of stone shepherds' huts, deserted at this season. This was the lunch stop. By this time I was so cold that food seemed entirely beside the point.

No one wanted to sit down on the rocky, deep-frozen ground. Standing, we chewed on some meat and bread, and Malu passed around a jar of *arak*. The liquor shot into my veins, warming my feet a degree or two. Ten minutes later we were on the move again.

Three more passes lay ahead: two at 4,750 meters (15,700 feet) and one at 4,700 (15,500). In between, there were rocks, more rocks, still more rocks, broad barren valleys full of rocks, and nearly invisible trail. The mist closed in again, parting occasionally to show us blockbuster vistas of snow-covered ranges. As we were coming down from the second pass, Harry asked, "How much farther?"

"Two hours," Shongshong replied. "From the other side of the next pass you can see Derge." These were heartwarming words, for it's always better if you can see your destination, even if it's a hundred miles away. The trip was supposed to last seven hours, but already we were going on eight.

We rode an hour more. Summitting the last pass brought us to a valley where the air seemed warmer—but bitter disappointment, for there was no sign of the town. I asked Shongshong, "How much farther?"

"Two hours," replied the stoic Tibetan.

It's customary in Tibet to dismount when going downhill, so we got off our horses and walked, propelled by the happiness of civilization nearly in our grasp. Down down down we went, until at last we came to a solitary house, where we stopped for tea and snacks. The guides, who had been on foot all day, ate their *tsampa* ravenously. John and Razat were so eager to get back that they started ahead while the rest of us were still resting. Harry trotted after them, but took a wrong turn; a little later Malu and I spotted him on a lookout looking baffled. "What are you doing up there?" shouted Malu, laughing.

Not much later, Harry was on the trail beside me, making good time with both feet and mouth. "It's just like the Long March!" he said.

After eleven hours on the trail, we reached the outskirts of town. *"Ga ah te,"* said villagers to Malu, giving the customary Derge greeting. Hard journey?

"Ga ma te," he lied. No, not hard.

Pamela Logan received a doctorate degree in aerospace science from Stanford University before changing career paths. An interest in martial arts training and photography led her to Tibet and resulted in her first book, Among Warriors: A Martial Artist in Tibet. *Returning to Tibet and taking an interest in ancient monasteries, she began leading international expeditions and established the Kham Aid Foundation to support monastery conservation work. She subsequently wrote* Tibetan Rescue: The Extraordinary Quest to Save the Sacred Art Treasures of Tibet, *from which this story was excerpted. Her life and work are chronicled at www.alumni.caltech.edu/~pam-logan/.index.html.*

RALPH WHITE

✦ ✦ ✦

A Walk on the Wild Side

He travels the hard way, bearing
forbidden messages.

LONG AGO, I FOUND MYSELF IN DHARAMSALA, INDIA, STAYING AT
the Tibetan Nechung Monastery, home of the only functioning
political oracle in the world. At certain ceremonial moments after
lengthy ritual preparations, the monk serving as the vehicle for the
oracle would go into trance wearing a 600-pound headdress. He
would then dance and speak to both the Kashag, the Tibetan
Parliament, and to the Dalai Lama himself. His words would offer
advice on pressing political matters. This was not a monastery with
many Westerners and I was fortunate to be there thanks to a personal connection.

It was the time of the Tibetan New Year and the monks began
their lengthy ceremony to invoke Pehar Gyalpo, the Nechung
Chogyam, fierce protector of both Tibet itself and the Dalai Lama.
I would wake in my small cell in the early, gray hour of the morning and hear the monks' prolonged, deep, baritone "oms" inter-
spersed with clashing cymbals and long, trumpet blasts. This was a
five-day ritual and as time went on the rhythm became increasingly shamanic. Moved by this event I asked the monks if I would be
permitted to join them for three mornings. They graciously agreed
and I sat quietly in a corner meditating while the ceremony con-

tinued—the celebrants in their high yellow hats and maroon robes, their enormous twelve foot trumpets ready for action.

At the conclusion of the Nechung ceremony I was sitting in my room one evening when a monk friend appeared at the door asking if he could bring the head monk inside. I was honored and welcomed him. He sat down on the small bed opposite me and began to tell me the tale of his flight from Tibet. When the political and military situation came to a head in 1959 and the Dalai Lama fled, the Chinese communists wanted the leaders of the Nechung Oracle very badly due to their important role in Tibetan political culture. A price had been placed on the head of the monk serving as the oracle and on the head monk himself, and both had been burned in effigy. They had barely escaped alive. As he spoke, I could feel the passion and outrage still burning beneath the head monk's composed and dignified bearing. I felt in him all the justified sorrow and anger at the way the Chinese had trashed the Tibetans' beautiful and ancient culture.

He reached the conclusion of his narrative and looked at me intensely. They had been waiting, he told me, for the right person to accomplish something of significance to the monastery. It was important to take some political material, highly illegal in China, into Tibet (to a place that I must leave unnamed). They felt I was the right person to do this. He had heard that I was planning to fly to Lhasa on the first plane of the year from Kathmandu. It was impossible for any Tibetan to carry this material as they would be searched too thoroughly. Therefore the only chance lay with a Westerner. Would I be willing to do it?

I knew as soon as he spoke that I would and I agreed with only a little hesitation. I calculated that I would take my chances at the airport and the worst that could happen would be arrest and deportation. On the day before my departure after a month in the monastery the head monk returned to my room and placed the white *kata* silk scarf around my neck as a blessing. He refused all payment for my stay and told me that while I was engaged in this attempt they would put me under the protection of the Nechung Chogyam.

However, March 1989 was the thirtieth anniversary of the uprising against the Chinese that had led to the flight of the Dalai Lama. Protests had begun to occur in Lhasa and news was appearing that monks were being shot dead at point blank range by Chinese police simply for holding up a piece of cardboard on which a crude Tibetan flag had been drawn. Too much information was appearing in the world media about this official policy of "merciless repression" and so the Chinese did what they usually do: they sealed the borders of Tibet and ordered all foreigners out of the country in forty-eight hours. Then the killing and torturing could continue uninterrupted.

All flights to Lhasa were canceled and it looked impossible to do what I had promised. Then, one day in Kathmandu I learned of the story of Joseph Rock, an Austrian American explorer in the early twentieth century who had taken an obscure route into Eastern Tibet in 1926 and written an article about it in the *National Geographic* of that year entitled "Journey to the Land of the Yellow Lama." As far as I knew no one had followed this route since but it would mean entering Eastern Tibet or Kham, home of the fierce Khampa warriors who had defended the border of Tibet for a thousand years.

These fighters had formed the core of the resistance to the Chinese for many years and they did not conform to the conventional peace-loving image of Tibetans. With their powerful build, their long, red-tasseled hair, cowboy hats and big earrings, they were considered some of the finest horsemen in Asia. They all, to a man, carried swords of varying length and were often crack shots. They had fought the Chinese in the 1950s and 60s

> A blow on the nose
> of a hated enemy
> Is surely more satisfying
> Than listening to the advice
> Of benevolent parties.
> —Khampa proverb

from their home in the Four Rivers, Six Ranges region of Eastern Tibet and, at high altitudes, man to man, they were considered unconquerable. That's why Mao had eventually bombed the major monasteries in Kham, before perpetrating countless atrocities against the innocent monks.

It was also why their home region was forbidden territory. From a copy of the *National Geographic* article given to me by a friend, which I devoured with fascination, it appeared that Joseph Rock, accompanied by a six man armed guard, had crossed this remote mountain region infested with bandits and entered the Lama Kingdom of Muli, then one of the least visited places on earth. Not much had changed since in that respect.

I decided to give it a try. I now had a back door into Tibet, and although I knew this journey would be dangerous and lonely, it promised an unforgettable experience in the service of a good cause—if I survived. I also had dreams at the time of a film about the forgotten war in Eastern Tibet and I wanted to see the location of this epic struggle for myself. I bought a second-hand backpack, a small tent and some dehydrated food at a trekking shop in Nepal and planned my journey. This would mean going to Bangkok and from there flying to Kunming, the capital of Yunnan province in Southwest China. From there I would need to make my way overland via Dali to Lijiang at the foot of the Tibetan snow range. From that point all travel would have to be done without the knowledge or approval of the Chinese authorities. It looked risky and exhausting but fascinating.

I left Nepal on the first available flight to Bangkok. I had a few days to wait in Thailand for the weekly flight to Kunming and already I could feel the knot in my solar plexus as I contemplated the journey ahead. Would I even get past Chinese customs and immigration on my arrival at Kunming airport? I did not relish the prospect of a Chinese communist interrogation, let alone a jail cell. When eventually I left Bangkok for the airport in the very early morning the sky was a distant pale blue with strange, disconcerting cloud formations. I felt very alone.

After months spent around the Tibetan community it was hard not to see China as a kind of demonic state possessed by the ugliest possible impulses. It felt like entering Tolkien's land of Mordor as we descended though the clouds and I was able to make out the first red brick, nondescript buildings at Kunming airport. There was some kind of nerve-wracking confusion at customs, and then suddenly I was through. From there I took a long bus ride to the town of Dali where I stayed in Guest House Number One and began to become familiar with the drab, almost inhuman nature of communist architecture. Even the guest house felt like a prison with its grimy, unadorned walls and unspeakable, maggot-filled toilets. After months in India and Nepal surrounded by colorful images of deities, beautiful clothing and gracious art, this was unbelievably ugly. The ubiquitous blue jackets and trousers of the people were depressing.

And then it was on to an even longer ride to my destination, Lijiang, at the foot of the Tibetan snow range. Here I would make my final preparations for the trip. But something unexpected was occurring. This was May 1989 and students had occupied Tiananmen Square to demand democracy. There was no English-language paper available and it was impossible to know what was happening. Was this a great moment of political breakthrough or was it going to produce appalling repression? No Chinese person would even talk about it and no Westerner had the faintest idea.

I was in a dilemma. The rainy season was about to begin and passage across the mountains into the Tibetan region of Muli, one of the three provinces of Kham, would soon become impossible. What was I to do? Tibet itself was under martial law and now it looked like China too might go the same way. It was impossible to determine the political outcome and so I decided to risk it and go into forbidden territory. I now had to make my way 300 kilometers to Lugu Lake up on the border of Yunnan, Szechuan, and Muli, from which point I would be able to strike out across the mountains. The only way to get there was a two-day journey by bus on dirt roads. However, the Chinese government forbade the sale of tickets to Westerners and, not for the last time, I had to persuade a gracious Chinese man to buy the ticket for me.

The journey was rough and muddy across big rivers, steep cliffs, and rain-lashed mountains. When the bus became stuck in mud all male passengers had to grab a tow rope and haul it out. Eventually we arrived at the lake, a spot of exquisite natural beauty with a small island at its center on which stood the evocative ruins of an old Tibetan monastery. At almost 9,000 feet this serene body of water perfectly mirrored the sky and clouds above in daylight, while at night intense meteor showers hurtled across the sky.

You could see the mountains of Muli in the distance—a jagged line of peaks way on the Western horizon. I looked in vain for some kind of a guide but nobody was planning to make that trip until after the rainy season. A Taiwanese man I met translated the opinions of the locals on the advisability of this journey: "Don't even think about it," they said, "the area is filled with bandits and leopards."

But the weather was beginning to change for the worse and I could wait no longer. I boarded the rickety daily bus around the lake to Yunming at the end of the road where the trek would begin. When I arrived, a prolonged torrential downpour began that made any kind of hiking impossible. To my utter surprise I found myself sharing a room at the local guest house with five young Germans who had managed to avoid detection despite their blond hair and strapping build. As the rain beat down relentlessly in that gray, desolate town I pondered my rather grim prospects. But then my new friends slowly began to inquire about my intentions. When they learned of the wild trip I planned they

> In "political" Tibet, the Tibetan government has ruled continuously from the earliest times down to 1951. The region beyond that to the north and east [Amdo and Kham in Tibetan]…is its "ethnographic" extension which people of Tibetan race once inhabited exclusively and where they are still in the majority. In that wider area, "political" Tibet exercised jurisdiction only in certain places and at irregular intervals for the most part, local lay or monastic chiefs were in control of districts of varying size. From the eighteenth century onwards, the region was subject to sporadic Chinese infiltration.
> —Hugh E. Richardson,
> *Tibet and Its History*

asked eagerly if they could join me. It felt like a stroke of providence and I agreed with relief. Perhaps they didn't match Rock's armed guard, but one of them was on leave from the German army, another a tri-athlete, and all of them were fit and strong.

As we walked out of town the next morning the tough part really began. The old backpack I had bought in Kathmandu was proving a poor choice, as the padding on the shoulder straps was far too thin and already they were cutting painfully into my flesh. We hiked all day towards the mountains through small valleys and it was up, up, up across mountain ridges and into dark forests. At dusk, as we descended exhausted into a new valley from the densely wooded slopes, we came across our first real village, Lichatsu. The inhabitants were stunned at the sight of us, yet after much initial concern and hesitation they proved wonderful hosts and we were invited to eat in one of the simple wooden houses. The scene inside was like something out of the sixteenth century. In the smoky darkness the women all sat to one side, an old granny naked above the waist, and the men cooked us eggs and potatoes in giant black cauldrons hung over a blazing fire.

Early next morning, after receiving some vague directions from the villagers, we headed deeper into the mountains. The forests seemed vast, the few trails confusing, the altitude depleting. Eventually we broke out of the trees and found ourselves on a relatively level plain. In the distance, but much closer than it had appeared from the lake, the strange, jagged ridge of the mountain entrance to the Tibetan world rose above us. That night we camped by a river and ate the last of our food. A tiny older man appeared on the riverbank and genially offered me a pipe of something green that I took to be tobacco but was never quite sure. For some reason my mind raced all night, despite my enormous fatigue, and I slept little if at all.

At dawn a man appeared from nowhere with a string of mules and began to load our packs on them. This was almost too good to be true. It appeared that he would lead us over the pass to Muli and we set off in high spirits with light steps, feeling almost freed from gravity without the weight of our packs. We climbed for hour after hour on a winding track, the forests gradually falling away, sheer rock faces and dramatic, craggy peaks appearing all around us. But the air was becoming very thin and despite the lighter loads it required serious sustained effort to keep going. Suddenly our guide stopped. Had we reached the pass? Was it just round the next corner? He indicated that this was as far as he would go and began to unpack the animals. Surely we must be close to the top, I thought.

It turned out to be another four hours of sheer torture. I staggered on gasping for air, trying to juggle my pack to relieve the cutting shoulder straps, pausing frequently. God knows how high we were. Nobody knew, there were no maps. On we went, past rushing waterfalls, through rain and drizzle, always another bend and another climb just when we thought this had to be the final one. I was lagging behind my younger companions and began to remember Rock's tales of bandits high up on the pass. Most of the men we had seen for days had carried rifles—it wasn't clear why—perhaps the leopards. I trudged on, each step agonizing, aiming to keep the blue and red rain jackets of my companions always in sight.

And then at last we reached the top. There was a modest stone wall or cairn marking the spot and as we threw ourselves down on the ground in the evening rain I experienced an enormous thrill. I had made it to the borders of Old Tibet, the fulfillment of a lifelong dream. There were no seven-foot Tibetan border guards of the kind I had read about as a boy but instead, to my amazement, there indeed was my first herd of yaks grazing two or three hundred yards away, their inscrutable faces barely acknowledging us. The sight of these almost mythic animals suddenly warmed my heart and I felt a huge, exhilarating rush of affirmation.

Now at least it was downhill. As we descended there was nothing but vast, silent, empty forests and distant mountain ranges. We stumbled as night began to fall and eventually concluded there was no way we would find a village that night. We camped with little if anything to eat and no water. In the morning, far below us, we could make out the shape of a small town down in the valley. This was now our fourth day of trekking since leaving the lake and Muli appeared at last to be in sight. After dropping another three or four thousand feet we began to encounter fields and at last, thankfully, a glimpse of water that looked drinkable, murky though it was. Eventually we reached the river and plunged in, exhausted yet inwardly strong, washing off the days of grime and sweat in the river's cool, rushing waters.

Finally we staggered up the far side of the steep valley to the town. What would we find? To my disappointment it appeared to be the usual colorless Chinese-influenced settlement with ramshackle buildings and inhabitants mostly in blue and green Mao-style suits. But the people were friendly enough—no communist commissars thankfully. However, where was the Tibetan culture? Then I met "the village idiot," a remarkable man. He was unable to speak properly but his sign language was brilliant. I mentioned the word "*gompa*," Tibetan for monastery, and he nodded his head vigorously, pointed into the distance and beckoned for us to follow him over the rocky bluffs on a small dirt track into another valley, puffs of white cloud high above us. And then suddenly there it was! A magnificent Tibetan monastery lay before us. I was stunned. It was covered in wooden scaffolding and as we approached I could see that it was being built from scratch. Inside the work was impeccable.

In Tibetan Buddhism the symbol of the cloud is of such far-reaching importance, that a glance upon Tibetan *thankas* (scrolls) or temple-frescoes would suffice to convince the beholder. The figures of Buddhas, Bodhisattvas (enlightened beings), saints, gods, and *genii* manifest themselves from cloud formations which surround their haloes. The cloud represents the creative power of the mind, which can assume any imaginable form. The white cloud especially (or even a cloud shining in delicate rainbow colors) is regarded as the ideal medium of creation for the enlightened or enraptured mind, which manifests itself on the plane of meditative vision as *sambhogakaya*, the mind-created "body of delight."

—Lama Anagarika Govinda,
*The Way of the White Clouds:
A Buddhist Pilgrim in Tibet*

As I looked around I could see the miserable ruins of the old monastery that must have been destroyed in the sixties during the Cultural Revolu-tion. And then on a hill above us I noticed a small temple and I could see a few monks gathered around it in their maroon robes. I ran excitedly up to meet them and they greeted me with amazed but friendly faces. There were about thirty-five monks and before long they had plied us with jasmine tea and a bowl of walnuts and shown us the sacred *thankas* and prayer wheels of their small home. I was thrilled. Here I was at last in a real live Tibetan monastery, far, far off the beaten path, perhaps the first Westerner to visit. Later, as we left the monks, the late afternoon sun was setting behind the mountain above them. They stood in a line along the temple wall above us waving silently, emanating a composed and quiet dignity. This was a dream come true. But now it was time to head deeper into Kham. I had learned that we were not in the town of Muli itself but in a smaller town named Wachan, further north, where in Joseph Rock's day the Lama King and living Buddha had maintained one of his temple-palaces. We had inadvertently come at least thirty miles out of our way and hiked over a hundred miles in four days. I was hoping now that life would start to get easier.

Nobody seemed to know anything at all about roads or direc-tions. So I decided to head northwest up a valley that appeared to run deeper into Tibetan territory. We hitched a ride in a pickup truck through a long, narrow valley and eventually began to climb a winding road to Sanchee, a logging town and one of the most god-forsaken spots I have ever encountered anywhere in the world. As we arrived, the locals gaped and we quickly made our way to the usual dingy local guest house and locked the door. But it was no use. Never in my life have I met people with such little respect for privacy. The inhabitants clamored at the dirty window, they pressed against the room door and knocked constantly. If someone opened the door twenty of them barged in and began to ask us questions. But not about who we were and where we came from. Instead it was how much did this pair of shoes and that watch cost. The whole town, it seemed, was trying to break down the walls of our room and examine the recesses of our packs.

My young companions had had enough. They had endured agonies of climbing and shared many moments of bewilderment with me. But they were looking for adventure, not to complete some crazed mission for a Tibetan monastery, and they didn't need this kind of intense aggravation. They decided to get out of this dive and hitch back towards Yunnan at first light. My heart sank, as I had enjoyed and benefited from their company, but I couldn't blame them.

By good fortune, a local teenager named Shinkaka emerged from nowhere and told me that there was a pass towards Daocheng, the next town of any size perceptible on my old British map. He volunteered to accompany me on the three-day hike. I couldn't believe my luck. Accordingly at the earliest opportunity I left that miserable town and headed once again up into the mountains. Above us were strange, black peaks that looked almost as if they were made from volcanic ash. We began for the first time to enter the territory of nomads with their black yak wool tents scattered along the mountainside. Although this was June an icy cold began to creep upon us at this high altitude. We pitched my small tent and as night fell I climbed inside my sleeping bag for warmth and lay there wondering if I was completely mad to be attempting this journey. In the morning, as we stumbled across the boulder-strewn, black-rocked moonscape at the pass, a sea of mountains spread out before us stretching as far as the eye could see in every direction.

The trail ran high above the tree line at a steady altitude. A wild and ferocious herd of yaks caused us to make a wide detour—those horns looked very sharp and they seemed to have the strength of bison and the agility of horses. Towards mid-afternoon we met our first human beings since crossing the pass—two men with mules and rifles. It turned out their home village was our destination for the day and towards sunset we descended into a small valley where I saw for the first time the gently tapering, stone, square, flat-roofed buildings, each like a mini Potala Palace, that the Tibetans build. They hospitably invited us to spend the night camped on the roof of their house. I was carrying twenty-five pictures of the Dalai Lama with me and it seemed appropriate to give one to each of them. It was clear immediately that I had made friends for life.

Outside the tiny Tibetan village the riverbanks were strewn with prayer flags and I began to feel that wonderful quality of warmth and generosity that I had glimpsed back at the monastery in Wachan. I slept well that night and next morning we headed up into the mountains again to cross the second pass. Up on the ridge, the track seemed to go on forever with no sign of habitation and, more worryingly, no water. We pressed on relentlessly, I at least inspired by the great mountain ranges stretching to both east and west. But the wind was fierce and the sun at this height burned harshly through the thin air.

Towards late afternoon we came across a collection of huts belonging to a group of yak herders. One of them was especially humorous and friendly and he invited us into his small hut to enjoy *chang* (barley beer), yak cheese, and the ever-present *tsampa*. When I emerged from the hut half an hour later I heard cries of "Gongga Shan! Gongga Shan!" and saw people pointing to the east. Far in the distance a magnificent peak in the form of a perfect white pyramid had appeared from amidst the clouds. It was the sacred mountain, a glimpse of which was said to be so rare that it was worth twenty years of meditation. I gazed in wonder at this beautiful sight, which had remained completely cloud hidden throughout our long trek down the ridge. Gongga Shan (also known as Minya Konka) had been "discovered" by Joseph Rock in 1931 and for many years was thought to be the highest mountain in the world as, unlike Everest, it rises straight up from the plains below. This glimpse of the perfect crystalline cone of the holy mountain sent shivers down my spine and I felt deeply moved. I was more than glad to take it as a blessing.

I had never seen such a deep valley before as the one that now began to open up below us. It seemed that the riverbed had to be six thousand feet below us and we trudged on and on, the light fading, down towards our goal—the town of Bezu, where, according to Shinkaka, I could find lodging, food, and a bus to Daocheng. Eventually at nightfall we arrived bone weary.

But this town was not what I expected. The grace and charm of a small Tibetan village were gone. The people were rude and unfriendly and there was neither shelter nor food available. It is hard to describe what it feels like to arrive exhausted at an unknown town in the heart of the eastern Himalayas and feel yourself surrounded by hostile people. Again there was that similar quality of intense materialism that I had noticed in the logging town. Young men only wanted to know how much you paid for your watch or your boots and ignored your sense of well-being. These Chinese-Tibetan borderlands contained such a mix of attitudes and values. Perhaps it was a romantic streak in me but it seemed that wherever traditional Tibetan culture remained strong the people had nobility and warmth, and wherever communist values had taken hold there was little but an intense concern with material possessions.

The following day, after more distasteful experiences with the locals, I headed across the river looking for the road to Daocheng. But there was only a rough path by the riverside and there was no alternative but to follow it and hope for the best. I hiked for hours up the valley in the blazing heat. After the high passes it felt dry and scorching and I saw no trace of vehicle tracks. Soon I began to feel extremely trapped. Ahead of me the valley seemed to come to a complete dead end as the river appeared to emerge from the foot of a sheer cliff. To each side steep mountainsides pressed in on me that I was too tired to climb and, besides, what would be the point? Behind me was a town filled with hostile inhabitants. I felt stuck and lost in a forgotten Himalayan valley in forbidden territory with no way out. A black mood of depression fell on me and I threw myself down on a rock. What on earth to do?

If ever my years of meditation practice came in handy it was then. I sat spine erect on the rock and watched my breath as I tried to center myself. Gradually, breath by breath, the feelings of despair slipped away and I resolved just to walk on. Within a quarter of a mile it became clear that the river, in fact, made a sharp ninety-degree turn at what I had thought was the end of the valley. Then two young Tibetan horsemen appeared and told me that yes, I was on the way to Daocheng, but it was seventy kilometers still and many mountains ahead. I felt cheered by the knowledge and hiked until I could go no further before asking permission to camp in a dry riverbed in front of a group of traditional stone houses. Playing my ace card again, I pulled out a picture of the Dalai Lama and presented it to a man standing at the front of one of the houses. He immediately smiled and gestured that I was welcome to camp there.

What a contrast to the previous night! Children and friendly adults emerged and helped me pitch my tent and light a fire. One man did in fact have a small tractor that could pull a cart in which passengers sat and he agreed to take me next morning to Daocheng for sixty yuan, perhaps the best four dollars I have ever spent. That night, as a soothing wind rustled through the leaves of the trees above my head, I relaxed for the first time in days.

The next morning my new friend appeared with a tiny tractor hauling a low, wheeled rectangular box in which both I and various Tibetan women sat for the four- or five-hour trip to the nearest town. After wending our way through the valley we climbed up high over another pass. Again the mountains of Kham stretched away to infinity in every direction, and then we began our descent towards Daocheng. The town was gray and windswept and a strange mix of Chinese and Tibetan. The tractor pulled up in front of the lone guest house. There was no one there. And then a young woman appeared. She took one look at me and let out a high-pitched scream. Clearly she had never seen a Westerner before. But after a few minutes she relented and rented me a bed in the usual dingy communal room. Now I wondered how I would get from here to Litang, birthplace of the Sixth Dalai Lama, the next stop on my route.

Dusk fell not long after my arrival and I fell into bed and tried to rest. I was dozing when I was startled by a loud, aggressive knock on the door. I looked at my watch. It was eleven o'clock at night. Bracing myself, I opened the door and found myself gazing at a weasel-faced Chinese policeman in a green uniform and his Tibetan colleague. The lead cop was extremely hostile, aggressive, and suspicious. My passport was scrutinized thoroughly but it was clear that no one could read anything except my Chinese visa. Eventually, after an hour of intense shouting of unintelligible questions, they left.

But it looked like the game was up. The police were clearly very, very unhappy to see me there and I expected to be arrested at dawn, as soon as they had communicated with headquarters. Dawn came, however, and nothing happened. Seizing my opportunity, I headed for a forlorn spot on the outskirts of town where I found a half-derelict set of buildings and a big logging truck. The driver agreed to take me for a small fee and we left, the truck grinding and growling its way through the many low gears needed to move over these forbidding mountains. We were on our way to the second highest town in the world at over 14,000 feet and we had an enormous load of huge logs.

As we began to pick up a little speed we rounded a corner and suddenly there was my first Khampa warrior. He was an elegant and vigorous looking young man riding a white horse with his Tibetan cowboy hat, red braided hair, and sword. When we got closer he saw me in the cab and gave me a huge smile as we passed. I was really moved. At last I was entering the world of the Khampas and as a result of that one man's simple but appreciative gesture I felt very, very welcome.

We arrived in Litang late at night in icy weather under an enormous star-filled sky. But there was nowhere to stay. I paced the tiny streets shivering, knocking desperately on doors and receiving no reply. The whole place, it seemed, was boarded up and locked down for the night. And then suddenly a Tibetan man with a warm manner appeared and beckoned me to follow him. He led me into a small guest house. We passed first one and then another room full of sleeping Tibetans on small, crude beds. At the back of the house we entered a small room near a fire with one narrow bed. He indicated that it was his but that I should take it, smiled and disappeared. I lay down to rest, relieved and grateful. At last I had arrived in the very world that I had set out to reach a month earlier.

Litang's great monastery in the heart of Kham has a dramatic history in the twentieth century. In the fifties, as the Chinese mounted their surreptitious invasion of Eastern Tibet, it had become a focal point of battles between the Khampa guerrillas and the communist troops. The monastery had been bombed, many monks were murdered atrociously and the head lama had been publicly hanged.

This is a forgotten piece of history but for me it was very vivid.

The next morning I bought a Khampa cowboy hat to protect me from the intense sun and cold and found myself standing next to two of the wildest looking dudes I have ever seen. With their long black hair half way down their backs, their shades, earrings, rakish hats, boots, and swords they looked like some kind of renegade half-breed hippy cowboys. I remembered the Khampa saying I had learned in Dharamsala: "A man without an earring will be reborn as a donkey" and checked my own turquoise earring that I had been sure to wear in this region.

I tried to keep a low profile in the town but I knew that eventually the police would arrive. The guest house itself was run by a charming older couple. Despite their blue Maoist clothes they were the soul of Tibetan hospitality, offering me food and tea and inquiring solicitously about my travel plans. Soon the familiar green uniformed Chinese policemen arrived with stern faces and ugly demeanor. Where had I come from? Where was I going? When was I leaving Litang and returning to Szechuan? After the usual hour of dumb smiles and grins and expressions of helpfulness on my part they left after securing a

> In his book, *Cavaliers of Kham: The Secret War in Tibet*, Michael Peissel describes the fierceness of the Khampas: "Howling like a pack of wolves, the men on horseback charged down, their braided hair swinging as their mounts rushed on. Their reckless speed allowed them to penetrate right into the village, forcing the Chinese snipers on the rooftops to stand up in order to shoot at them.... [They] took no prisoners, left not one Chinese soldier alive. Close on 500 Chinese bodies were thrown into the river the following day. With sinister efficiency, in a few hours 200 Khampas, hastily recruited seven days previously, had exterminated an entire garrison of three times that many well-trained veterans of Mao's army."
>
> —JO'R and LH

promise from me that I would depart the following morning for the four-day journey to Chengdu.

The intensity of my situation now began to weigh heavily on me. I lay on my simple cot, my solar plexus in a knot. With the tightening surveillance that came with this more traveled region did it make any sense at all to continue? I thought of my girlfriend back in Virginia who had first introduced me to the Nechung Monastery, and gained some strength from contemplating her love and support. Perhaps wisdom dictated a return to China—after all, it was amazing that I had made it this far and I already had memories that would last a lifetime. I walked up a hillside and sat in the piercing sunlight as I tried to compose my thoughts and priorities. I gazed long and hard over that high valley, turning over all the options, looking for inspiration. The more I thought about it, the more I felt that having come this far it made no sense to turn back before I had achieved my objective. Despite the stress and anxiety, and with considerable trepidation, I resolved to go on.

I informed my gracious hosts in the guest house that I would be leaving for Szechuan at five in the morning. Delightful and caring as ever they got up with me in the bitter cold and boiled water for me to take on my trip. I said my slightly guilty goodbyes, headed out of the door into the icy, pitch black night and gazed out on the broad valley with its enormous dome of crystal stars. My plan was to walk west through the town and hike two or three miles up the mountain where I would conceal myself until the first vehicles began their journey in the morning deeper into Tibetan territory. Then I would try and hitch a ride. I walked alone through the silent, freezing town, the only sound the eerie echoes of my own footsteps. There was only one small light in the center of town and I was concerned that a barking dog might awaken the people inside whom I suspected to be police. I tried to tiptoe around this isolated lamp, my heart in my mouth, and my spirits lifted when I passed it without incident. I clamped my Khampa hat more firmly down on my head to ward off the night cold and strode into the hills. By first light Litang had become a distant sight down in the valley and I wrapped myself in my sleeping bag and hid behind a stone wall to await the first trucks. The first two vehicles ignored me but the third, a pickup driven by two young Chinese men pulled up. I offered them the familiar few dollars, threw my pack in the back, and climbed in the cab with a rush of exhilaration. Thank God.

They drove like maniacs, leaving a high dust plume behind them in the thin air. On we went in the early morning sunlight. Then suddenly, they stopped in a great silent valley where a small dirt road led off at right angles. I got out, waved them goodbye, and watched their dust plume disappear in the distance. I looked around me. The sun had not yet risen over the tops of the mountains, and down in the valley was a tranquil, deserted turquoise lake. Here I was in the most remote place I had ever been dropped in all my years of hitch-hiking, but I felt free and happy.

It seemed there was no choice but simply to walk on. I put on my pack and, with a quiet inner joy despite the vast empty silence around me, started walking deeper into Tibet. I hadn't gone far when I saw a group of mounted nomads slowly driving their yaks towards the lake. They crossed the road just fifty feet ahead of me. A beautiful Tibetan girl of about seventeen, with long hair braided with turquoise and coral and high boots, rode slowly past me on a white horse. A little way in the distance, her father and brothers, rifles slung across their backs, moved gracefully in their saddles. As I gazed at this vision of feminine beauty she seemed to me like a symbol of the old Tibet, proud, free, untouched by the horrors of materialistic communism. I stood silently by the roadside and felt a deep reverence for the fading beauties of traditional Tibetan culture.

Then they were gone and I walked on down the valley and before long I was able to flag a ride further west towards my destination. As the truck rumbled past beautiful aquamarine lakes set like precious stones below high, snow-capped mountain peaks, I noticed pilgrims making their way to Lhasa, prostration by prostration, their knees protected by leather pads, their clothes ragged and torn, their faces weatherbeaten, their spirits undaunted and invincible. In the distance, set right in the heart of the valley, my eye fell on a large stupa, a place of deep sanctity around which pilgrims had gathered. I was coming home to sacred Tibet.

I would like to describe more fully what followed but for reasons of security and protection for all involved it is impossible. Suffice it to say that after my final ride I lay beside a rushing river, half hidden by an old stone bridge, wondering how to complete my journey. With a mind filling with dark thoughts, I could see no way to make the connections I needed in this remote spot. Then children began to gather round me to play and my spirits lifted. After a couple of hours a Tibetan man approached me and beckoned mysteriously to follow him through a maze of tiny village alleys. He disappeared suddenly through a hole in a long wall and I followed him. To my amazement, I stepped into the center of a small but ancient monastery where I was able to hand on the material I had carried. I was assured that traders left every two weeks for the heart of Tibet, and that they would carry this precious cargo to its final destination. I had achieved my objective and it was an immense relief.

I now had to get back to China without detection. It was a bumpy, crowded, and smoke-filled bus ride of endless dusty days winding across arid mountainsides. After a number of close scrapes, I arrived in Kanding which Mao himself in his memoirs describes as the border of Tibet even though the communists have gone on to claim that Chinese territory extends hundreds of miles to the west. As the bus gradually descended the winding road towards the town I was struck by the exceptional ugliness of the place. Every building seemed poorly constructed and devoid of charm with virtually the whole town built in an ungainly sprawl. But as we neared the town center below us I could see one magnificent building at its heart, surrounded on all sides by a warren of narrow streets. I wondered what it was, and expected never to know the answer.

As we pulled up at the bus station, the driver announced completely unexpectedly with a logic that only Chinese transport understands that we would stop for four hours in this curious place. Well, I thought, this is my last stop in Tibetan culture and I'm going to try and find that building. As I walked through the marketplace, large, powerful looking Khampas lounged around looking curiously at my Tibetan shirt and cowboy hat. I guessed roughly where the curious building might be and threaded my way towards it.

I turned a corner in a maze of back alleys and suddenly there it was—an exquisite monastery combining perfectly the pagoda-like architecture of China with the magnificent colors and forms of Tibet. As I approached, three monks appeared and invited me in. Within the courtyard there was a huge door that I took to be the entrance to the temple. Would I like to enter? As the monk swung open the doors a thirty-foot gilded statue of the Buddha appeared with twenty-foot Bodhisattvas seated on each side. Realizing these would be my last moments among Tibetan spiritual imagery, not knowing what news awaited me of political turmoil back in China, I decided to do a final meditation, expressing gratitude for my safe emergence from a month in forbidden territory. I closed my eyes in silent contemplation and reverence and gave thanks for all those forces, seen and unseen, that had enabled me to complete this journey.

Opening my eyes after fifteen minutes I stood to leave. As I did so my eye fell on a striking statue just to the right of a Bodhisattva. I looked at it quizzically. Where had I seen this fierce figure before? Then it suddenly dawned on me. Turning to the monk who had greeted me I asked "Nechung Chogyam?" He nodded vigorously. It was indeed none other than the Nechung protector whose image I had last seen in Dharamsala months earlier when the senior monk of the Nechung monastery had promised that they would put me under the deity's protection for the duration of this task. Perhaps it was simply synchronicity but I was in no mood for such speculation. To me it felt like a blessing and I was flooded by profound feelings. There could be no sweeter conclusion to my walk on the wild eastern side of Tibet and, as I headed back to that dingy bus station, my heart was singing.

Ralph White is the editor of Lapis *magazine and co-founder of the New York Open Center, the city's leading venue for holistic learning since 1984. Born in Wales, he read* Seven Years in Tibet *at the age of fourteen, which instilled in him an unshakable desire to visit the country. He has organized numerous programs in New York on Tibetan culture and spirituality and is also a writer and lecturer. He introduced and edited* The Rosicrucian Enlightenment Revisited, *and wrote the foreword to the Travelers' Tales book,* The Way of the Wanderer.

PART FIVE

THE LAST WORD

Mestizo

*Race, culture, religion: reality is more
complex than our imaginings.*

IT'S SWELTERING IN NEW YORK, NOTHING LIKE THE DRYNESS OF
the Lhasa summer. The music on the CD must be kept low, because
it's long after midnight; even the gloomier stretches of Upper
Manhattan don't like noise at night. I might as well let Streisand
sing. About women. About where it's written what they are meant
to be. About letting her imagination float across the mountains and
the seas.

And can she sing. What richness, what purity of sound, what
shaving of the quarter tones...an aesthete's ecstasy, a nostalgic's
prophylactic against misery. Forget that indulgent orchestration. Just
revel in the woman's tone, her passion, her reach.

Her reach. Her global reach.

"Is that the religion which women cannot practice?"

It was the third time we had met in her apartment. Past the
Potala, right at the fork, across the roundabout, and into the Chinese
part of Lhasa. Left at the second alleyway after the Golden Yaks.

"Is that the what?" I said. It wasn't very good English, and I was
only there on the pretext that I spoke English well. Even with it,
meeting in her place seemed to be stretching the borders of safe

risk. Once a week, Thursday nights. It had taken me a while to find
my way there. No one seemed to be watching and I always waited
until night, but tourists rarely visited this part of town, west of the
Yaks, so it made no odds; I was conspicuous anyway.

There was a door in the wall across the courtyard, across a sward
of splinters left by the glasscutters who worked there during the day.
Probably Chinese, I thought viciously, who knew all about hard
work and private enterprise but hadn't discovered the broom.

Beyond the door in the wall was a second tiny courtyard leading
to two rooms cut out of a former outhouse. The first was lined with
gilt knicknacks and kitsch calendars. What I could see of the second
was lined with books.

"Youtai religion," she explained. The Chinese term for Jews and
Judaism. "Women cannot practice."

There is only one place I know where that statement has been
formulated. She can't have seen it. They don't show that sort of film
in Tibet. They show Hong Kong martial arts films and Hindi
movies and dubbed action films with Sylvester Stallone. Nothing
too troubling for the mind. Mostly about violence, mostly about
men. And endless twenty-six part TV marathons about their liberation from feudal landlords by fresh-faced youth dressed in the
plain, faded green of the PLA, so popular that on Thieves' Island on
the south side of the city you can now hire a private room in a
restaurant and be served by girls in the same 1950s uniforms, only
newly creased, without the fadedness, and wearing revolutionarily
bright-red lipstick.

And anyway all the cinemas in town except for two have closed
now, because some smart planner in the Party worked out that
wealthy people don't stage demonstrations and tripled all the
salaries. So now everyone has bought a VCR, even the Tibetans. But
she still didn't have one. So she can't have seen it. And she clearly
didn't know that the ban on Jewish women studying had passed by
most communities fifty years ago. This was a one-source piece of
knowledge, and that source could only be...

"Yen-tel," she said. "Yen-tel."

She came back from the other room with *A Collection of the*

World's 1,000 Best Films. At least I think it was called that, but I can't read Chinese. But there, under 1982 or 1983, it was: Directed by Barbra Streisand, Produced by Barbra Streisand, Starring Barbra Streisand, *Yentl*, the story of the Jewish girl who won't accept that the study of the religion is not allowed for her. The girl whom Bashevis Singer had told of, in his wicked, impenetrable, and subversive way, the girl who had disguised herself as a boy in order to study, and who in her desperation to maintain the illusion had ended up in a wholly fabricated sexless marriage. And who after years and years had been turned into a sepia-toned Hollywood epic for which, even for this, they still hadn't given Babs a copper Yak, let alone an Oscar.

My Thursday evening pupil was not far off Barbra's age. Once, I had heard my pupil sing, a spiritual she had learned in its entirety from a Japanese film in which a Negro, as she put it, had died falling from a cliff for some reason I couldn't grasp, singing. She had sung divinely, and I had sat there on her sofa amongst the nylon cushions and the plastic flowers and discreetly cried. But she didn't have a film star's looks. The horn-rimmed spectacles, the scraped-back hair, the asexual garb, the absence of adornment, severity of appearance. At first, three weeks before, in the Snowlands Restaurant where she had asked if I would teach her, she had seemed more like an Asiatic Rosa Klebb. She embodied the Chinese puritan, the ones who were already too committed to abandon woolen stockings for skin-tight polyester suits and nylons when the market had arrived, or, rather, had been pushed in. Or the ones who gambled that the state bureaucracy was a safer bet than the main-street stores and nightclubs that they maybe had realized even then were sure as spring tide to come.

She didn't only look like a stern-faced Chinese cadre: she was a Chinese cadre. A very high-up Chinese cadre. In my very last lesson I finally dared to ask, "What do you do?"

"You would not understand," she said, "I have seen films. I know what Americans in offices do. Especially New York. They work, all the time. It's a different system here. We do nothing. We play mahjong and we do nothing. It's different here."

Her gamble had been right, of course: she did nothing all day and still got paid. Handsomely by local standards, 2,000 kuai a month, I'd bet. Of course she had been right: the Party wouldn't dare to break the iron rice bowl in Tibet, the life-long social safety net. Tibet is one place where it doesn't mind paying for compliance, at least among officials. Anyway, she had placed her bet both ways: she had long since told her husband to leave, and had paid her way into part-ownership of a high-class nightclub, in which Sichuanese migrant girls in scanty outfits—Tibetan girls, she said, just don't know how to do it—served liquor to Chinese soldiers and office staff drinking up their altitude-allowances and remoteness-bonuses, but still left with plenty to squander in brothels on their way to their bare and lonely one-bulb rooms in China's western outpost.

That's a smart cadre. Play both ways.

She served more tea. Chinese leaf tea, almost colorless, bitter but refreshing in the intense cold now that the sun had long gone down. I was still trying to exonerate my religion. It was just a custom in some communities, I stammered hopefully, it has no written basis. "They were the ones who killed Yishu," she declared. The Chinese word for Jesus. So now I knew from whom she had learned her English: it must have been the officially sanctioned foreign English teachers, the same covert Protestant evangelists who had told me that all Tibetans were damned to hell. I had killed Jesus, so I understood why I should go there, but what the Tibetans had done I wasn't sure. But the missionaries weren't there to explain these things to foreigners, they had more pressing work to do.

She looked through the book and wrote some notes on films we found. *Bullit. Star Wars. Vertigo.* Her pen was lavishly inlaid with fake lapis lazuli, an excess of plastic opulence. "Presented to Tibet's Cadres by the Central Authorities' Representative Delegation on the 30th Anniversary of Peaceful Liberation" it had faintly etched on it. It ran out of ink again. I lent her mine.

"I was in it," I said. "The tailor. The apprentice tailor."

She took no notice, she was writing in her notebook. A long description of her father's life lay across its pages, written in a grotesque cursive that knew no horizontals, and she was copying

my corrections to what had been her homework from the week
before. He had been a landless laborer in the Yunnanese southwest
sixty years before, and had fled to join Maoist guerrillas in the hills
after beating the landlord's donkey to death by mistake. But it was-
n't his oppressed credentials that had brought him to high office
under the new regime: it was the happenstance that he had learned
Tibetan in his youth from driving animals to market across the
mountains in Tibet. First a translator for the arriving army as it followed the passes he had so often crossed, then some years of education in the cadre's school, and finally a county leader, or as she put
it, a district magistrate. This woman ate dictionaries for breakfast.

She reads everything, the Tibetan girl from the Snowlands told
me later. All she does is read. No one of us knows as much as her.
And she's read all of the *Water Margins*. And not just the *Dream of the
Red Chamber*, either. Other things too, she said. She hardly goes out,
she just reads.

I remembered the Dostoevsky I had recognized amongst the rows
and rows of Chinese novels, next to the photo of her taken as a
student twenty years ago at college, with the red neck-scarf that
marked her party future. It was printed on that lightly plastic-coated
paper at that time used for posters, too large for any private photograph, with some caption printed underneath: she must have been
a propaganda model distributed across the country. My god, she had
been beautiful then. Joyous, gleaming, flush with the promise of
revolution. Now rows and rows of bookshelves towered around
the dusty memorabilia of a thrilling youth. There were cheap ency-
clopedias leaning against the empty fish tank, and picture books of
other countries stacked beside the songbird's cage. And all across
the glass-topped table were ornate cups and boxes filled with plastic flower stems and fountain pens whose bulbs no longer would
accept ink.

She passed me the next installment of her homework. This time
it was not about her father. It was about her mother. And her mother had been even poorer than her husband, and had become a much
higher cadre than either him or their ever-so-accomplished daugh-

ter. Something really high, but this was not for telling, not even in the quest to acquire more vocabulary. All I knew was that the mother had been born of poor farmers in the hills just to the west of the Drichu, and had traveled into Lhasa behind the army which her husband was then translating for. Swept up in that great movement she had ended up by the seventies as a leader in Tibet.

That was when I realized. West of the Drichu were the heartlands of Tibet. My pupil couldn't write it, she couldn't read it, she could only speak it with effort, she surely wore no *chupa* and she didn't eat parched barley flour. But her mother was Tibetan. And on weekends and late at night perhaps, or sometimes in her dreams maybe, the daughter was Tibetan, too.

The Tibetan language likes to play with unequal pairings and conflicting negatives: *ra ma lug, lha ma yin*—neither beast nor bird, goat nor sheep, neither god nor human. They do not describe such people as half this, half that, but as *rgya ma bod*: neither Chinese nor Tibetan. I watched her write more new words into her vocabulary list and wondered if I was looking into the mixed, the hybrid, the non-dual, the undivided, the commingled, the neither-being-nor-not-being described in the Higher Sutras. Then I remembered I was looking at the Cadre Who Played Both Ways, who was weaned on Marx and who graduated on Bashevis Singer.

In the Upper Manhattan apartment Barbra is still singing of her long-lost father and the window from which she can see only a patch of sky. It is nearly day. I wonder what my pupil is doing now. Whether she had to answer questions about the unofficial evening classes. Whether she kept her resolve to sell the nightclub holding. Whether she is still writing in her notebook, hoping for some Western teacher to come one day to check the endless pages of cursive confessional. Whether she dreams she is Tibetan. Whether she still thinks Jews are all misogynists. Why she never asked who the tailor was.

Hollywood and Bashevis Singer gave Yentl a glorious ending, by having her escape the misery of her homeland and the fiction of her marriage by taking a boat to America. Being great writers of fiction and crafters of dreams, they never told us if she was happy when she got there. Or if she retained the love of her religion and her language after the first few years had passed. Or if the culture left behind survived. They didn't describe the Land of Individual Freedom where men survive by roaming Manhattan streets at nighttime counting coke cans out of garbage bins at fifteen dollars a day, where Barbra had in childhood been unhappy.

The half-goat, half-sheep grazes both the pastureland and the mountainsides; she doesn't run away to sea. The one migrates in chase of dreams; the other adapts. The one enchants, the other discards outward charms. With her the future lies.

Robbie Barnett was born in London in 1953 and first visited Tibet in 1987. The following year he founded the Tibet Information Network, an independent news and research service. Since 1998 he has been teaching at Columbia University in New York, and since 2000 running a summer language program for foreign students at the university in Lhasa. He started his career as an actor in 1975 and appeared in Roberts Brothers' Circus, Circus Hoffman, Billy Smart's Big Top, and the Spanish State Circus before going on to work with the Royal National Theatre, The Muppet Show, *and the BBC, as well as on several major films, including* Yentl.

Recommended Reading

Here are a few choice books which are either excerpted or are referenced in the text, or worthwhile reading in their own right.

Allen, Charles. *The Search for Shangri-La: A Journey Into Tibetan History*. London: Time Warner UK, 1999.

Avedon, John F. *In Exile in the Land of Snows: The Dalai Lama and Tibet Since the Chinese Conquest*. New York: Perennial, 1998.

Balf, Todd. *The Last River*. New York: Crown Publishers, 2000.

Barnett, Robert, (ed.). *Resistance and Reform in Tibet: Tibet 40 Years On, 1950-1990*. Bloomington: University of Indiana Press, 1994.

Barnett, Robert and Mickey Spiegel. *Cutting Off the Serpent's Head: Tightening Control in Tibet 1994-95*. New York: Human Rights Watch; London: Tibet Information Network, 1996.

Bernstein, Jeremy. *In the Himalayas: Journey through Nepal, Tibet, and Bhutan*. New York: Touchstone, 1989.

Bhum, Pema. *Six Stars with a Crooked Neck: a Tibetan Memoir of the Cultural Revolution*, translated by Lauren Hartley. Dharamsala, India: Tibet Times Newspaper, 2001.

Brackenbury, Wade. *Yak Butter and Black Tea: A Journey Into Forbidden China*. Chapel Hill, NC: Algonquin Books, 1997.

Buckley, Michael. *Cycling to Xian and Other Excursions*. Vancouver, BC: Crazyhorse Press, 1988.

Buckley, Michael. *Tibet: The Bradt Travel Guide*. London: Bradt Guides, 2003.

Chan, Victor. *Tibet Handbook: A Pilgrimage Guide*. Chico, Calif.: Moon Publications, 1994.

David-Neel, Alexandra. *Magic and Mystery in Tibet*. New York:

Penguin, 1975.

David-Neel, Alexandra. *My Journey to Lhasa.* Boston: Beacon Press, 1993.

Davis, Wade. *Shadows in the Sun: Travels to Landscapes of Spirit and Desire.* Washington, DC: Shearwater, 1998.

Dowman, Keith. *The Sacred Life of Tibet.* London: Thorsons Publishers, 1998.

Erickson, Barbara. *Tibet: Abode of the Gods, Pearl of the Motherland.* Berkeley, Calif.: Pacific View Press, 1997.

Feigon, Lee. *Demystifying Tibet: Unlocking the Secrets of the Land of the Snows.* Chicago: Ivan R. Dee Publisher, 1998.

Foltz, Richard. *Religions of the Silk Road: Overland Trade and Cultural Exchange from Antiquity to the Fifteenth Century.* New York: St. Martin's Press, 1999.

Goldstein, Melvyn C. and Matthew T. Kapstein (eds.). *Buddhism in Contemporary Tibet: Religious Revival and Cultural Identity.* Berkeley: University of California Press, 1998.

Goldstein, Melvyn C. *The Snow Lion and the Dragon: China, Tibet and the Dalai Lama.* Berkeley: University of California Press, 1997.

Govinda, Lama Anagarika. *The Way of the White Clouds: A Buddhist Pilgrim in Tibet.* Boston: Shambhala, 1988.

Greenwald, Jeff. *The Size of the World: Once Around without Leaving the Ground.* New York: Ballantine, 1997.

Gyatso, Palden. *Fire Under the Snow: Testimony of a Tibetan Prisoner.* London: The Harvill Press, 1997.

Harrer, Heinrich. *Seven Years in Tibet.* New York: Putnam, 1996.

Harrer, Heinrich. *Return to Tibet: Tibet After the Chinese Occupation.* New York: Putnam, 1998.

Hedin, Sven. *My Life as an Explorer.* New York: Kodansha, 1996.

Hopkirk, Peter. *The Great Game: The Struggle for Empire in Central Asia.* New York: Kodansha America, 1994.

Iyer, Pico. *Video Night in Kathmandu: and Other Reports from the Not-So-Far-East.* New York: Vintage, 1989.

Johnson, Russel. *Tibet's Sacred Mountain: The Extraordinary Pilgrimage to Mount Kailas.* Rochester, VT: Inner Traditions/Park Street Press, 1999.

Kanamaru, Atsushi (ed.). *Mapping the Tibetan World*. Reno, Nev.: Kotan Publishing, 2000.

Knaus, John Kenneth. *Orphans of the Cold War: America and the Tibetan Struggle for Survival*. New York: Perseus Books Group, 1999.

Lama, Dalai and Howard C. Cutler. *The Art of Happiness: A Handbook for Living*. New York: Riverhead Books, 1998.

Landor, A. Henry Savage. *An Explorer's Adventures in Tibet*. La Crescenta, Calif.: Mountain N' Air Books, 2000.

Laird, Thomas. *Into Tibet: The CIA's Secret Expedition to Lhasa*. New York: Grove, 2002.

LeSueur, Alec. *Running a Hotel on the Roof of the World: Five Years in Tibet*. London: Summersdale, 1998.

Logan, Pamela. *Among Warriors: A Woman Martial Artist in Tibet*. New York: Vintage Departures, 1996.

Logan, Pamela. *Tibetan Rescue: The Extraordinary Quest to Save the Sacred Art Treasures of Tibet*. North Clarendon, VT: Tuttle, 2002.

Maraini, Fosco. *Secret Tibet*, translated by Eric Mosbacher and Guido Waldman. London: Harvill, 1998.

Matthiessen, Peter. *The Snow Leopard*. New York: Penguin, 1996.

McCue, Gary. *Trekking in Tibet: A Traveler's Guide*. Seattle: The Mountaineers, 1999.

Meyer, Karl Ernest and Shareen Blair Brysac. *Tournament of Shadows: The Great Game and the Race for Empire in Central Asia*. Washington, DC: Counterpoint/Perseus, 1999.

Peissel, Michael. *Cavaliers of Kham: The Secret War in Tibet*. New York: Little, Brown & Co., 1972.

Peissel, Michael. *The Last Barbarians: The Discovery of the Source of the Mekong in Tibet*. New York: Henry Hold, 1997.

Piburn, Sidney (ed.). *The Dalai Lama, A Policy of Kindness*. Ithaca, NY: Snow Lion Publications, 1990.

Richardson, Hugh E. *Tibet and Its History*. Boston: Shambhala, 1984.

Ridgeway, Rick. *Below Another Sky: A Mountain Adventure in Search of a Lost Father*. New York: Henry Holt, 2000.

Rinpoche, Guru. *The Tibetan Book of the Dead*, translated by Francesca Fremantle and Chogyam Trungpa. Boston: Shambhala

Publications, 1975; New York: Random House, 1988.

Schaller, George B. *Tibet's Hidden Wilderness: Wildlife and Nomads of the Chang Tang Reserve*. New York: Harry N. Abrams, 1997.

Schaller, George B. *Wildlife of the Tibetan Steppe*. Chicago: University of Chicago, 1998.

Schell, Orville. *Virtual Tibet: Searching for Shangri-La from the Himalayas to Hollywood*. New York: Henry Holt, 2000.

Schmidt, Jeremy. *Himalayan Passage: Seven Months in the High Country of Tibet, Nepal, China, India, & Pakistan*. Seattle: The Mountaineers, 1991.

Shakya, Tsering. *The Dragon in the Land of Snows: A History of Modern Tibet Since 1947*. New York: Columbia University Press, 1999.

Snellgrove, David L. and Hugh Richardson. *A Cultural History of Tibet*. Boston: Shambhala Publications, 1995.

Swift, Hugh. *Trekking in Nepal, West Tibet, and Bhutan*. San Francisco: Sierra Club Books, 1989.

Taring, Rinchen Dolma. *Daughter of Tibet*. London: Wisdom, 1986.

Thurman, Robert A. *Circling the Sacred Mountain: A Spiritual Adventure through the Himalayas*. New York: Bantam, 1999.

Walker, Wickliffe W. *Courting the Diamond Snow: A Whitewater Expedition on Tibet's Forbidden River*. Washington DC: National Geographic Society, 2000.

Ward, Tim. *The Great Dragon's Fleas*. Berkeley, Calif.: Celestial Arts, 1993.

Wheeler, Tony. *Lonely Planet Unpacked*. Melbourne: Lonely Planet, 1999.

Wignall, Sydney. *Spy on the Roof of the World*. New York: Lyons & Burford, 1997.

Wright, Alison. *Spirit of Tibet: Portrait of a Culture in Exile*. Ithaca, NY: Snow Lion Press, 1998.

Index

Ali 134
Andrade, Father 136

Bardo Thödol (The Tibetan
    Book of the Dead) 202
Bardo Trang 98
Barga 122
Barkhor bazaar 35
Bell, Sir Charles 26
Bezu 266
British invasion 174
Buddhism 23, 32
Burang 121
bus travel 88

caves 109, 140, 157
Celestial Burial 193
ceremonies 144
Chang Thang 133
Chetur La 14
Chogyam 255
Chökorgye Monastery 168
Chomolungma 153
clouded leopard 40
cycling 105, 120, 128

dakinis 141
Dalai Lama 17
Dali 259
Daocheng 268
Deng Xiaoping 64
Dharamsala, India 255
Do-ngak Chöling 152
Drepung monastery 106
Drira Phuk 98
Drölma La 99

earthquake 27
education 74
Everest 153

four-wheel-drive tour 131
frescoes 216

Ganden 12
Golmud 90
Gongga Shan 266
Gossul Gompa 118
Gotshangpa, Gyalba 99
Guge 131
Guge history 137
Gurla Mandata 115, 126
Guru Rimpoche 152
Gyantse 173

Han 63
Hebu 13
Hedin, Sven 124, 210
Himalayas 40

Jokhang temple 32, 83
Jomolangma 153

Kama Chu 40, 52
Kanding 273
Kelsang Potrang 144
Kham 257
Khampa warriors 257
Khampas 270
Kharta Chu 46
Kirimtse 212
kora 35, 96

Lake Manasarovar 113, 123
Lhamo Latso 164
Lhasa 7, 59, 87, 105, 143, 163, 193
Lichatsu 261
Litang 269
Lugu Lake 259

Makalu 40
Mallory, George 55
Manasarovar (see Lake Manasarovar)
merit 33
Metoktang Valley 165
Milarepa 167
Minya Konka 266
Mount Kailash 96
Muli 259
murals 138

Nechung Monastery 255
Nechung Oracle 256
Nenying Gompa 173
Norbulingka 16, 143
Nyak-Tso Lake 204

Palpung 247
Pang La 42
Pangong Lake 204
Pangong Range 204
Pemogang 212
Pethang Ringmo 55
pilgrimage 33, 96, 168, 196
Potala Palace 193

Qing Dynasty 67
Qomolangma Nature Preserve 49

Rakshas Tal 124
Red River Valley 174
Red Temple 138
Rock, Joseph 257
Rongbuk 151
Rongphu 152

sailing 113
Samye 10
Sanchee 264
Schell, Orville 68
schools 72
Shao La 49
Siwatshal Dutro 99

Tatopani 227
temple manners 29
Thango La 92
Tibet Autonomous Region
   (TAR) 45
Tibet Information Network 25
Toling Gompa 141
trekking 10, 96, 165, 184, 196,
   258, 261
Tsaparang 136
Tsaparang Dzong 140
Tseqgu 167

Wachan 264
Woka Taktse 171
Wuchi Mountain 247

Yamantaka Chapel 139
Yangönpa 116
Yaobang, Hu 77
Yarlung River 11
Yatung 222
Yogurt Festival 145
Younghusband, Sir Francis 175
Yueba 46

Zanda 131, 141
Zhangmu 227
Zhotön 145
Zhukar La 14

Index of Contributors

Allen, Charles 96–104, 137

Banks, Barbara 3–6
Barnett, Robbie 277–284
Bass, Catriona 8
Blazdell, Philip 121
Brewster, Valerie 100
Buckley, Michael 109, 131–142,
    173–183
Buddha 198

Coburn, Broughton 59–62
Craig, Sienna 187

David-Neel, Alexandra 184–191
Davis, Wade 40–58

Eigen, William 36, 133, 200
English, Kevin 105–112

Gill, Mike 33
Govinda, Lama Anagarika ix,
    196–211, 263
Greenwald, Jeff 235-245

Habegger, Larry 34, 111, 233
Haber, Daniel B. 230
Harrer, Heinrich xv-xviii, 16–31
Hedin, Sven 113–119
Hessler, Peter 63–84

Iyer, Pico 193–195

Jenkins, Mark 163–172
Joyce, Tom 44, 89, 151–162

Khadka, Rajendra S. 227–234

Lama, H. H. the Dalai 21, 23
Lama, Sangita 227–234
Le Sueur, Alec 32–39
Logan, Pamela 247–254

Maraini, Fosco 212–224
Marchant, Garry 127, 174, 178
McCue, Gary 45, 114, 129, 145
Milarepa 82, 239
Möller, Maria 7–9

Norris, Tim 13, 50, 72, 76, 78

O'Reilly, James 5, 42, 153, 228

Phuntsok, Tenzin 92

Richardson, Hugh E. 260
Rockhill, William 11

Schaller, George B. 64
Schmidt, Jeremy 120–130
Swenson, Karen 143–147

Taring, Rinchen Dolma 167, 208

Ward, Tim 87–95
Wheeler, Tony 98
White, Ralph 255–274
Wong, Edward 10–15
Wright, Alison 249

Acknowledgments

We would like to thank our families and friends for their usual forbearance while we are putting a book together. Many thanks also to Tim and Sean O'Reilly, Susan Brady, Krista Holmstrom, Raj Khadka, Alex Brady, Jennifer Leo, Michele Wetherbee, Patty Holden, Judy Johnson, Kelly Knowles, and Keith Granger. Heartfelt thanks to all others who made important contributions, including John Ackerly, Robbie Barnett, Marybeth Bond, Michael Buckley, Gaye Carlson, Brot Coburn, Lesley Friedel, Lodi Gyari, Heinrich Harrer, His Holiness the Dalai Lama, Usha Lama, Alec Le Sueur, Gary McCue, Tim Norris, Lesley Fridell, Rev. Seumas O'Reilly, Chhime Rigzin, Gary Sheppard, and Tim Ward.

Special thanks from James to Wenda, for always saying "Go," and Ahna, Noelle, and Mary for visiting me in my dreams when I'm far away.

Special thanks from Larry to Paula, Alanna, and Érne for brightening every day.

Frontispiece excerpted from *The Way of the White Clouds: A Buddhist Pilgrim in Tibet* by Lama Anagarika Govinda. Copyright © 1966 by Lama Anagarika Govinda. Reprinted by permission of Georges Borchardt, Inc., agent for the author.

"A Tibetan Picnic" by Barbara Banks published with permission from the author. Copyright © 1996 by Barbara Banks.

"Chasing Monks" by Maria Möller published with permission from the author. Copyright © 2003 by Maria Möller.

"The Pilgrim's Way" by Edward Wong reprinted from the April 28, 2002 issue of *The New York Times*. Copyright © 2002 by the New York Times Company. Reprinted by permission.

"Tutor to the Dalai Lama" by Heinrich Harrer excerpted from *Seven Years in Tibet* by Heinrich Harrer. Copyright © 1953 by Heinrich Harrer. Reprinted by permission of the Marsh Agency.

"Around the Johkang" by Alec Le Sueur excerpted from *Running a Hotel on the Roof of the World: Five Years in Tibet*. Copyright © 1998 by Alec Le Sueur. Reprinted by permission of Summersdale Publishers Ltd.

"The Realm of the Clouded Leopard" by Wade Davis excerpted from *The Clouded Leopard* by Wade Davis. (Published in the United States under the name *Shadows in the Sun: Travels to Landscapes of Spirit and Desire.*) Copyright © 1998 by Wade Davis. First published by Douglas & McIntyre Ltd. Reprinted by permission of Island Press and Douglas & McIntyre Publishing Group.

"The Sew-Tel Hotel" by Broughton Coburn published with permission from the author. Copyright © 2003 by Broughton Coburn.

"Tibet through Chinese Eyes" by Peter Hessler reprinted from the February 1999 issue of *The Atlantic Monthly*. Copyright © 1999 by Peter Hessler. Reprinted by permission of the author.

"Like a Rolling Stone" by Tim Ward published with permission from the author. Copyright © 2003 by Tim Ward.

"On the Sacred Mountain" by Charles Allen excerpted from *The Search for Shangri-La: A Journey Into Tibetan History* by Charles Allen (Time Warner Books). Copyright © 1999 by Charles Allen. Reprinted by permission of Time Warner Books UK and Sheil Land Associates Ltd.

"A Meeting with a Monk" by Kevin English published with permission from the author. Copyright © 2003 by Kevin English.

"The Holy Lake" by Sven Hedin excerpted from *My Life as an Explorer* by Sven Hedin. Copyright © 1925 by Boni and Liveright, translation © 1953 by Alfhild Huebsch. Reprinted by permission of Kodansha America, Inc.

"Bicycles to Burang" by Jeremy Schmidt excerpted from *Himalayan Passage: Seven Months in the High Country of Tibet, Nepal, China, India, & Pakistan* by Jeremy Schmidt. Copyright © 1991 by Jeremy Schmidt. Reprinted by permission of The Mountaineers, Seattle, WA.

"The Lost Kingdom of Guge" and "Red River Valley" by Michael Buckley excerpted from *Heartlands* (Summersdale Publishers, 2002) by Michael Buckley. Copyright © 2002 by Michael Buckley. Published by permission of the author.

"At the Norbulingka" by Karen Swenson reprinted from the April 16, 1998 issue of *The Wall Street Journal*. Reprinted by permission of the author and The Wall Street Journal. Copyright © 1998 by Dow Jones & Company, Inc. All rights reserved.

"The Space Between" by Tom Joyce published with permission from the author. Copyright © 2001 by Tom Joyce.

"Instant Karma" by Mark Jenkins originally appeared in the June 2000 issue of *Outside* and in *The Hard Way* by Mark Jenkins, published by Simon & Schuster. Reprinted by permission of the author. Copyright © 2000 by Mark Jenkins.

"Approaching Lhasa" by Alexandra David-Neel excerpted from *My Journey to Lhasa* by Alexandra David-Neel. Copyright © 1927 by Harper and Row, Publishers, Inc. Renewed 1955 by Alexandra David-Neel. Reprinted by permission of HarperCollins Publishers, Inc.

"Mondays Are Best" by Pico Iyer excerpted from *Video Night in Kathmandu: and Other Reports from the Not-So-Far-East* by Pico Iyer. Copyright © 1988 by Pico Iyer. Used by permission of Alfred A. Knopf, a division of Random House, Inc.

"Journeys with a Buddhist Pilgrim" by Lama Anagarika Govinda excerpted from *The Way of the White Clouds: A Buddhist Pilgrim in Tibet* by Lama Anagarika Govinda. Copyright © 1966 by Lama Anagarika Govinda. Reprinted by permission of Govinda Trust.

"The Visions of the Dead" by Fosco Maraini excerpted from *Secret Tibet* by Fosco Maraini, translated by Eric Mosbacher and Guido Waldman, published by Harvill Press. Copyright © 1998 by Casa Editrice Corbaccio s.r.l., English translation © The Harvill Press, 2000. Used by permission of The Random House Group Limited.

"Zone X in Zhangmu" by Sangita Lama and Rajendra S. Khadka published with permission from the authors. Copyright © 2003 by Sangita Lama, translation copyright © 2003 by Rajendra S. Khadka. A slightly different version first appeared in the *Nepali Times*, Kathmandu, Nepal.

"A Day in the Life of Ghang Sik Dondrup" by Jeff Greenwald excerpted from *The Size of the World: Once Around without Leaving the Ground* by Jeff Greenwald. Copyright © 1995 by Jeff Greenwald. Reprinted by permission of the author.

"Rebuilding Palpung" by Pamela Logan excerpted from *Tibetan Rescue: The Extraordinary Quest to Save the Sacred Art Treasures of Tibet* by Pamela Logan. Copyright © 2000, 2002 by Pamela Logan. Reprinted by permission of Tuttle Publishing.

"A Walk on the Wild Side" by Ralph White published with permission from the author. Copyright © 2003 by Ralph White.

"Mestizo" by Robbie Barnett published with permission from the author. Copyright © 2003 by Robbie Barnett.

Additional Credits (arranged alphabetically by title)

Selection from "A Most Maligned Drink" by Catriona Bass copyright © 2003 by Catriona Bass.

Selections from "At Large in the Common World" by William Eigen published with permission from the author. Copyright © 2003 by William Eigen.

Selections from *Daughter of Tibet* by Rinchen Dolma Taring copyright © 1970, 1986 by Rinchen Dolma Taring. Reprinted by permission of John Murray (Publishers) Ltd.

Selections from the Foreword by George Schaller excerpted from *Trekking in Tibet: A Traveler's Guide* by Gary McCue copyright © 1991, 1999. Reprinted by permission.

Selections from "Glimpses of Tibet" by Larry Habegger published with permission from the author. Copyright © 2003 by Larry Habegger.

Selection from "Lhasa Notes" by Mike Gill published with permission of the author. Copyright © 2003 by Mike Gill.

Selection from "Not Quite Made in Tibet" by Daniel B. Huber copyright © 2003 by Daniel B. Huber.

Selection from "Notes from the Roof" by James O'Reilly published with permission from the author. Copyright © 2003 by James O'Reilly.

Selection from "Postcard from Tibet" by Valerie Brewster copyright © 2003 by Valerie Brewster.

Selection from "Riding in the Rain Shadow" by Sienna Craig reprinted from the Summer 1998 issue (Volume VII, Number 4) of *Tricycle: The Buddhist Review*. Copyright © 1998 by The Buddhist Ray, Inc. Reprinted by permission.

Selections from "The Road to Gyantse" by Garry Marchant published with permission from the author. Copyright © 2003 by Garry Marchant.

Selection from "Shell Game" by Alison Wright published with permission from the author. Copyright © 2003 by Alison Wright.

Selection from *The Search for Shangri-La: A Journey Into Tibetan History* by Charles Allen copyright © 1999 by Charles Allen. Reprinted by permission of Little Brown and Company UK.

Selection from *Tibet and Its History* by Hugh E. Richardson copyright © 1984 by Hugh E. Richardson. Reprinted by permission of Shambhala Publications.

Selection from *Tibet: The Bradt Travel Guide* by Michael Buckley copyright © 2003 by Michael Buckley. Published by permission of the author.

Selection from "Tibetan Roads" by Gary McCue published with permission from the author. Copyright © 2003 by Gary McCue.

Selections from "Tibet Journals" by Tim Norris published with permission from the author. Copyright © 2003 by Tim Norris.

Selection from "Travel in Tibet" by Philip Blazdell published with permission from the author. Copyright © 2003 by Philip Blazdell.

Selections from *Trekking in Tibet: A Traveler's Guide, 2nd Edition* by Gary McCue published by The Mountaineers. Copyright © 1991, 1999 by Gary McCue. Reprinted by permission of the author and The Mountaineers, Seattle WA.

Selections from "Walking the Mount Kailash Circuit" excerpted from *Lonely Planet Unpacked* by Tony Wheeler. Copyright © 1999 by Tony Wheeler. Reprinted by permission of Lonely Planet Publications.

Selections excerpted from *The Way of the White Clouds: A Buddhist Pilgrim in Tibet* by Lama Anagarika Govinda copyright © 1966 by Lama Anagarika Govinda. Reprinted by permission of Govinda Trust.

Selections from "Yeti, Flying Saints, and Boys with Guns" by Tom Joyce published with permission from the author. Copyright ©2003 by Tom Joyce.

About the Editors

James O'Reilly, president and publisher of Travelers' Tales, wrote mystery serials before becoming a travel writer in the early 1980s. He's visited more than forty countries, along the way meditating with monks in Tibet, participating in West African voodoo rituals, and hanging out the laundry with nuns in Florence. He travels extensively with his wife, Wenda, and their three daughters. They live in Palo Alto, California.

Larry Habegger, executive editor of Travelers' Tales, has been writing about travel since 1980. He has visited almost fifty countries and six of the seven continents, traveling from the frozen Arctic to equatorial rain forest, the high Himalayas to the Dead Sea. In the early 1980s he co-authored mystery serials for the *San Francisco Examiner* with James O'Reilly, and since 1985 their syndicated column, "World Travel Watch," has appeared in newspapers in five countries and on WorldTravelWatch.com. As series editors of Travelers' Tales, they have worked on almost seventy titles, winning many awards for excellence. Habegger regularly teaches the craft of travel writing at workshops and writers conferences, and he lives with his family on Telegraph Hill in San Francisco.

TRAVELERS' TALES

THE SOUL OF TRAVEL

Footsteps Series

THE FIRE NEVER DIES
**One Man's Raucous Romp
Down the Road of Food,
Passion, and Adventure**
By Richard Sterling
ISBN 1-885-211-70-8
$14.95

"Sterling's writing is like spit-fire, foursquare and jazzy with crackle...."
—*Kirkus Reviews*

LAST TROUT
IN VENICE
**The Far-Flung Escapades
of an Accidental
Adventurer**
By Doug Lansky
ISBN 1-885-211-63-5
$14.95

"Traveling with Doug Lansky might result in a considerably shortened life expectancy...but what a way to go."   —Tony Wheeler,
Lonely Planet Publications

ONE YEAR OFF
**Leaving It All Behind for a
Round-the-World Journey
with Our Children**
By David Elliot Cohen
ISBN 1-885-211-65-1
$14.95

A once-in-a-lifetime
adventure generously shared.

THE WAY OF
THE WANDERER
**Discover Your True Self
Through Travel**
By David Yeadon
ISBN 1-885-211-60-0
$14.95

Experience transformation through travel
with this delightful, illustrated collection by
award-winning author David Yeadon.

TAKE ME
WITH YOU
**A Round-the-World
Journey to Invite a
Stranger Home**
By Brad Newsham
ISBN 1-885-211-51-1
$24.00 *(cloth)*

"Newsham is an ideal guide. His journey, at
heart, is into humanity." — Pico Iyer, author
of *Video Night in Kathmandu*

KITE STRINGS OF
THE SOUTHERN
CROSS
**A Woman's
Travel Odyssey**
By Laurie Gough
ISBN 1-885-211-54-6
$14.95

— ★ ★ ★ —

ForeWord Silver Medal Winner
— *Travel Book of the Year*

THE SWORD
OF HEAVEN
**A Five Continent Odyssey
to Save the World**
By Mikkel Aaland
ISBN 1-885-211-44-9
$24.00 *(cloth)*

"Few books capture the soul
of the road like *The Sword of Heaven*,
a sharp-edged, beautifully rendered memoir
that will inspire anyone."   —Phil Cousineau,
author of *The Art of Pilgrimage*

STORM
**A Motorcycle Journey
of Love, Endurance,
and Transformation**
By Allen Noren
ISBN 1-885-211-45-7
$24.00 *(cloth)*

— ★ ★ ★ —

ForeWord Gold Medal Winner
— *Travel Book of the Year*

Travelers' Tales Classics

COAST TO COAST
A Journey Across 1950s America
By Jan Morris
ISBN 1-885-211-79-1
$16.95

After reporting on the first Everest ascent in 1953, Morris spent a year journeying by car, train, ship, and aircraft across the United States. In her brilliant prose, Morris records with exuberance and curiosity a time of innocence in the U.S.

TRADER HORN
A Young Man's Astounding Adventures in 19th Century Equatorial Africa
By Alfred Aloysius Horn
ISBN 1-885-211-81-3
$16.95

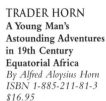

Here is the stuff of legends —tale of thrills and danger, wild beasts, serpents, and savages. An unforgettable and vivid portrait of a vanished late-19th century Africa.

THE ROYAL ROAD TO ROMANCE
By Richard Halliburton
ISBN 1-885-211-53-8
$14.95

"Laughing at hardships, dreaming of beauty, ardent for adventure, Halliburton has managed to sing into the pages of this glorious book his own exultant spirit of youth and freedom."
—*Chicago Post*

UNBEATEN TRACKS IN JAPAN
By Isabella L. Bird
ISBN 1-885-211-57-0
$14.95

Isabella Bird was one of the most adventurous women travelers of the 19th century with journeys to Tibet, Canada, Korea, Turkey, Hawaii, and Japan. A fascinating read for anyone interested in women's travel, spirituality, and Asian culture.

THE RIVERS RAN EAST
By Leonard Clark
ISBN 1-885-211-66-X
$16.95

Clark is the original Indiana Jones, relaying a breathtaking account of his search for the legendary El Dorado gold in the Amazon.

Travel Humor

NOT SO FUNNY WHEN IT HAPPENED
The Best of Travel Humor and Misadventure
Edited by Tim Cahill
ISBN 1-885-211-55-4
$12.95

Laugh with Bill Bryson, Dave Barry, Anne Lamott, Adair Lara, and many more.

THERE'S NO TOILET PAPER...ON THE ROAD LESS TRAVELED
The Best of Travel Humor and Misadventure
Edited by Doug Lansky
ISBN 1-885-211-27-9
$12.95

★ ★ ★

Humor Book of the Year —Independent Publisher's Book Award

ForeWord Gold Medal Winner— Humor Book of the Year

LAST TROUT IN VENICE
The Far-Flung Escapades of an Accidental Adventurer
By Doug Lansky
ISBN 1-885-211-63-5
$14.95

"Traveling with Doug Lansky might result in a considerably shortened life expectancy...but what a way to go."
—Tony Wheeler, Lonely Planet Publications

Women's Travel

A WOMAN'S PASSION FOR TRAVEL
More True Stories from A Woman's World
Edited by Marybeth Bond & Pamela Michael
ISBN 1-885-211-36-8
$17.95

"A diverse and gripping series of stories!" —Arlene Blum, author of Annapurna: A Woman's Place

A WOMAN'S WORLD
True Stories of Life on the Road
Edited by Marybeth Bond
Introduction by Dervla Murphy
ISBN 1-885-211-06-6
$17.95

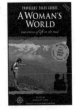

Winner of the Lowell Thomas Award for Best Travel Book— Society of American Travel Writers

WOMEN IN THE WILD
True Stories of Adventure and Connection
Edited by Lucy McCauley
ISBN 1-885-211-21-X
$17.95

"A spiritual, moving, and totally female book to take you around the world and back." —Mademoiselle

A MOTHER'S WORLD
Journeys of the Heart
Edited by Marybeth Bond & Pamela Michael
ISBN 1-885-211-26-0
$14.95

"These stories remind us that motherhood is one of the great unifying forces in the world" —San Francisco Examiner

Food

ADVENTURES IN WINE
True Stories of Vineyards and Vintages around the World
Edited by Thom Elkjer
ISBN 1-885-211-80-5
$17.95

Humanity, community, and brotherhood comprise the marvelous virtues of the wine world. This collection toasts the warmth and wonders of this large, extended family in stories by travelers who are wine novices and experts alike.

FOOD (Updated)
A Taste of the Road
Edited by Richard Sterling
Introduction by Margo True
ISBN 1-885-211-77-5
$18.95

Silver Medal Winner of the Lowell Thomas Award for Best Travel Book— Society of American Travel Writers

HER FORK IN THE ROAD
Women Celebrate Food and Travel
Edited by Lisa Bach
ISBN 1-885-211-71-6
$16.95

A savory sampling of stories by some of the best writers in and out of the food and travel fields.

THE ADVENTURE OF FOOD
True Stories of Eating Everything
Edited by Richard Sterling
ISBN 1-885-211-37-6
$17.95

"These stories are bound to whet appetites for more than food."

—Publishers Weekly

Spiritual Travel

THE SPIRITUAL GIFTS OF TRAVEL
The Best of Travelers' Tales
Edited by James O'Reilly and Sean O'Reilly
ISBN 1-885-211-69-4
$16.95

A collection of favorite stories of transformation on the road from our award-winning Travelers' Tales series that shows the myriad ways travel indelibly alters our inner landscapes.

PILGRIMAGE
Adventures of the Spirit
*Edited by Sean O'Reilly & James O'Reilly
Introduction by Phil Cousineau*
ISBN 1-885-211-56-2
$16.95

—— ✦✦✦ ——

*ForeWord Silver Medal Winner
— Travel Book of the Year*

THE ROAD WITHIN
True Stories of Transformation and the Soul
Edited by Sean O'Reilly, James O'Reilly & Tim O'Reilly
ISBN 1-885-211-19-8
$17.95

—— ✦✦✦ ——

Best Spiritual Book — Independent Publisher's Book Award

THE WAY OF THE WANDERER
Discover Your True Self Through Travel
By David Yeadon
ISBN 1-885-211-60-0
$14.95

Experience transformation through travel with this delightful, illustrated collection by award-winning author David Yeadon.

A WOMAN'S PATH
Women's Best Spiritual Travel Writing
Edited by Lucy McCauley, Amy G. Carlson & Jennifer Leo
ISBN 1-885-211-48-1
$16.95

"A sensitive exploration of women's lives that have been unexpectedly and spiritually touched by travel experiences.... Highly recommended."
—*Library Journal*

THE ULTIMATE JOURNEY
Inspiring Stories of Living and Dying
James O'Reilly, Sean O'Reilly & Richard Sterling
ISBN 1-885-211-38-4
$17.95

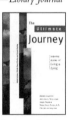

"A glorious collection of writings about the ultimate adventure. A book to keep by one's bedside—and close to one's heart." —Philip Zaleski, editor, *The Best Spiritual Writing series*

Adventure

TESTOSTERONE PLANET
True Stories from a Man's World
Edited by Sean O'Reilly, Larry Habegger & James O'Reilly
ISBN 1-885-211-43-0
$17.95

Thrills and laughter with some of today's best writers: Sebastian Junger, Tim Cahill, Bill Bryson, and Jon Krakauer.

DANGER!
True Stories of Trouble and Survival
Edited by James O'Reilly, Larry Habegger & Sean O'Reilly
ISBN 1-885-211-32-5
$17.95

"Exciting...for those who enjoy living on the edge or prefer to read the survival stories of others, this is a good pick."
—*Library Journal*

Special Interest

365 TRAVEL
A Daily Book of Journeys, Meditations, and Adventures
Edited by Lisa Bach
ISBN 1-885-211-67-8
$14.95
An illuminating collection of travel wisdom and adventures that reminds us all of the lessons we learn while on the road.

THE GIFT OF RIVERS
True Stories of Life on the Water
Edited by Pamela Michael
Introduction by Robert Hass
ISBN 1-885-211-42-2
$14.95
"*The Gift of Rivers* is a soulful compendium of wonderful stories that illuminate, educate, inspire, and delight."
—David Brower, Chairman of Earth Island Institute

FAMILY TRAVEL
The Farther You Go, the Closer You Get
Edited by Laura Manske
ISBN 1-885-211-33-3
$17.95
"This is family travel at its finest." —*Working Mother*

LOVE & ROMANCE
True Stories of Passion on the Road
Edited by Judith Babcock Wylie
ISBN 1-885-211-18-X
$17.95
"A wonderful book to read by a crackling fire."
—*Romantic Traveling*

THE GIFT OF BIRDS
True Encounters with Avian Spirits
Edited by Larry Habegger & Amy G. Carlson
ISBN 1-885-211-41-4
$17.95
"These are all wonderful, entertaining stories offering a *bird's-eye view!* of our avian friends."
—*Booklist*

A DOG'S WORLD
True Stories of Man's Best Friend on the Road
Edited by Christine Hunsicker
ISBN 1-885-211-23-6
$12.95
This extraordinary collection includes stories by John Steinbeck, Helen Thayer, James Herriot, Pico Iyer, and many others.

THE GIFT OF TRAVEL
The Best of Travelers' Tales
Edited by Larry Habegger, James O'Reilly & Sean O'Reilly
ISBN 1-885-211-25-2
$14.95
"Like gourmet chefs in a French market, the editors of Travelers' Tales pick, sift, and prod their way through the weighty shelves of contemporary travel writing, creaming off the very best."
—William Dalrymple, author of *City of Djinns*

Travel Advice

SHITTING PRETTY
How to Stay Clean and Healthy While Traveling
By Dr. Jane Wilson-Howarth
ISBN 1-885-211-47-3
$12.95

A light-hearted book about a serious subject for millions of travelers— staying healthy on the road—written by international health expert, Dr. Jane Wilson-Howarth.

THE FEARLESS SHOPPER
How to Get the Best Deals on the Planet
By Kathy Borrus
ISBN 1-885-211-39-2
$14.95

"Anyone who reads *The Fearless Shopper* will come away a smarter, more responsible shopper and a more curious, culturally attuned traveler."

—Jo Mancuso, *The Shopologist*

GUTSY WOMEN
More Travel Tips and Wisdom for the Road
By Marybeth Bond
ISBN 1-885-211-61-9
$12.95

Second Edition—Packed with funny, instructive, and inspiring advice for women heading out to see the world.

SAFETY AND SECURITY FOR WOMEN WHO TRAVEL
By Sheila Swan & Peter Laufer
ISBN 1-885-211-29-5
$12.95

A must for every woman traveler!

THE FEARLESS DINER
Travel Tips and Wisdom for Eating around the World
By Richard Sterling
ISBN 1-885-211-22-8
$7.95

Combines practical advice on foodstuffs, habits, and etiquette, with hilarious accounts of others' eating adventures.

THE PENNY PINCHER'S PASSPORT TO LUXURY TRAVEL
The Art of Cultivating Preferred Customer Status
By Joel L. Widzer
ISBN 1-885-211-31-7
$12.95

Proven techniques on how to travel first class at discount prices, even if you're not a frequent flyer.

GUTSY MAMAS
Travel Tips and Wisdom for Mothers on the Road
By Marybeth Bond
ISBN 1-885-211-20-1
$7.95

A delightful guide for mothers traveling with their children— or without them!

Destination Titles:
True Stories of Life on the Road

AMERICA
Edited by Fred Setterberg
ISBN 1-885-211-28-7
$19.95

FRANCE (Updated)
Edited by James O'Reilly,
Larry Habegger &
Sean O'Reilly
ISBN 1-885-211-73-2
$18.95

AMERICAN SOUTHWEST
Edited by Sean O'Reilly
& James O'Reilly
ISBN 1-885-211-58-9
$17.95

GRAND CANYON
Edited by Sean O'Reilly,
James O'Reilly &
Larry Habegger
ISBN 1-885-211-34-1
$17.95

AUSTRALIA
Edited by Larry Habegger
ISBN 1-885-211-40-6
$17.95

GREECE
Edited by Larry Habegger,
Sean O'Reilly &
Brian Alexander
ISBN 1-885-211-52-X
$17.95

BRAZIL
Edited by Annette Haddad
& Scott Doggett
Introduction by Alex
Shoumatoff
ISBN 1-885-211-11-2
$17.95

HAWAI'I
Edited by Rick &
Marcie Carroll
ISBN 1-885-211-35-X
$17.95

CENTRAL AMERICA
Edited by Larry Habegger
& Natanya Pearlman
ISBN 1-885-211-74-0
$17.95

HONG KONG
Edited by James O'Reilly,
Larry Habegger &
Sean O'Reilly
ISBN 1-885-211-03-1
$17.95

CUBA
Edited by Tom Miller
ISBN 1-885-211-62-7
$17.95

INDIA
Edited by James O'Reilly
& Larry Habegger
ISBN 1-885-211-01-5
$17.95

IRELAND
Edited by James O'Reilly,
Larry Habegger &
Sean O'Reilly
ISBN 1-885-211-46-5
$17.95

SAN FRANCISCO
Edited by James O'Reilly,
Larry Habegger &
Sean O'Reilly
ISBN 1-885-211-08-2
$17.95

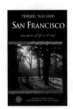

ITALY (Updated)
Edited by Anne Calcagno
Introduction by Jan Morris
ISBN 1-885-211-72-4
$18.95

SPAIN (Updated)
Edited by Lucy McCauley
ISBN 1-885-211-78-3
$19.95

JAPAN
Edited by Donald W. George
& Amy G. Carlson
ISBN 1-885-211-04-X
$17.95

THAILAND (Updated)
Edited by James O'Reilly
& Larry Habegger
ISBN 1-885-211-75-9
$18.95

MEXICO (Updated)
Edited by James O'Reilly
& Larry Habegger
ISBN 1-885-211-59-7
$17.95

TIBET
Edited by James O'Reilly,
Larry Habegger, & Kim
Morris
ISBN 1-885-211-76-7
$18.95

NEPAL
Edited by Rajendra
S. Khadka
ISBN 1-885-211-14-7
$17.95

TUSCANY
Edited by James O'Reilly, &
Tara Austen Weaver
ISBN 1-885-211-68-6
$16.95

PARIS
Edited by James O'Reilly,
Larry Habegger &
Sean O'Reilly
ISBN 1-885-211-10-4
$17.95

**BRIDGEPORT
PUBLIC LIBRARY**

1230124872